We Will Not Be Silenced

We Will Not Be Silenced

The Academic Repression of Israel's Critics

Edited by
William I. Robinson and Maryam S. Griffin

This edition © 2017 AK Press (Chico, Oakland, Edinburgh, Baltimore)
ISBN: 978-1-84935-276-5
E-ISBN: 978-1-84935-277-2
Library of Congress Control Number: 2016948842

AK Press
370 Ryan Ave. #100
Chico, CA 95973
USA
www.akpress.org
www.akuk.com
akpress@akpress.org

The above address would be delighted to provide you with the latest
AK Press distribution catalog, which features books, pamphlets, zines,
and stylish apparel published and/or distributed by AK Press. Alternatively,
visit our websites for the complete catalog, latest news, and secure ordering.

This book is printed on paper suitable for recycling and made from fully
managed and sustained forest sources. Logging, pulping and manufacturing
processes are expected to conform to the environmental standards of the
country of origin.

Typeset by Stanford DTP Services, Northampton, England

Printed in the USA.

Contents

Foreword

Cynthia McKinney

Former Member of the United States Congress

I remember it as if it were yesterday, although it really happened almost 15 years ago.

Not many people wanted to touch me after, from my position as Member of Congress from the State of Georgia, and member of the House Committees on International Relations and Armed Services, I demanded an investigation of the tragic events of September 11, 2001. After all, the people of the US had invested trillions of dollars into a military and intelligence infrastructure that failed four times on one day and I felt that my constituents deserved an explanation of what went wrong and if, as was promised to them, we were going to work together as a country to prevent a reoccurrence, we had to have an independent investigation and explanation of what exactly had happened on that day. After learning that both President George W. Bush and Vice President Dick Cheney had contacted Congressional leaders asking that they *not* support any investigation of the tragic events of that day, I became outraged and wrote an Op Ed that was carried in several newspapers. In that Op Ed, I mentioned that the National Transportation Safety Board routinely investigated train derailments and airplane crashes. So, why not an investigation of the events of September 11? I went on a Bay Area California radio program and repeated my call for an independent investigation.

And then, several weeks later, out of the blue, I was the main topic of national conversation, with the *hasbara* unleashed against me. (*Hasbara* roughly translates to "propaganda" in Hebrew. It can loosely be thought of as a virulent, organized public relations smear campaign unleashed by devotees of Israel, in some cases, even paid for by the state of Israel, carried out by what Professors Robinson and Griffin, in their Introduction to this book, refer to as the "Israel Lobby.") It was like a switch was flipped by somebody, and all of a sudden, the light was shone on me, exposing a brilliantly painted neon-glow bull's-eye on my back. I became the focus of ridicule, stigma, and ultimately silencing, by the likes of CNN, *Washington Post*, *New York Times*, local Georgia news outlets, and even some alternative progressive news and opinion outlets on the internet for which I had earlier served as one of their go-to persons. Inexplicably, after raising the investigation issue, I was soon accused of being a conspiracy theorist, anti-Semitic, and a holocaust denier.

After losing my Congressional seat in the *hasbara*-induced election-time whirlwind, I was invited by the Africana Studies Department at Cornell University to serve as a Rhodes Fellow, which meant that I got to spend one week on the Cornell campus, interacting with the students, lecturing about my Congressional experiences. Before I even reached the school, the campus newspaper began playing the anti-Semitism card against me. By the time I reached the campus, quite an effective frenzy had been created. Certain students followed me everywhere I went on campus taunting me as if I were a caged animal and the students were cruel animal tamers, accustomed to using the lash to whip their prey into submission. This same group of students also each had a notebook from which they read as they attempted to shut down every classroom appearance that I made. These students were loud, boisterous, unruly, and completely in charge inside and outside the classrooms as the authorities that had invited me onto the campus were in utter cowardice mode, remaining silent as I was forced to awake each day to face yet another blistering test of my dignity.

These "playbook" students were the first to raise their hands to ask the same questions; the first to bum-rush the microphones, leaving the other students with non-*hasbara* questions, flat-footed, slow, seemingly inept, and unable to ask their questions. These *hasbara* students even orchestrated disrupting my institution-wide public lecture by being dragged by campus security out of the auditorium where that capstone lecture took place. I was told that the students even arranged a meeting with members of the Board of Trustees to complain about my presence on campus. Finally, the Rhodes Fellowship was defunded and I was the last Rhodes Fellow on the Cornell University campus. The irony of my Cornell experience is that I was invited by the Africana Studies Department and my intention was to speak about the situation in Haiti; Israel was nowhere on my agenda. But, because of the actions of the *hasbara* students, the issue of Israel (and Palestine) occupied a place that was front and center.

My experience on the Cornell University campus is not unlike that of the professors and students in this book who chronicle their experiences when Constitutional rights, academic freedom, and scholarly curiosity are not allowed to exist. The pro-Israel totalitarian groupthink enforced by the *hasbara*'s internet, radio, TV, and print media warfare has completely rewritten the rules of academic engagement – destroying professional and institutional independence in the process. US universities are as much under attack as is any battlefield in the US/Israel/NATO-led war of terror. Indeed, terror has now entered US university classrooms.

My all-time favorite speech is that of President John F. Kennedy who chose the occasion of the 1963 graduation ceremony of American University to make a profound policy statement. In a speech entitled, "A Strategy of Peace," lasting fewer than 30 minutes, President Kennedy uttered the word "peace" over 30 times. Here is what he had to say about the importance of the university as a place of research, bold thinking, and important policy debate:

> "There are few earthly things more beautiful than a university," wrote John Masefield in his tribute to English universities – and his words are equally true today. He did not refer to towers or to campuses. He admired the splendid beauty of a university, because it was he said, "a place where those who hate ignorance may strive to know, where those who perceive truth may strive to make others see." I have, therefore, chosen this time and place to discuss a topic on which ignorance too often abounds and the truth too rarely perceived – and that is the most important topic on earth: peace.

President Kennedy chose the location of a US university to challenge the very military-industrial complex about which his predecessor, President Eisenhower, had issued a warning. A few months later, President Kennedy's brains were blown out in full public view, thus ending any Administration-led efforts to make peace with the Soviet Union, the major US geopolitical rival at that time. The ground has shifted underneath US campuses that are losing their competitive edge in free thinking. Professors Robinson and Griffin, and all of the contributors to this anthology, are trying to stop the "fracking" that is causing this by exposing the illegal drilling being done to undermine the foundation of academic freedom and integrity. US universities are one of the new battlefields putting academic freedom and institutional integrity at risk.

I want to personally thank Professor Robinson for allowing me to tell my own story as I endorse this vitally important book. I encourage you to read it and study it and then act in any way that you can to preserve the venue of the US university as a locus of questioning "conventional" wisdom so that a new and better wisdom can be created and become the new conventional. It is this very questioning that has resulted in huge strides being made for humankind. The choice is totally ours: remain mired in the constrictions of a particular groupthink enforced by a political special interest or advance the goal of freedom, liberation, and justice, thus possibly elevating the status of all of humankind.

I look forward to returning to a US classroom to discuss my experiences, or even to teach as I have earned a Ph.D. since leaving Congress. Unfortunately, such phone calls of invitation to me continue to be few and far between.

Preface

Richard A. Falk

United Nations Special Rapporteur for Occupied Palestine (2008–14)
Professor Emeritus of International Law at Princeton University

It is impossible to understand the effort to silence and punish academic critics of Israel and the student-led Boycott, Divestment, Sanctions (BDS) campaign of the Palestinian solidarity movement without some awareness of its connections with the twists and turns of the underlying Israel-Palestine relationship. What is most at stake is the evolving struggle by the Palestinian people to achieve their fundamental rights as this struggle interacts with Israel's expansionist ambitions. These ambitions collide with international diplomacy built on the idea that peace will come about once an independent Palestinian state is established. Also relevant is the political context in the Middle East. The recent turn of events in the region has greatly diminished the interest of the Arab world, Europe, and the United States in finding a solution for the conflict. This in turn has removed pressures on Israel to accept the idea of a Palestinian state more or less coterminous with the 1967 borders of Israel. Such a context should not be understood as implicit support for the two state solution as the only, or even the best, outcome for the Palestinians. A sustainable peace based on the equality of the two peoples should reflect a fair compromise with respect to overlapping claims of self-determination, nothing more, and certainly nothing less.

What these developments on the ground have meant over the course of the last decade is an Israeli shift in tactics away from the interstate warfare of its first decades of existence to the conduct of a counterinsurgency war that is waged against the Palestinians generally, but focuses on Hamas and Hezbollah, non-state adversaries. As Americans first learned in Vietnam (assuming that the memories of the war against Philippines resistance fought at the end of the nineteenth century have faded) is that in this kind of war "the people" become the enemy, and when modern weaponry is used by the state, it inevitably gives rise to two sets of outcomes: repeated patterns of war crimes and an anti-war backlash in Western democratic societies, especially among students and more politically engaged scholars and intellectuals. In this respect, there is an intimate connection between Israel's military onslaughts against the vulnerable and subjugated civilian population of Palestine and its gathering political resolve to impose a one-state solution on the Palestinians based on an apartheid scheme of permanent annexation and oppressive control.

There is a further often unnoticed element of the overall situation that adds to this surge of supportive solidarity with the Palestinian people: the shift in Palestinian tactics away from armed struggle and terrorism, and toward a reliance on diplomacy and non-violent forms of resistance. Although the Palestinian leadership is split, both branches share this transformation of tactics. Even Hamas has made it repeatedly clear that if Israel withdraws to the 1967 borders it will sign onto a long-term ceasefire arrangement. This may not bring sustainable peace, but it seems a far preferable alternative to the lethal brew of apartheid and counter-insurgency warfare that has been the experience of the period since the Lebanon War of 2006 when Israel first appalled world public opinion by deliberately targeting the civilian neighborhood of south Beirut, followed by three devastating massive attacks on the totally vulnerable 1.7 million Palestinians living in Gaza, and locked into the combat zones, during the last six years.

Especially here in America, where the government is seen as an unconditional ally of Israel, funding its war machine to an unprece-dented degree, there has in recent years occurred a pushback by way of criticism of Israel's policies and practices, both as occupier and as practitioner of cruel forms of counterinsurgency warfare. In earlier periods, there was also controversy surrounding Israel's policy, and efforts by pro-Israeli forces to disrupt and discourage such criticism and pushback, seeking to dominate the political space by insisting upon the supposedly undeniable moral superiority of Zionist claims. Those who defended Israel against criticism shouted their denunciations or posed questions prepared in advance that sought to subvert the presentation if deemed critical of Israel. But they did not directly question the viability of academic freedom with respect to discussions of Israel-Palestine relations from various viewpoints, although with the proviso that as far as campus visitors and events were concerned, the pro-Israeli events were numerous, and the pro-Palestinian ones were rare exceptions.

Over the last decade the tone and game plans of both sides have changed, as has the campus atmosphere. Strong critics of Israeli behavior have become totally disillusioned with the diplomatic track, contending that the steady expansion of the settlement phenomenon combined with rightward drift of internal Israeli politics together with Palestinian moves toward non-violent forms of resistance has made it imperative for civil society to take the lead in pushing for peace by escalating support for more pressure. In turn, the powerful Israeli lobby has turned its guns on all those who dare to join in this Legitimacy War being waged against Israel, branding them as biased and one-sided, and if Jewish, self-hating Jews, and if not, as anti-Semites or both. Note especially that the Israeli lobby, with its many well-funded organizational components, no longer expends energy on prevailing in, or even influencing, the substantive debates, but is using its unhealthy leverage to punish, marginalize, intimidate, and suppress activities that are seen as somehow harmful to Israel's current unilateralist agenda.

My own experience seems relevant, especially with respect to my role as United Nations (UN) Special Rapporteur for Occupied Palestine in the period from 2008 to 2014. I should explain that this position is the one truly independent voice that the Palestinian people possess within the UN and in relation to the media that has the mandate of setting the record straight on Israeli violations of international humanitarian law (especially, the Geneva Conventions) and international human rights standards in relation to occupied Palestine. As Special Rapporteur (SR), while affiliated with the University of California at Santa Barbara, I reported annually for six years to the General Assembly in New York and to the Human Rights Council in Geneva, and helped call world attention to the most serious violations of international law, including the expansion of unlawful settlements and outposts, de facto annexation of occupied territory, extreme forms of collective punishment in Gaza and through the demolition of homes, consistent reliance on excessive force in relation to security, and abusive detention procedures and prison conditions. I was, as might be expected, attacked by Israeli diplomatic representatives, as well as by their American counterparts and international allies, including such faux human rights advocates as Susan Rice and Samantha Power, and even by the UN Secretary General, Ban Ki-Moon, but this is not the place to go into the geopolitics of Israeli support at the UN.

More relevant and more insidious was the work of ultra-Zionist non-governmental organizations (NGOs) that linked their public defamatory denunciations of my efforts to bear truthful witness to the realities of the occupation with a variety of campaigns to ensure that college campuses would be off limits for critics of Israel, and especially for faculty. The Simon Wiesenthal Center in Los Angeles, for instance, publishes a list of the ten most dangerous anti-Semites in the world each year, and while I was still doing my UN job, listed me as the third most dangerous, ranked only behind the Supreme Guide of Iran and the Prime Minister of Turkey. It was a hurtful jibe given wide publicity, although it did make me realize that my UN role was worthwhile despite having to contend with a torrent of defamatory denunciations. Another tormenter of mine was UN Watch, an NGO based in Geneva that, during my tenure as SR, devoted much of its energies to spreading defamatory lies about my views on various issues *other than* criticisms of Israel, such as the 9/11 attacks and the Boston marathon bombing. Their tactics included sending defamatory formal letters to UN diplomats and high officials demanding my denunciation and dismissal. Particularly disconcerting was the readiness of these prominent public officials to shore up their pro-Israel credentials by joining in the attack on my reputation without ever bothering to check with me or on the accuracy of the accusations.

What makes this tawdry experience relevant to this book is that these efforts to discredit in an international context were followed up, especially by UN Watch, openly and behind the scenes, in a variety of academic settings, some undoubtedly unknown to me. I spoke in this period at universities as disparate as the American University in Beirut, McGill, McMaster, Norfolk, Sydney, Australian National University (ANU), as well as at an array of American universities, including Stanford, Columbia and even Princeton where I had spent 40 years as a member of the faculty, as well as several units of the California state system. The typical tactic was to organize a letter writing campaign as well as to send well-crafted letters to the president of the institution and university board of directors setting forth a series of reasons for regarding me as an unworthy speaker, and suggesting that if the relevant event was not cancelled, donations would stop. Despite varying degrees of wobbling, none of these speaking events was cancelled, nor was there any attempt to challenge me on substance. Nevertheless, the objections to my presence on campus did have unfortunate effects. It effectively turned audience, and especially media attention, from the message to the messenger, confronting me with a variety of questions about my views on various issues other than Israel/Palestine. It also signaled to student groups and faculty that it would be a damaging hassle to invite a controversial critic of Israel to the campus and might even affect faculty tenure and appointment decisions, without, of course, ever being disclosed. The most insidious aspect of this assault on academic freedom is what is done covertly to please the lobby, to avoid friction, and to advance an unacknowledged Zionist agenda, that is, the person not invited, not hired, the conference not planned or funded.

There were also more direct impacts on my professional life. At the initiative of the dean at the time, I had been negotiating with the UCLA Law School with respect to locating a rather large project on climate change and democracy within its confines, together with a partial teaching relationship. When my views on Israel/Palestine were brought to his attention, he abruptly terminated the negotiation, contending late in the day that there was insufficient office space available to house the project. I cite this case as one illustration of the insidious back door approaches to purging universities of those who seem not to be "politically correct" in the eyes of the Israel Lobby.

Another similar experience occurred at Kings College School of Law in London where I had been recruited to be a visiting Fellow, a research appointment, on a recurring, annual, half-time, year-to-year basis. When I arrived for the first year, my host faculty member informed me, with evident embarrassment, that the provost vetoed any further appointments because of my views on Israel.

Even a respected and prominent human rights NGO played along with the defamatory tactics of UN Watch. After the national office of Human Rights Watch (HRW) received a letter denouncing me as anti-Semitic I was abruptly asked to resign my membership in the local HRW Santa Barbara Committee without even being told the real reason. I was only told that the UN position I held at the time created a conflict of interest, although I had the job for several years, and the letter from UN Watch was not even mentioned. Of course, after my dismissal UN Watch boasted that their pressure convinced HRW that I was too anti-Semitic even to be acceptable for an NGO critical of Israel. When UN Watch predictably gloated afterwards that HRW had dismissed me because I was too anti-Semitic and extreme even for them, I asked the Executive

Director of HRW to clarify my resignation, but he refused, allowing UN Watch to claim uncontested credit for their shabby victory without even a dissent. I interpreted such behavior as testifying to the power of Zionist forces within HRW. This negative branding by HRW, a liberal powerhouse, had professional fallout. It rendered more credible efforts to exclude me from speaking engagements, visiting appointments, and other forms of access to university dialogue on controversial issues.

I mention my personal difficulties at such length because it has been an unpleasant experience that I felt directly and endured, despite being insulated by tenure throughout most of my career and the protective environment of established universities. Putting the issue differently, I was as invulnerable to Zionist pushback as it is probably possible to be, and yet suffered this variety of indignities and interferences with normal academic activities. As the testimonies in this collection powerfully demonstrate, those with greater vulnerability are made to suffer far more harm to their professional life, reputation, and career, as well as to be made a scapegoat in the wider effort to turn the tide of opinion and activism within American campus communities.

Returning to substantive concerns, this issue of silencing debate and inhibiting non-violent activism is particularly pernicious with respect to academic freedom in the United States. On no question of public policy is critical discussion and debate more urgently central to sustaining claims of democratic credentials than with respect to American foreign policy toward the Middle East, with particular attention to Israel/Palestine. The American so-called "special relationship" with Israel has the effect of turning a blind eye to whatever Israel does even when it collides with obvious national interests in the region, as well as disposing the government toward disastrous military interventions of which the Iraq example is only the most notorious. To the extent that universities have a vital role in preparing students to be engaged citizens as well as members of the workforce, it is crucial to keep the campus open and *unafraid*. When Israel Lobby groups collect names and pictures of students who take part in BDS activities in a society where jobs are hard to come by, it fosters inhibitions and creates a variety of incentives to lie low rather than to follow the path of conscience. When students in college courses are being encouraged to complain to ADL, Campus Watch, Stand With Us, and others about teachers who criticize Israel, the Orwellian overtones are evident.

I am proud to be associated with this admirable group of engaged citizens and distinguished academics who have suffered due to acting on the courage of their convictions. Perhaps some of their initiatives reflected an imprudent response that exhibited their emotional agitation, but it takes heat as well as light to respond appropriately to situations of life and death for vulnerable people. In some ways, borrowing from another powerful initiative rooted in the lives of the men and women of America, we can say "Palestinian Lives Matter" as the moral motivational force behind our words and actions. What the testimonials in this collection have in common is the contention that moral passion is a valuable dimension of academic life, and deserves to be protected against those forces that would shut it down. We need all the eloquence, analysis, and commitment at our disposal, as well as the support of all those who believe in the critical role of academic freedom, to spread this vital message even if it means crossing the boundaries of "civility" at times.

Finally, as has been pointed out by others, anti-Semitism as ethnic hatred is a diabolical force that is real and should be denounced whenever it is genuinely present. However, to follow the Israel Lobby in "playing the anti-Semitic card" to insulate Israeli policies and practices from scrutiny is to do two serious disservices. Firstly, to deflect justifiable criticism of Israel despite its policies of long-term dispossession and oppression that have made Palestinians "strangers" in their own land, and secondly, to muddy the waters of anti-Semitism by confusing hatred of Jews with disapproval of Israel's behavior.

This concern has been intensified greatly by the US State Department adopting a definition of anti-Semitism that is responsive to the Israel Lobby and is under consideration by the Board of Regents entrusted with administering higher education in the University of California system. To evade charges of undermining academic freedom, the State Department appends these bland words to its essential attempt to blend criticism of Israel and related activism as instances of anti-Semitism: "However criticism of Israel similar to that leveled against any other sovereign state cannot be regarded as anti-Semitism." Who is to monitor "similar to," and what can that possibly mean without an accompanying assessment of the context. It would be necessary to inquire into what Israel has been doing in overt defiance of the constraints of international law and morality that has generated the criticism and activism. It would also be relevant to take account of the official links between the US Government by way of unconditional diplomatic support and the use of taxpayer revenue to subsidize Israel's budget. Such defining realities make Israel dissimilar from other countries, and this makes reasonable an equivalent level of criticism and non-violent opposition. But as it stands, especially if imitated by academic institutions, such a definition of anti-Semitism is certain to exert an intimidating influence on academic freedom with respect to Israel, especially as accompanied by a militant campaign to criminalize participation in BDS advocacy activities.

If the air is cleared, academic freedom restored to its proper role, it may be that universities can become a more constructive influence on public policy debate as well as a site of struggle on Israel/Palestine. It is my experience that those being denounced as anti-Semites actually favor a just and sustainable peace for both peoples consistent with their overlapping claims of self-determination, the most fundamental of all human rights that inheres in both Jews and Palestinians. In this respect, we cannot redo the historical experience of Palestine over the course of the last century, but we can do our very best to encourage a future based on the equality, rights, and dignity of both peoples.

Introduction: Academic Repression on US University Campuses

William I. Robinson and Maryam S. Griffin

A storm is raging on college and university campuses across the United States.

A worldwide campaign in support of the Palestinian freedom struggle has taken off in recent years, spurred on in this age of global digital media by omnipresent images of Israeli brutality against the Palestinians and the everyday humiliations of its occupation of Palestinian lands, now in its fifth decade. As awareness has grown over Israeli violations of Palestinian human rights and of international law, as well as US government and transnational corporate complicity in these violations, so too has the movement in solidarity with the Palestinian people.

Ground zero for this movement in the United States is college and university campuses. Some 25 years after the fall of apartheid in South Africa, the movement to end apartheid and settler colonialism in Israel/ Palestine has spread among a new generation of campus activists. The issue has inflamed passions and engulfed students, faculty, administrators, and even government officials in conflicts over free speech and academic freedom.

At the core of these conflicts is the attempt by what we will call here the Israel lobby to intimidate those on and off campus who have the courage to take a stand for Palestinian freedom. As the veil is lifting and the tide of public opinion begins to turn with increased awareness of the occupation, Israeli war crimes, and US complicity, the lobby has drastically stepped up its campaigns to silence and repress those who have spoken out for Palestinian freedom. It has systematically targeted persecution scholars, academics, and students who speak out on campuses and in our communities against Israeli policies and for Palestinian rights. Scholars have been turned away for jobs, denied tenure and promotion, rejected for funding, expelled from institutions, maligned and vilified. Student organizations have faced harassment and sanctions. Individual students have been threatened with expulsion. Some have even been criminally investigated and prosecuted.

The lobby consists of a network of individuals and organizations aligned with the Israeli government that actively works to stifle any criticism of Israel or US support for it and to silence any mention of Palestinian rights. We use the term lobby despite certain limitations; there is no ideal term to describe this network of loosely coordinated, overlapping, and interlocked advocacy groups, some of whose leaders have held high-level positions in the US government and occupy key positions in think tanks, universities, media outlets, political parties, and civil society organizations.

As with other lobbies that seek to influence the US political system and policy, both domestic and foreign, the Israel lobby seeks to shape a US policy toward Israel, Palestine, and the Middle East in a way favorable to the Israeli state's objectives. However, what distinguishes the Israel lobby from others is the breadth and depth of its influence over policy toward Israel and toward the Israel-Palestine conflict, as well as the resources and pressure that it brings to bear on those who criticize Israel or come out in public support for Palestinian freedom, as we will discuss in more detail below and as the testimonials in this anthology bear out. It is important to note in this regard that the lobby is not united by religion or ethnicity but rather by its political agenda and its determination to ostracize, censor, and punish anyone who criticizes Israel or advocates for the Palestinians.

There is a considerable literature on the Israel lobby in the United States.[1] Perhaps the landmark study among these is *The Israel Lobby and US Foreign Policy*, published in 2007 by political scientists John Mearsheimer of the University of Chicago and Stephen Walt of Harvard University. "It is difficult to talk about the lobby's influence on American foreign policy, at least in the mainstream media in the United States, without being accused of anti-Semitism or labeled a self-hating Jew," wrote Mearsheimer and Walt. "It is just as difficult to criticize Israeli policies or question US support for Israel in polite company. America's generous and unconditional support for Israel is rarely questioned, because groups in the lobby use their power to make sure that public discourse echoes its strategic and moral arguments for the special relationship [between Israel and the United States]." They went on to observe:

The lobby rewards or punishes politicians largely through an ability to guide the flow of campaign contributions. Organizations in the lobby also put pressure on the executive branch through a number of mechanisms, including working through government officials who are sympathetic to their views. Equally important, the lobby has gone to considerable lengths to shape public discourse about Israel by putting pressure on the media and academia and by establishing a tangible presence in influential foreign policy think tanks. Efforts to shape public perceptions often include charging critics of Israel with anti-Semitism, a tactic designed to discredit and marginalize anyone who challenges the current relationship [of steadfast US government support for Israel].[2]

As if intentionally to lend credence to one of the book's claims, upon publication of their study, Israel advocacy organizations promptly labeled Mearsheimer and Walt "anti-Semitic."[3]

Mearsheimer and Walt identified as key organizations in the lobby the American Israel Political Affairs Committee (AIPAC), the American Jewish Congress, the Zionist Organization of America, the Israel Policy Forum, the American Jewish Committee, the Anti-Defamation League, Americans for a Safe Israel, Hadassah, the Jewish Institute for National Security Affairs, the Middle East Forum, and the Washington Institute for Near East Policy, among others, as well as at least three dozen pro-Israel Political Action Committees, or PACs, organizations notorious in the money-driven US political system for raising and spending money to elect or defeat candidates in national, state, and local elections. While a number of these organizations are active in campaigns to silence and repress critics of Israel on US college and university campuses, there is a second tier of several dozen organizations that liaise with the major Washington-based lobby groups and that have formed a tightly-knit network, the "Israel on Campus Coalition."

In a shocking and deeply disturbing expose of the inner workings of this Coalition (see Chapter 1 of this anthology) University of California professors Goldberg and Makdisi document how the lobby monitors campus political life and mounts coordinated campaigns of harassment and repression against their designated targets, employing "character assassinations, selective misquotation, the willful distortion of the record, the fabrication of falsehoods, and an utter disregard for the truth." The targets of such censorship campaigns, as they show and as become clear in the 14 testimonials we publish here, are students and faculty who criticize Israel or support Palestinian freedom in and out of the classroom, but also university administrators and local and state politicians. Administrators are pressured and sometimes even blackmailed with a cutoff of financial donations by wealthy pro-Zionist donors to censor and discipline the offending party, while politicians are lobbied to apply pressure on university officials – although it must be observed that pro-Zionist academics, administrators, and politicians are often themselves a part of these campaigns.

Meanwhile, in the years since Mearsheimer and Walt's landmark study was published, several new books, articles, and reports have appeared on the battles raging in the United States and worldwide in support of Palestinian freedom and on the lobby and its repressive activities. In 2015, the New York-based legal advocacy organization, the Center for Constitutional Rights, and Palestine Legal, a non-profit organization that is, according to their website, "dedicated to protecting the civil and constitutional rights of people in the US who speak out for Palestinian freedom," published a seminal report, *The Palestine Exception to Free Speech*, documenting the "chilling and censoring of Palestine advocacy in the United States."[4] In that same year, Jewish Voice for Peace, a faith-based Jewish organization that calls for an end to Israeli occupation and apartheid and supports the boycott of Israel (see below), published its own report, *Stifling Dissent: How Israel's Defenders Use False Charges of Anti-Semitism to Limit the Debate Over Israel on Campus*.[5] In addition, several scholarly studies and conferences have in recent years addressed the censorship and repression that targets supporters of Palestinian rights in the United States.[6]

Beyond these reports, books, and public fora, there are many important studies on Palestine for those interested in the historical and political background.[7] Rather than duplicate what is already available, this book seeks to provide a special window, through *first-hand testimonial accounts*, into how the Israel lobby has worked on US campuses to suppress free speech and academic freedom. These testimonials tell the story of academics, scholars, and students who have been victim to the repression of the Israel lobby in the United States. Some of these cases of persecution have been aired publicly – in the press and social media – while other cases have gone poorly publicized, if at all, often as a result of an intentional blackout. Academics who become targets of the lobby's aggressive tactics are affected unevenly. This makes it difficult for certain kinds of stories to get attention even in the absence of a media blackout because it may be difficult for targeted individuals to come forward without fear of reprisals. As we shall see in these testimonials, the tactics of Israel advocacy organizations vary, from calls for outright institutional sanction to more subtle aggressions that nonetheless have a cumulative effect of creating a hostile work environment or career-long stress. Even the exact same tactics take different tolls depending on the status of the targeted individual. Instructors with precarious appointments such as single term lecturers and graduate students are far more vulnerable than tenured faculty, as are individual students over student groups that may draw on collective resources. The impacts of persecutions are similarly felt differentially across race, gender, and other social categories, with Palestinians, Arabs, Muslims, and other racially or ethnically oppressed groups – and especially women from these groups – often placed in particularly vulnerable situations, so that fight-back can often place additional pressures on those that are already the most overburdened.

As this tide turns, many of those whose stories are here told have been able to triumph over academic repression, in both direct and indirect ways. Others, however, have yet to be granted redress for the persecution they have suffered. We want this edited collection to be a beacon of inspiration that scholars and students who face such persecution are not alone and that, with collective struggle linked to the larger community, we can beat back repression on our campuses; that even if there are risks in speaking out, academic freedom and justice can triumph.

Zionism and Palestine

Why has the Palestinian struggle against colonialism and apartheid inflamed such conflict and passionate emotion, and also generated widespread fear of speaking out among those who believe in freedom, justice, and self-determination? After all, there was not the same level of fear in the United States among those who spoke out against apartheid in South Africa decades earlier. The intimidation experienced by supporters of justice for Palestinians results in part from the way the political issue has been deeply misunderstood by a significant portion of the US and international public. Popular misperceptions over the nature of this conflict are, in large part, a deliberate outcome of the narrative that has been propagated for seven decades by the Zionist movement – a narrative that has enjoyed the explicit approval of and recitation by the US government alongside its steadfast political, military, and economic support for Israel. The Zionist narrative, however, has come under increasing challenge as the international public has become more aware of the colonial nature of the Israel-Palestine conflict and global movements in solidarity with Palestinians have proliferated.

The creation of Israel as an ethnically exclusive "Jewish state" was part of the new wave of European colonialism that swept Africa, the Middle East, and Asia in the late nineteenth and early twentieth centuries. At the same moment that the peoples of those regions achieved decolonization and freedom in the post-World War II era, Palestine was being recolonized and remains one of the last vestiges worldwide of that late nineteenth and early twentieth century wave of European settler colonialism. It was in the context of European overseas colonial empires that the Zionist movement emerged in the late nineteenth century as a particular blend of colonialism and the racial nationalisms that swept Europe. Racial nationalism called for the creation of "ethnically pure" nations in the West and deployed racial supremacist ideologies to justify these colonial projects. Examples of the ideology of settler colonialism bolstered by racial nationalism included Manifest Destiny in the United States, which provided a convenient rationale for US Western expansion, the seizure of Mexican and Indian territories, and, later on, the invasion and colonization of Puerto Rico, Cuba, the Philippines, and the South Pacific islands. Ironically, as Jewish-American scholar Norman Finkelstein has shown in his historical research, the Nazi call for a "racially pure Aryan" Germany sprung from the same ideological well of racial nationalism.[8] Zionism called for the establishment of an "ethnically pure" Jewish state, although, to this day, the Zionist movement involves a confused and contradictory discourse that conflates religion, nationality, and ethnicity.

Early Zionists were drawn from the European Jewish middle class and intelligentsia who called for the emigration of Jews from their various homelands and resettlement in a new Jewish state. Zionist leaders lobbied European colonial powers to support such a state in exchange for Zionist support for colonization and imperial design. The father of Zionism, the Austrian Theodor Herzl, first approached the German Kaiser, and then the Russian Czar, and later the Pope for an imperial alliance with his movement, before successfully lobbying the British to support the creation of Israel as a British colonial outpost. "England, with her possessions in Asia should be most interested in Zionism for the shortest route to India by way of Palestine," he said. "England's great politicians were the first to recognize the need for colonial expansion ... and so I must believe that here in England the idea of Zionism, which is a colonial idea, should be easily and quickly understood."⁹ Most Jewish people in Europe at the time paid little attention to Zionism, preferring to fight anti-Semitism in their own countries or to immigrate to the United States.

The rise of power of the Nazis and the horrific holocaust that ensued, however, led to a massive increase of European Jewish migration to Palestine in the 1930s and 1940s. The British had taken over Palestine as a colonial protectorate with the collapse of the Ottoman Empire at the close of World War I. Under British colonial auspices, and with critical US support, the United Nations – which at the time had no African or Asian member states, not to mention that the Palestinians themselves were never even consulted – approved in 1947 a Partition Plan. The Plan called for granting 55 percent of historic Palestine to the Jewish settlers, who, at the time, comprised 35 percent of the residential population and owned 6 percent of the land, and the remaining 45 percent of land for an independent Arab state. The Zionists proceeded to create Israel through a military campaign of terrorism and ethnic cleansing – what Israel calls its "war of independence" – that involved the massacre of thousands of Palestinians, the permanent destruction of over 400 Palestinian villages, and the uprooting and expulsion of 750,000 Palestinians from their homeland.¹⁰

When this war came to a close in 1948, the newly established State of Israel controlled nearly 80 percent of historic Palestine. The remaining 20 percent was seized by Israel following the 1967 Israeli invasion of the West Bank, the Golan Heights, East Jerusalem, and the Gaza Strip. These lands have come to be known as the Occupied Palestinian Territories, or OPT, and the portion of them that has not been directly annexed by Israel remains under a 49-year (and counting) military occupation. Since 1948, Palestinians have endured ongoing ethnic cleansing, colonization, racial discrimination, and military occupation, in violation of international law and despite repeated condemnation by the international community, including the United Nations (UN) and human rights organizations.

The official Zionist narrative portrays Israel as a democratic and heroic underdog facing hostile Arabs. It claims that granting Jewish immigrants their own state to the exclusion of Palestinians was just compensation for historic anti-Semitism in Europe and as well is God's will – a land promised 4,000 years ago, as stated in the Old Testament, to Jewish people. It has been Israel's leading Jewish historians themselves who in recent years have researched government and military archives that have been declassified to draft what is known in Israel as the "new historiography." This historical research belies the official narrative and demonstrates how Israel was founded on the calculated and cynical ethnic cleansing of the Palestinians.

Today, Israel is an international outlaw state and an apartheid state. The UN General Assembly has continuously ratified every year since its approval in 1948 UN Resolution 194, which establishes the right of all those Palestinians expelled in 1948 to return to their homes and to receive compensation. And UN Resolution 242, approved in 1967 and continuously ratified by the international community each year since then, declares Israel's occupation of the OPT illegal and calls for Israel to withdraw to its pre-1967 borders. Israel is also in violation of other articles of the UN Charter and several dozen resolutions of the UN Security Council, the Geneva Conventions, the International Convention on the Suppression and Punishment of the Crime of Apartheid, international humanitarian law, and International Court of Justice advisory opinions. It has been repeatedly condemned by every major international human rights organization for the ongoing denial of Palestinian rights, for committing numerous war crimes, for illegal detentions, torture, extra-judicial killings, forced relocation and exile, among other violations.

In 2009, 15 years after the fall of South African apartheid, the South African Human Sciences Research Council sent a high level international delegation to the OPT to investigate the charge of Israeli practices of colonialism and apartheid as defined by international law.[11] Regarding colonialism, the report found that Israel's policy is demonstrably to fragment the West Bank and annex part of it permanently to Israel using Jewish-only residential colonies, which is the hallmark of settler colonialism. Israel, the report observed, has appropriated land and water in the OPT, merged the Palestinian economy with its own, and imposed a system of domination over Palestinians to ensure their subjugation to these measures. Regarding apartheid, it found that Israel's laws and policies in the OPT fit the definition of apartheid in the International Convention on the Suppression and Punishment of the Crime of Apartheid. Israeli law conveys privileges to Jewish settlers and disadvantages Palestinians in the same territory on the basis of their respective identities, which function as racialized identities (Jews and Palestinians) in the sense provided by international law. In sum, the report observed that Israel's policies are a corollary to five of the six "inhumane acts" listed by the Convention. It concluded that: the three pillars of apartheid in South Africa are all practiced by Israel in the OPT. These include demarcating the population into distinct racial groups and according superior rights, privileges, and services to one; segregating the population into different geographic areas allocated by law to different racial groups; and imposing a "matrix of draconian 'security' laws and policies" to suppress any opposition to the regime and reinforce the system of racial domination.

Racism and discrimination are actually built into Israel's legal and institutional structure. In fact, according to the State of Israel there is no such thing as an Israeli nationality because, according to the Israeli High Court, "there is no Israeli nation separate from the Jewish people,"[12] defined as Jewish people residing in Israel and the OPT as well as those living anywhere in the world, whether or not they have ever been to Israel or have any connection whatsoever to the country. Such a system, *by definition*, excludes Palestinians from the nation of their birth and their ancestors.

In the OPT, there is one legal and administrative system – Israeli civil law – applied to the Jewish settler population, which number now about 750,000, and another – military law – applied to the Palestinian population. Inside Israel itself, Palestinians (the latter make up 20 percent of the population) are subject to institutional discrimination.[13] "In defining itself as the Jewish state," observes Saree Makdisi,

> Israel establishes a major distinction between what it calls "nationality" and what it calls "citizenship"; and it is the only state that explicitly identifies itself not as the state of its actual citizens, but rather as the state of a people, most of whom have no connection to it, let alone any intention of ever living there.

This distinction between "citizenship" and "nationality," he notes "has proven rhetorically useful to Israel; it can declare that it treats all its citizens equally, for example, because most forms of discrimination in the state are not established on the basis of citizenship as such, but rather on the basis of nationality."[14]

US Support for Israeli Colonialism and Apartheid

The outrage over such a blatantly racist system, the atrocities of Israeli colonialism, military occupation, and apartheid has shocked the sense of social justice and equality of a growing number of people among the international public, ourselves included, and spurred them into solidarity with the Palestinian freedom struggle. Yet the Israel lobby in the United States and around the world routinely condemns this solidarity as "anti-Semitism." This is no less ludicrous a claim than it would be to characterize criticism of human rights violations in Egypt, Syria, or Iran as "anti-Muslim" or condemnations of apartheid in South Africa as "anti-White." It is as well a claim that, in the view of renowned Jewish-American scholar and Israel critic Norman Finkelstein, intentionally manipulates the Nazi holocaust experience and Jewish suffering.[15]

If such a claim for the informed observer is a fairly obvious attempt to delegitimize opposition to Israeli apartheid and support for Palestinian rights – and to rationalize intimidation and repression by the lobby – it has nonetheless gained traction as a result of the support it has enjoyed from none other than the US State Department. The State Department revised its definition of anti-Semitism earlier this century to include the so-called "three Ds": "*demonizing Israel*," a category that includes "drawing comparisons of contemporary Israeli policy to that of the Nazis" and "blaming Israel for all inter-religious or political tension"; *double standard* for Israel, which involves "applying double standards by requiring of it a behavior not expected or demanded by any other democratic nation" and "multilateral organizations focusing on Israel only for peace or human rights investigations"; *delegitimizing Israel*, which includes "denying the Jewish people their right to self-determination, and denying Israel the right to exist."[16]

This definition has many flaws, which stem from the conflation of state, religion, and ethnicity, as we have already observed, so that criticizing a state's practices and policies is portrayed as an act of religious or ethnic hatred. The main point is that, in turn, Israel advocacy organizations draw legitimacy from the State Department's "new definition" to silence those who criticize Israeli state practices and come out in support of Palestinian freedom by labeling them *ipso facto* "anti-Semitic." The chilling effect of this charge often has the intended effect of imposing censorship and *self-censorship* on would-be critics. Jewish Voices for Peace has documented and condemned this manipulation of anti-Semitism, highlighting in particular "bullying inside the Jewish community" against the increasing number of Jews on and off campus who have come out against Israeli apartheid and occupation and in favor of the global boycott, divestment and sanctions movement (see below):

> By framing much activism on behalf of Palestinian rights and criticism of Israel as "anti-Semitic," these Israel advocates cause confusion over what is truly anti-Jewish versus political positions that cause discomfort to the Israeli government and its supporters. Students and faculty who are targeted for their political beliefs hesitate to participate in public discourse out of fear of the consequences of exercising their right to free speech. Each new complaint, and every campaign against a faculty hire, invited speaker, or student protest succeeds in raising an uproar on campus – and increasing tension and fear around speaking out on issues relating to Israel and Palestine. Israel advocacy organizations use these efforts to wear down administrators, intimidate faculty, and frighten students. Students who are already targeted by strict scrutiny and surveillance, particularly those from Palestine, Arab and/or Muslim communities, adjunct and untenured faculty and progressive Jewish students bear the brunt of this bullying.[17]

This State Department "redefinition" of anti-Semitism is consistent with the US role as the principle sponsor of the Israeli state and its policies. Between 1949 and 2015 the United States provided Israel with a whopping $124.3 billion in economic and military aid and currently averages some $3 billion annually, not including special appropriations and other forms of financial support, such as loan guarantees.[18] If these were taken into account, the figure would be more than $4.3 billion annually, according to Mearsheimer and Walt.[19] Each time Israel has launched one of its routine military assaults on the Gaza Strip, the United

States has resupplied the Israeli Defense Force. It has supplied white phosphorous and cluster bombs, barbarous weapons that are banned by international treaties and whose use constitutes war crimes, yet which the Israeli military has unleashed on Palestinian civilians with impunity. Its support has made possible the development in Israel of a military-security-industrial complex – Israel has the sixth largest army in the world and is a leading international arms dealer.[20] Washington has also turned a blind eye to Israel's clandestine programs for the development of Weapons of Mass Destruction (WMD), including the production of Israel's nuclear weapons arsenal (estimated at some 300 warheads) and an active chemical and biological weapons program, making a mockery of US claims to pursue the non-proliferation of these weapons.

"The most singular feature of US support for Israel," say Mearsheimer and Walt, "is its increasingly unconditional nature."[21] Between 1972 and 2011 the United States vetoed no less than 42 UN Security Council resolutions critical of Israel, including those calling on Israel to halt its massacres in Gaza, condemning illegal settlements in the OPT and the killing by Israeli security forces of UN employees, deploring Israeli policies and practices in the occupied territories, and calling on Israel to abide by the Geneva Convention, among others.

It is doubtful that Israeli colonialism and apartheid would endure without such steadfast US support. It is for this reason that we have chosen to limit the testimonials in this book to the Israel lobby and academic repression specifically in the United States. There are natural limits to all books and writers have to find a point in which the content is circumscribed; readers should be aware that the patterns of repression documented in these testimonials is widespread in many countries around the world. Yet Israel would surely be forced to abandon its oppression of the Palestinians and reach a just and democratic resolution, we believe rather quickly, were there to be a fundamental change in US policy and economic support.

Mearsheimer and Walt believe the astonishing influence of the Israel lobby on US policy can be accounted for in large part by the support base the lobby enjoys within the Jewish-American community and its major organizations as well as support from Christian Zionists and the neo-conservative movement. We believe, however, that an equally important factor is the role that Israel plays as a regional platform for US interventionist policies in the Middle East and as a key transnational corporate outpost in that region, especially for the arms industry, informatics, and global finances, although we must defer such discussion for elsewhere.

Meanwhile, Jewish-Americans are distancing themselves in increasing numbers from Israeli policies and practices and as a consequence are attacked by the lobby as "self-hating Jews." The organization Jewish Voice for Peace (JVP) is emblematic of the shifting sentiment within the Jewish-American community. The organization "opposes anti-Jewish, anti-Muslim, and anti-Arab bigotry and oppression." It "seeks an end to the Israeli occupation of the West Bank, Gaza Strip, and East Jerusalem; security and self-determination for Israelis and Palestinians; a just solution for Palestinian refugees based on principles established by international law; an end to violence against civilians; and peace and justice for all peoples of the Middle East." JVP members, declares the organization's mission statement, "are inspired by Jewish tradition to work together for peace, social justice, equality, human rights, respect for international law, and a US foreign policy based on these ideals."

The charge of "self-hating Jew" finds its counterpart in the particularly venomous aggression the lobby unleashes on Palestinian faculty and students, as well as on Middle Eastern and Muslim faculty and students more generally. As Islamophobia escalates in the United States and around the world, the lobby's aggression intensifies the already existing climate of hostility against Muslims and Middle Easterners. Naturally, this aggression mirrors the Israeli government's treatment of scholars and students in Palestine itself.

While this book focuses on testimonies of academics from US universities, the forces that operate domestically to silence and punish supporters of justice for Palestinians act in concert with the forces that deny the most basic elements of academic freedom to Palestinians in Palestine. Israeli movement restrictions impede and delay the ability of Palestinian professors and students in the OPT to reach their schools and universities. Checkpoint traffic and random stops often force academics and students to miss class or exam sessions and corrode the integrity of their overall education. Israel also denies them the right to travel to universities abroad; such practices led the Obama administration, for example, to cancel in 2012 a program to provide scholarships for Gazan students to study in West Bank universities, which may be the only places that offer certain careers. As well, the Israeli military routinely raids universities, harassing and arresting faculty and students. Palestinians in East Jerusalem, occupied since 1967, suffer massive disparities in the allocation of educational resources as compared to their non-Palestinian counterparts in West Jerusalem. Palestinian citizens of Israel face such structural disparities as under-funding of schools in predominantly Palestinian areas and the refusal to offer courses or even textbooks in Arabic, as well as explicit racial discrimination; Palestinian students, for example, are prohibited from publicly expressing their political opinions and are denied housing by bigoted landlords.[22]

The Academic and Cultural Boycott of Israel and *Lobby* Tactics on Campus

In 2004 the International Court of Justice (ICJ) issued a historic advisory opinion on the illegality of Israel's Wall in the OPT, which has become known as the Apartheid Wall. The Wall is twice as high as the Berlin Wall. It runs for some 700 miles through Palestinian territory, with watchtowers, electric fences, fortified checkpoints, cameras, trenches, sensors, and military patrols. It effectively locks Palestinians into military zones from which they cannot leave and turns the West Bank into a giant open-air prison. In 2005, in the wake of the ICJ advisory ruling, Palestinian civil society organizations, under the banner of the Palestinian BDS National Committee (BNC) – in which BDS stands for Boycott, Divestment, Sanctions – called on people around the world to launch boycotts, implement divestment initiatives, and demand sanctions against Israel until Palestinian rights, including that of self-determination, are recognized in full compliance with international law. The Palestinian BNC explicitly took as its inspiration the similar movement for boycott, divestment, and sanctions against South Africa, which was critical in bringing about the fall of apartheid in that country.

The Palestine campaign, known as the BDS movement, has taken off around the world. Hundreds, perhaps thousands, of trade unions, churches, faith-based and social justice organizations, cultural associations, professional societies, and student groups have passed resolutions in support of BDS. Thousands of scholars, artists, academic and student associations have endorsed the academic and cultural Boycott of Israel, a subset of the BDS movement among academics and cultural workers.[23] In the United States, some of the many endorsers include: the American Studies Association, the American Anthropological Association, the Association for Asian American Studies, the Association for Humanist Sociology, the National Association of Chicana and Chicano Studies, the Native American and Indigenous Studies Association, the Middle East Studies Association, the National Women's Studies Association, and both the undergraduate and the graduate student associations at the University of California (our own home university) along with dozens of other student associations on US campuses across the country.

The worldwide upsurge of support for BDS has taken defenders of Israeli apartheid by surprise. In the United States, Israel advocacy organizations have invested enormous resources and political capital in an effort to counter this worldwide solidarity movement for justice for Palestine. For instance, Sheldon Adelson, the Las Vegas-based multi-billionaire casino magnate and owner of the Israeli newspaper *Israel Ha Yom*, held a secret summit in June 2015 that raised some $50 million to fight the BDS movement. According to press reports, the meeting brought in representatives from some 50 Jewish organizations who made fund-raising pitches to wealthy donors. Adelson said the funds raised were to go to operations on US university campuses to fight the BDS movement and to "researchers" who would supply information about groups on campuses critical of Israel and recommend possible legal avenues to block their activities.[24] State and local governments, and even the federal government, have attempted to criminalize support for the BDS. Repression by lobby organizations appears to be targeting students and scholars in particular because college and university campuses have become the epicenter of this burgeoning movement in solidarity with Palestinians and in support of the BDS. According to the report *The Palestine Exception to Free Speech* (see above), the Center for Constitutional Rights and Palestine Legal responded in 2014 alone to over 200 incidents of censorship and repression against individuals and groups on US campuses advocating Palestinian rights. "These numbers understate the phenomenon, as many advocates who are unaware of their rights or afraid of attracting further scrutiny stay silent and do not report incidents of suppression," the report stated. "The overwhelming majority of these incidents ... targeted students and scholars, a reaction to the increasingly central role universities play in the movement for Palestinian rights."[25]

The report went on to document the tactics employed by the *Israel lobby* to suppress support for Palestinian rights. These include: false and inflammatory accusations against students and faculty of anti-Semitism and support for terrorism; official denunciation against advocates in response to outside lobby groups; bureaucratic barriers imposed by university officials to hamper student organizing; cancellation and alteration of academic and cultural events; administrative sanctions against students and faculty members; threats to academic freedom; lawsuits, legal threats, and legislation; and criminal investigations and prosecutions.

The testimonies collected in this book illustrate how the Israel lobby and their supporters – or university administrators who have been cowed by the lobby – employ all these tactics against faculty members and students. We open the selection with an article by Professors David Goldberg and Saree Makdisi of the University of California on the chillingly cynical, corrupt, and repressive nature of the tactics deployed against campus critics by Israel lobby organizations. What then follows are 14 testimonials by individual faculty members and student organizations from campuses across the United States. We hope here to capture, in the way that only a first-person testimonial can, the breadth and depth of the censorship, slander harassment, and repression meted out to defenders of Palestinian rights as well as the tenacious resistance against intimidation. However, we can only include here a *small portion* of the many hundreds of stories in this drama. It should be noted, as well, that we two editors are solely responsible for the content of this Introduction.

Finally, the phrase that we chose for our title, "We will not be silenced," has multiple significances. It is not uncommon to see clothing emblazoned with a variant of this phrase, "we will not be silent," for sale to activists in Palestine and also in the United States. The phrase has enjoyed a recent resurgence after it was printed on t-shirts, in English, Arabic, and Spanish, by the anti-war organization, Critical Voice. The t-shirts became very popular after Palestinian-Iraqi blogger Raed Jarrar was prevented from boarding a JetBlue flight because he was wearing the same t-shirt, with the phrase written in Arabic. The phrase carries with it a bittersweet message that our ideas and beliefs in freedom and justice are stronger than all of the military, monetary, cultural, and political forces that attempt to alienate, slander, punish, and crush any opposition to injustice. The history of this phrase dates back to its popularization, in the early 1940s, by the White Rose – a non-violent movement of students and their professor, who were dedicated to resisting the Nazis in Germany. Much like today's anti-Zionist intellectuals, the White Rose movement opposed militarism, totalitarianism, and oppression, and they used the written word as their primary "weapon." And much like today's anti-Zionist intellectuals, they were hunted and attacked for wielding such powerful and thus dangerous ideas of freedom. In selecting this phrase, and the powerful history it invokes, for our title, we mean to locate our book and the voices it presents within a seasoned tradition of speaking truth to power and resisting craven attempts to suppress ideas that undermine oppressive regimes and oppose injustice everywhere in the world. Like the White Rose movement, we will not be silent; without justice for everyone, "we will not leave you in peace!"

Notes

1. Among these are former US Congressman Paul Findley's best-seller, *They Dare to Speak Out: People and Institutions Confront Israel's Lobby* (Chicago: Chicago Review Press, 2003, third edition); James Petras, *The Power of Israel in the United States* (Atlanta: Clarity Press, 2006); Alison Weir, *Against Our Better Judgment: The Hidden History of How the US Was Used to Create Israel* (Louisville, KY: CreateSpace, 2014); Grant S. Smith, *Big Israel: How Israel's Lobby Moves America* (Washington, DC: Institute for Research: Middle Eastern Policy, 2016).

2. John J. Mearsheimer and Stephen M. Walt, *The Israel Lobby and US Foreign Policy* (New York: Farrar, Straus, and Giroux, 2007), pp. 9, 16.

3. See, for example, discussion in Gal Beckerman, "Mearsheimer and Walt are Ready for their Closeup," *Forward*, February 28, 2013, http://forward.com/opinion/172014/walt-and-mearsheimer-are-ready-for-their-close-up/. All websites last accessed December 15, 2015.

4. The full report can be accessed at https://ccrjustice.org/the-palestine-exception. The home page of the Center for Constitutional Rights is https://ccrjustice.org/. That of Palestine Legal is http://palestinelegal.org/.

5. The full report can be accessed at https://jewishvoiceforpeace.org/stifling-dissent/.

6. See, for example, Piya Chatterjee and Sunaina Maira (eds.), *The Imperial University: Academic Repression and Scholarly Dissent* (Minneapolis: University of Minnesota Press, 2014); Beshara Doumani (ed.), *Academic Freedom After September* 11 (New York: Zone Books, 2006). In 2015, Steven Salaita, who in a high-profile case lost his appointment at the University of Illinois as a result of his criticism of Israeli repression against Palestinians, published a detailed account of his own experience, *Uncivil Rights: Palestine and the Limits of Academic Freedom* (Chicago: Haymarket, 2015). Salaita has contributed a chapter to the present anthology.

7. These studies number in the hundreds and cannot be listed here. For those interested in an eye-opening and accessible account of the occupation, see Saree Makdisi, *Palestine Inside Out: An Everyday Occupation*, with a foreword by Alice Walker (New York: W.W. Norton, 2008).

8. Normal G. Finkelstein, *Image and Reality of the Israel-Palestine Conflict* (London: Verso, 2003, second edition), see in particular chapter one, "Zionist Orientations: The Theory and Practice of Jewish Nationalism."

9. To which, by the way, then-British colonial minister Joseph Chamberlain agreed to offer Zionism a colony anywhere "in the English possessions where there were no white people as of yet." As quoted in Abdullah Schleifer, *The Fall of Jerusalem* (New York: Monthly Review Press, 1972), p. 23.

10. Among the many studies, see the eminently readable and eye-opening account by one of Israel's foremost historians, Ilan Pappé, *The Ethnic Cleansing of Palestine* (London: Oneworld Publications, 2007, second edition).

11. See the Council's web page at www.hsrc.ac.za/en/media-briefs/democracy-goverance-and-service-delivery/report-israel-practicing-apartheid-in-palestinian-territories. The pdf of the full report is available at www.alhaq.org/attachments/article/236/Occupation_Colonialism_Apartheid-FullStudy.pdf.

12. As cited in Makdisi, *Palestine Inside Out*, p. 12.

13. Although we cannot go into detail here, there is another layer of racism and discrimination in Israel, against immigrants from countries in the Global South, such as from Ethiopia or the Philippines, and against the generally darker-skinned Jews who are not white or of European descent, this latter know as Ashkenazi Jews.

14. Makdisi, *Palestine Inside Out*, p. 145. The Jewish National Fund, a quasi-governmental agency, has argued in justifying its discrimination against Palestinians: "the distinction between Jews and non-Jews that is the basis of the Zionist vision [is] in complete accord with the founding principles of Israel as a Jewish state" (as cited by Makdisi, p. 284). Makdisi states: "Israel can either be a Jewish state, or it can be a state of equal citizens, Jewish and non-Jewish. It is literally impossible for it to be both. Israelis therefore face a choice: they can go on insisting that Jews ought to have rights that non-Jews are denied, or they can relinquish the privileges of Jews and allow Israel to become a state of all its citizens" (p. 284).

15. Norman G. Finkelstein, *The Holocaust Industry* (London: Verso Press, 2003, second edition).

16. See State Department web page www.state.gov/j/drl/rls/fs/2010/122352.htm.

17. *Stifling Dissent*, p. 2.

18. Jeremy M. Sharp, Congressional Research Service Report to Congress, *US Foreign Aid to Israel*, June 10, 2015.

19. Mearsheimer and Walt, *The Israel Lobby*, pp. 26–7.

20. See, for instance, Stephen Graham, "Laboratories of War: Surveillance and US-Israeli Collaboration in War and Security," in Elia Zureik (ed.), *Surveillance and Control in Israel/Palestine: Population, Territory, Power* (New York: Routledge, 2011), pp. 133–52; and J. Cook, "Israel's Booming Secretive Arms Trade," *Aljazeera*, August 16, 2013, at www.aljazeera.com/indepth/features/2013/08/201381410565517125.html.

21. See Mearsheimer and Walt, *The Israel Lobby*, p. 37, and see chapter two, "The Great Benefactor" for details on myriad forms of US support for Israel.

22. This is an extremely limited snapshot of the many ways that Israeli policies and practices deny Palestinians academic freedom, not to mention the internationally guaranteed human right to education. See, for example, the Institute for Middle East Understanding's report, *Israeli Violations of Academic Freedom & Access to Education* (February 6, 2014), http://imeu. org/article/israeli-violations-of-palestinian-academic-freedom-access-to-education.

23. For more details, see the official BDS website, http://bdsmovement.net/ bdsintro. With regard specifically to the call for an academic boycott, the website explains: "In calling for this institutional boycott, academic boycott is a powerful, yet non-violent, tactic through which scholars can exert political and moral pressure on Israel to change its policies towards the Palestinians. The PACBI Guidelines for the International Academic Boycott of Israel are quite clear in that sense. [The BDS movement] rejects on principle boycotts of individuals based on their identity (such as citizenship, race, gender, or religion) or opinion [unless] an individual is representing the state of Israel or a complicit Israeli institution. Mere affiliation of Israeli scholars to an Israeli academic institution is therefore not grounds for applying the boycott. The boycott neither targets individuals nor academic freedom. It does target institutions, and individuals who act in official capacity, that are complicit in the occupation and oppression of Palestinians in Israel and in the Occupied Territories. Israeli academic institutions have intimate connections with the military, security, and political establishments in Israel. More than that, they have actively contributed to strengthen Israel's domination. In calling for this institutional boycott, academic boycott is a powerful, yet non-violent, tactic through which scholars can exert political and moral pressure on Israel to change its policies toward the Palestinians."

24. Nathan Guttman, "Secret Sheldon Adelson Summit Raises Up to $50M for Strident Anti-BDS Push," *Forward.com*, June 9, 2015, http://forward.com/news/israel/309676/secret-sheldon-adelson-summit-raises-up-to-50m-for-strident-anti-bds-push/.

25. Ibid., p. 5.

1

The Trial of Israel's Campus Critics

David Theo Goldberg and Saree Makdisi

Editors' note: We open the collection of testimonials with the following article, written by David Goldberg, Professor of Comparative Literature and Criminology, Law and Society at the University of California-Irvine, and Saree Makdisi, Professor of English and Comparative Literature at the University of California-Los Angeles. The article was originally published in the September/October 2009 edition of *Tikkun* magazine. In it, Goldberg and Makdisi document and expose the inner working of the Israel lobby on US college and university campuses through the creation by leading lobby organizations of an "Israel on Campus Coalition." The tactics employed by this Coalition, they show, "plumb the depths of dishonor and indecency and include character assassination, selective misquotation, the willful distortion of the record, the fabrication of falsehoods, and an utter disregard for the truth."

The Israeli-Palestinian conflict remains one of the most visible political issues on campuses around the nation. A rising level of concern about the continuing Israeli occupation of Palestinian territory (now in its fifth decade), as well as the precarious position of Israel's beleaguered Palestinian minority, have been countered by increasingly strident, even furious, attempts to silence or stifle criticism of Israeli policy on American college campuses.

Tensions have been heightened especially in the wake of Israel's January 2009 re-invasion of Gaza, the consequent mobilization of protest, and the growing campaign for boycott, divestment, and sanctions. As the tide of public opinion in the United States and around the world continues to turn against Israel's policies of occupation and repression, the response to criticisms of Israeli policy on campus are growing uglier. Off-campus organizations – many tied to the most assertive Israeli lobby in Washington – are playing a growing role in on-campus debates. Campus activities, as a result, have been wired directly into national politics, and have become more contentious and infinitely more bitter. And the situation is likely to continue to get worse as Israel's image continues to deteriorate and as its defenders grow more anxious and resort to ever more desperate measures to turn things around.

It is an extraordinary fact that no fewer than thirty-three distinct organizations – including AIPAC [American Israeli Public Affairs Committee], the Zionist Organization of America, the American Jewish Congress, and the Jewish National Fund – are gathered together today as members or affiliates of the Israel on Campus Coalition. The coalition is an overwhelmingly powerful presence on American college campuses for which there is simply no equivalent on the Palestinian or Arab side. Its self-proclaimed mission is not merely to monitor our colleges and universities. That, after all, is the commitment of Campus Watch, which was started by pro-Israel activists in 2002. It is, rather (and in its own words), to generate "a pro-active, pro-Israel agenda on campus." There is, accordingly, disproportionate and unbalanced intervention on campuses across the country by a coalition of well-funded organizations, who have no time for – and even less interest in – the niceties of intellectual exchange and academic process. Insinuation, accusation, and defamation have become the weapons of first resort to respond to argument and criticism directed at Israeli policies. As far as these outside pressure groups (and their campus representatives) are concerned, the intellectual and academic price that the scholarly community pays as a result of this kind of intervention amounts to little more than collateral damage.

We have become increasingly concerned at the ways in which scholarly critics of Israeli policy have been cavalierly and maliciously misrepresented, mostly through ad hominem attacks on their characters, reputations, and careers. We are troubled also by the ways in which academic programs – most notably Middle East Studies programs at major universities – are being attacked as bastions of irresponsible radicalism and anti-American activity. Our concern has been heightened especially in view of the outside pressure being brought to bear on university administrations, some of which seem to have yielded to coercion, even while trying to "balance" calls for responsibility with commitments to academic freedom. Some senior university administrators seem willing to take for granted the misrepresentations and fabrications by boisterous supporters of Israel, and have done so merely on the strident assertion of those making these claims. This is a curious position to take in the name of "balance," a notion about which we will have more to say in a moment.

These are not altogether new developments, of course, as the dire threat to a number of academic careers and institutional programs in recent years, particularly in Middle East studies, will attest. Scholars whose work is critical of Israeli policies have been denied jobs, denied tenure (or faced a threat to their prospects for tenure), and in general have had their lives made difficult – not because of academic criteria, but because of political interference from extra-academic forces. Outside political intervention by those who advocate unflinching support for Israel have plunged one American program or campus after another into crisis. The University of California is only the latest in a string of such campuses,[1] following incidents at Columbia University, Barnard College, Yale University, Wayne State University, and DePaul University.

Trumped-up Furor at UCLA

For several weeks this spring, considerable pressure was brought to bear on UCLA and especially on its Center for Near Eastern Studies. As the crisis came to a head, Stanley Kurtz, in a *National Review Online* article, predicted that UCLA's Center was on the way to becoming today's *bête noir* of the academy, just as Columbia's Middle East Studies program had been for Israel's strident supporters a few years ago. Kurtz is one of a trio (Martin Kramer, a senior faculty member at Tel Aviv University, and Daniel Pipes round out the group, and David Horowitz is a kind of associate) who repeatedly chide and harry academic scholars for their criticisms of Israeli policy.

It is crucial to note that Kurtz's prediction was fueled by completely falsified accounts of an event the UCLA Center sponsored in 2009, by ongoing attacks on faculty members who have spoken critically of Israeli policy, and by thoroughly misleading characterizations of them intended at the very least to make others think twice before speaking out.

In January 2009, UCLA's Center for Near Eastern Studies hosted "Human Rights and Gaza," a panel discussion on campus to address the situation in Gaza in the context of human rights and international humanitarian law. One of us attended as an audience member; the other spoke on the panel, alongside professors Richard Falk, Lisa Hajjar, Gabriel Piterberg, and Susan Slymovics (as chair). Each of the panelists had published extensively on this topic, and Richard Falk was, of course, the UN Special Rapporteur on Human Rights in the occupied Palestinian territories, and hence a global authority on this matter.

The panel discussion was only one of three events on Gaza that took place at UCLA around the same time. The other two, sponsored by the UCLA Israel Studies program, were explicitly intended to bring Israeli perspectives, including that of the Israeli Consul in Los Angeles, to campus, and to justify the bombardment of Gaza. "Human Rights and Gaza," by contrast, was not designed to present a Palestinian perspective (indeed, three of the five participants were Jewish, and one an Israeli); rather, it was meant to restore a sense of intellectual balance and historical context, by offering, in an academic format, a space in which established scholars could address the growing concerns (on campus and more broadly) about the human rights of a population under devastating attack by the Israeli military. That the panel was concerned with violations of human rights and international humanitarian law perhaps explains why no advocate of those violations was added to the panel (after all, advocates of legal and human rights violations are not often forthcoming).

The talks by the four speakers were largely uneventful, being interrupted by pro-Israeli jeers just once and briefly. The question and discussion period grew a bit more heated and contentious. But it was hardly uncivil, save for a mostly irrelevant rant read by an insistent member of the Socialist Workers Party who refused to stop even when she was asked to by the chair, and by a couple of Israeli supporters becoming heated. This provoked one ironic and misinterpreted response from one of the panelists to a comment from the floor about the murderous nature of all Arabs (for which the panelist but not the audience member offered an apology).

Now if you read the characterizations of this event published in various outlets – from the *Jewish Journal of Los Angeles* to the *National Review*, the *Wall Street Journal*, and the *Los Angeles Times* – you would take away a very different view of things. Repeated descriptions of the event *by those who admit that they did not attend it* have characterized the proceedings as akin to a "beer hall political rally" and an anti-Semitic lynch mob, and have gone so far – by the time Stanley Kurtz joined the chorus – as to charge the panel, apparently working on behalf of Hamas, as having led an increasingly frenzied crowd in chants of "F-ck Israel" and "Zionism is Nazism."

Plain Facts: What Actually Took Place at UCLA

Both of us were present throughout the entire event, we have listened in the wake of these absurd accusations to the publicly available podcasts of the talks, and we have checked with others present. Nothing could be further from the truth.

A testament to the civility of the evening was made evident by the appearance of a campus policeman beside the front stage as discussion grew a little heated. His very presence seemed to cool tempers, and he exchanged smiles and greetings with some audience members. While there was applause at various points, laughter at others – how different from most academic panels – at no time was there chanting or invective hurled by the audience (that either of us, or anyone we talked to, witnessed) or by panelists at Israel or at any other state. No panelist called for or led the audience to chant or collectively to chastise Israel. In fact, the most uncomfortable expression of the evening was heard repeatedly at the front stage after the event had ended. A well-known Israeli provocateur from the UCLA neighborhood (neither a student nor a faculty member), who had once been involved in a scuffle with the UCLA campus rabbi (of all people), was marching up and down hissing wildly beneath her breath at one of the speakers on the panel, calling him out by first name and insisting in a tone laced with invective that he should be ashamed of himself.

How, then, have hearsay, exaggeration, and sheer fabrication managed to replace a sturdy, robust account of the event based on actual facts? Two accounts of the panel were published shortly after it took place.

The first was by a professional journalist writing for *UCLA Today*, the campus newspaper of record, on January 22. It characterized the forum as "a well-attended public event," and went on to summarize the main arguments of the papers. It made no mention of jeers, chants, or other untoward behavior (because there were none). It is remarkable that in all the discussion of the panel that has subsequently taken place, there are, as far as we can tell, only two links to this article on the entire internet.

How the Internet Loves Malicious Fictions

The second article, which has proliferated widely through the enchantment of the internet, was written by the education/research director of Stand With Us (one of the most vociferous components of the Israel on Campus Coalition), who sometimes identifies herself as a member of the faculty of UC Irvine (which in fact she is not). Under the headline, "Reviving 1920s Munich Beer Halls at UCLA," she presents an incoherent and rambling account of the talks that fails to convey accurately any of what was actually said (which can be easily verified by comparing her article to the podcasts of the talks at www.international.ucla.edu/cnes/podcasts). She also liberally adds unsupported and indeed unsupportable assertions and wild exaggerations into the mix (e.g., saying that the event amounted to "an academic lynching of Israel," claiming that the speakers "expressed hope that Israel would lose against Hamas," and comparing the talks by four academically distinguished and well-published scholars to "the anti-Semitic rabble rousing of 1920s Munich beer halls").

These baseless assertions (even a quick listen to the podcasts will confirm that that is what they are) have gone on to frame and color the way in which the event has been represented and characterized in almost all of the subsequent discussions. Not only has most of the subsequent discussion been based on this one article, no one relying on it has pointed out its provenance or the inherently unreliable testimony of the author, or the gap between the article and the actual talks as embodied in the live recordings publicly available to anyone in the podcasts. Thus, subsequent discussions – by, it bears repeating, *people who admit that they were not actually at the event* – have followed the pattern taken by the children's game, "telephone." A message is passed on from person to person until, having gone around the room, it bears only a passing resemblance to the original utterance. Only in this case not only does the original message (itself already faulty, given the source) deteriorate, but further layers of exaggeration and hyperbole are added to it at each pass.

Pearls of Misinformation

Judea Pearl, a professor of computer science at UCLA and one of Israel's most ardent defenders in Los Angeles, helped to ratchet up the misrepresentations of the event. Pearl began writing about the Gaza panel first in the *Wall Street Journal* (February 3, 2009), then in another article in the *Jewish Journal of Los Angeles* (February 18, 2009), and then in yet another piece, in the *Los Angeles Times*. In his first piece he asserts without evidence or justification that the event was essentially "a Hamas recruiting rally" intended – *by Hamas*, the reader could be led to believe – to score "another inroad into Western minds." By the time he published the piece in the *Jewish Journal*, Pearl had embellished his account further, adding the utterly fictitious allegation that the panelists "led the excited audience into chanting 'Zionism is Nazism,' 'F-ck, f-ck Israel,' in the best tradition of rhino liturgy."

What is most interesting about Pearl's many accounts of the event, however, is not their hyperbolic nature, but rather the fact that *he was not at the event which he has described in such lurid and varying terms in three different published accounts*. His source (as he acknowledges in one of his articles, though not the others) is the Stand With Us article. Later, referring back in seamless circularity to this series of articles sealing itself from the truth, another writer in the *Jewish Journal* (Tom Tugend, published on February 25, 2009) comes to refer to the event as "the by now notorious UCLA symposium." Character assassination by self-referencing fabrication!

The mischaracterizations and fabrications of Pearl's account, themselves building on the unsteady foundation provided by those in the Stand With Us piece, have been repeated ad nauseam by others as the gospel truth. For example, although it is highly unusual – if not altogether unheard of – for a university president to criticize his own faculty for expressing their views in an academic setting, in public comments at a Los Angeles synagogue the president of the University of California, Mark Yudof, did just that, chastising the scholars participating in the Center for Near Eastern Studies panel, according to what he had learned of it from Pearl's misrepresentation of the event. Stanley Kurtz's main "evidence" for his characterization of the panel in the *National Review Online* article also comes from Pearl. In short, the fabrications have become the public record of note, the "truth" of the matter.

A Wider Pattern: Barnard College, UC Santa Barbara

This broader logic, too, follows a disturbing pattern. In a campaign (initiated by an angry alumna living in a Jewish settlement in the West

Bank) against a tenure case at Barnard College two years ago, professor Nadia Abu el-Haj was accused of shoddy scholarship by those who had never read her work. She was falsely charged with writing about Israeli archaeology while knowing no Hebrew, and of falsifying the history of archaeology to anchor an argument about Palestinians' historical claim to the Holy Land (she makes no such argument). Analogous mischaracterizations have been made about the scholarship of other vocal critics of Israel's policies and actions toward Palestinians, equally based on false, misleading, or nonexistent evidence – or sheer fancy. Public fabrications of other events, including letters of complaint to chancellors, some at sister-UC campuses, have stuffed false, damaging, and demeaning language into the mouths of the critics of Israeli policy; twisted arguments and intentions to something altogether unrecognizable; and sometimes garbled, while refusing to discuss in any way, the substance of the criticisms expressed. Like a growing list of others, we [the authors of this chapter] have both repeatedly been subjected to "the treatment."

The most recent episode of this kind of distortion involves Professor William Robinson of the Sociology Department at UC Santa Barbara. During the Israeli bombardment of Gaza in January 2009, Robinson forwarded to his class on "Sociology of Globalization" material that drew comparisons between the Nazi assault on the Warsaw Ghetto and the Israeli assault on Gaza. Two Jewish students in the class, after apparently talking with the Anti-Defamation League, filed a complaint against Robinson for "violating the Faculty Code of Conduct" and dropped the class. It turns out that Abraham Foxman, director of the Anti-Defamation League, met (under misleading pretexts) with senior UC Santa Barbara administrators and began to pressure them to investigate and censure Robinson. Foxman also apparently threatened to encourage Jewish donors to the university to withdraw their financial support unless Robinson was censured. Stand With Us – the same outfit that played such a damaging role in the UCLA incident – likewise became actively involved, organizing a massive letter writing campaign and threatening to bring pressure to bear to cut off donations to the campus.

The most troubling aspect of this case is not that the Anti-Defamation League made the accusation or that Stand With Us jumped into the fray so eagerly, but rather that the UC Santa Barbara administration took the accusation seriously, and apparently succumbed to outside political pressure to have Professor Robinson investigated (http://sb4af.

wordpress.com). Evidence mounted of numerous violations of university procedures in the conduct of the investigation. This included, most disturbingly, key committee members (themselves known supporters of Israeli policy) discussing the case privately with Foxman who, it should be emphasized, had no standing to be involved in the investigation at all.

And yet the investigation apparently pressed on, in the face of mounting faculty, student, and external criticism of the university's violations of academic freedom and of its own investigative policies. It was only in mid-June 2009, six months after the case was initiated, that Professor Robinson received notice that all charges against him were being dropped. No reason was cited, but the remarkable mobilization of students and faculty against the investigation – culminating in an uncontested UC Santa Barbara Academic Senate vote to investigate the administration's own mishandling of the entire affair – no doubt played a key role.

Political Effects: The Case of Charles Freeman

Perhaps because many of the same organizations, like the Anti-Defamation League, are involved in both cases (via the Israel on Campus Coalition), the situation in the academy has now dovetailed with that outside the academy, and in the world of actual, hard politics centered on Washington. In the recent speech in which he explained his sudden withdrawal from the chairmanship of the National Intelligence Council, for example, Ambassador Charles Freeman said, "It is apparent that we Americans cannot any longer conduct a serious public discussion or exercise independent judgment about matters of great importance to our country as well as to our allies and friends." In a message published March 10, 2009, on Foreignpolicy.com, Freeman blamed this situation, and his own departure from public life amid a swirl of unfounded allegations, mischaracterizations, distortions, and fabrications, on the dominant elements within the Israeli lobby in Washington.

The tactics of the Israel lobby plumb the depths of dishonor and indecency and include character assassination, selective misquotation, the willful distortion of the record, the fabrication of falsehoods, and an utter disregard for the truth. The aim of this lobby is control of the policy process through the exercise of a veto over the appointment of people who dispute the wisdom of its views, the substitution of political correctness for analysis, and the exclusion of any and all options for decision by Americans and our government other than those that it favors.

We should all find alarming that what is taking place in the academy today is an extension of what takes place on Capitol Hill and in the corridors of (real) power. What is at stake is the process of representation, which shapes memory, disposition, and arguably – in the long run at any rate – the policy process itself. Many of the same tactics are being used in both situations; and they share the aim to monopolize legitimacy by tarnishing all criticism and questioning it as inherently illegitimate and malevolent.

The Most Assertive Israeli Lobby: Dishonorable Tactics, Avoidance of Debate

It is worth pointing out that those who resort to the sorts of unbridled and unfounded charges exemplified by the attacks on the UCLA Gaza panel or the Robinson affair at UC Santa Barbara rarely if ever actually engage the arguments of Israel's critics. Counter-arguments are hardly ever mounted, counter-evidence almost never thought necessary. The rhetoric of response is predictable, and it takes the shape of the familiar litany of exhausted assertions that are inevitably recited *en bloc*, without any reference to what is actually being said; what evidence is being offered; what reasons, arguments, facts, figures, and citations are being assembled.

Thus any criticism of Israel and Zionism is treated as criticism of Jews (even if made by Jews, who are then obviously self-hating), and therefore anti-Semitic or worse, as Judea Pearl asserts in his piece in the *Los Angeles Times* of March 15, 2009. Israel is merely protecting the security of its people; any state under rocket attack would do the same. Hamas, like Hezbollah, is a terrorist organization and Israel, like the United States, has the right to protect itself by all means necessary (a right that in such accounts the Palestinians never seem to possess). And it's not fair – or, better yet, it's inherently anti-Semitic – to single out Israel for criticism when there are places in the world that are far less democratic and far more violent toward their residents than Israel (Darfur, the cause célèbre of many pro-Israeli organizations, is often trotted out as an example, though usually without it being noted that the United States does not support, arm, and subsidize the Sudanese government or give its illegal actions political cover in the UN Security Council, let alone that there is no one in the United States – much less dozens of well-funded organizations and an armada of campus outfits – actively condoning the atrocities in Darfur).

The Pro-Israel Propaganda Handbook

It is not surprising, then, given its provenance, that the Stand With Us report on "Gaza and Human Rights" expresses what pro-Israel campus activists refer to using the Hebrew word "hasbara." This means, essentially if not literally, "propaganda." The *Hasbara Handbook: Promoting Israel on Campus*, which is distributed to campus activists by organizations like Stand With Us (e.g., click "Guides for Activists" on www.middle-east-info.org), explains that it is often better to score points than to engage in actual arguments, and offers an explanation for how, in its own words, "to score points whilst avoiding debate." Point-scoring, the *Hasbara Handbook* explains, "works because most audience members fail to analyze what they hear. Rather, they register only a key few points, and form a vague 'impression' of whose argument was stronger." Part of the strategy is to recycle the same claims over and again, in as many settings as possible. "If people hear something often enough," the document points out, "they come to believe it."

The *Hasbara Handbook* offers several other propaganda devices, all of which can be seen vividly at play in the coverage of the UCLA Gaza panel and other similar events, including, again, the Robinson affair. "Creating negative connotations by name calling is done to try to get the audience to reject a person or idea on the basis of negative associations, *without allowing a real examination of that person or idea*," the handbook states with remarkable bluntness, in advocating that tactic. It also suggests using the opposite of name calling, to defend Israel by what it calls the deployment of "glittering generalities" (words like "freedom," "civilization," "democracy") to describe the country; manipulating the audience's fears ("listeners are too preoccupied by the threat of terrible things to think critically about the speaker's message"); and so on. The point of all this is not to use arguments backed by reason and evidence. It is, instead, to *manipulate* (the handbook's own term) an audience precisely in order *not* to examine arguments, *not* to think critically about what is being said. Which is a rather remarkable approach for a book intended for a university audience.

This is precisely, almost to the letter, the approach taken by most of the attacks on scholarly critics of Israeli policy. It matters little what is actually being discussed by critics; the familiar stock-in-trade responses will be brought to bear to terminate the discussion. Or a campaign to silence the critics will be promoted by making life uncomfortable for them or threatening the withdrawal of support for their institutions, or most extremely threatening their very careers, or their very employability (as happened with Norman Finkelstein at DePaul). The less successful the initial attempt to close things down, the louder the next round of condemnation, the more heated the invective, the more extreme the charges, the more gratuitous the escalation. Thus escalates the crescendo of attacks aimed at the UCLA panelists, which now basically has them taking orders directly from Hamas, and leading a chanting mob of anti Semites.

We have both been subjected to similar accusations, in person and in print, mangling what we mean, putting words in our mouths we neither uttered nor thought, meanly misquoting or decontextualizing or partially citing what we write. It matters not that we have repeatedly and publicly endorsed nonviolent forms of protest and counter-action to Israel's violence; that we believe in justice, law, and human rights; that we would have all the people in the promised land enjoy its promise rather than some suffer strangulation at the hands of the others.

Unbalanced Calls for "Balance" Undercut the Very Idea of the University

Why then can strident supporters of Israel repeatedly resort to these tactics and be taken so seriously without engaging – indeed, while altogether avoiding – actual debate? Critics of the critics of Israeli policy repeatedly call for "balance," assuming that every panel by their opponents – but not the ones they organize themselves – should have counter-voices. Of course, the fact that every one-sided panel may be countered by one equally one-sided on the other side suggests that campuses can achieve a broader semblance of balance in other ways, as UCLA Chancellor Gene Block rightly noted in response to attempts by Israel's supporters to silence Israel's critics. We don't hear too many calls for economics departments having to hire Marxist political economists, or (in the opposite political direction) biology departments having to hire intelligent designers, in the name of "balance." Not to worry, we are not attempting to open up new cans of worms! We mean only to point out how one-sided the calls in the case of Israel-Palestine are, how unbalanced in the name of balance. Indeed, how off-balance.

We certainly don't recall hearing from these quarters any condemnation of the one-sidedness of, say, Alan Dershowitz [retired Harvard law professor and a leading public defender of Israel]. Nor do we hear at a minimum any expression of concern by those so volubly condemning Hamas rockets fired at southern Israel for the devastation wrought by the Israeli bombardment of civilian men, women, and children taking shelter in schools and UN compounds during the recent assault on Gaza.

And when Benny Morris, Israel's most renowned revisionist historian, famously insists that if you have to kill or be killed, it would be better to kill, we hear no pro-Israeli voices objecting in the name of "balance" that these are hardly the only options. Posing the issues reductively and solely as ones of survival in terms of physical self-defense so skews the issues as to essentially end the possibility of any debate. But perhaps that's the very point of the claim (as the *Hasbara Handbook* points out).

When President Jimmy Carter was invited to speak by various campuses, including one of our own, after the publication of his book *Palestine: Peace Not Apartheid*, Alan Dershowitz insisted in the name of "balance" that he share the stage or follow the former president's appearance. No doubt Professor Dershowitz speaks to many groups on his own, pushing *his* one-sided position. We don't hear calls that his audiences have access to an immediate counter-view. If balance is required in public of a former US president, is it not also to be applied to a "one-sided" professor? And then what – every lecture on every issue on every campus is to be followed by a counter-lecture? The very idea is absurd. Likewise perhaps with public forums such as *National Review Online*. In his article, Stanley Kurtz makes a good deal of the lack of balance by public forums giving voice to Israel's critics. And yet he does so in a forum hardly known for publishing pro-Palestinian pieces. Be careful what you call for!

In *The Trial*, Kafka writes that "the charges are never made frivolously, and that the Court, once it has brought a charge against someone, is firmly convinced of the guilt of the accused and can be dislodged from that conviction only with the greatest difficulty." Israel's campus critics are accused without notice, condemned without evidence, convicted without recourse, and sentenced without representation. Israel's most vocal American proponents serve as policeman and accuser, judge and jury. In the end, those convicted are reduced to nothing more than shadow figures, straw persons set afire by the flaming terms of accusation.

Those undertaking to place off bounds all criticism of the Israeli state or military regarding treatment of Palestinians by automatically and offhandedly denouncing such criticism as anti-Semitic trivialize any legitimate charge of real anti-Semitism. This accusatory trivialization confronts such strident supporters with a quandary. They seek to de-exceptionalize Israel by insisting that critics do not equally condemn Sudan or China or North Korea for violations of human rights. And yet they exceptionalize the Israeli state by seeking to shield it from any criticism whatsoever. No good ever comes from a state rendered or rendering itself immune from criticism, as the instances cited by Israel's supporters prove without qualification.

True to our nature, however, academics as such should live to push ideas, to press difficult points, to debate the ins and outs. As Edward Said repeatedly pointed out, academics and intellectuals have a responsibility not just to speak in clearly articulated ways but also to air ideas even about difficult subjects, to venture where others might avoid going. The misrepresentations formulated by Israel's most vociferous supporters are designed to narrow not just what can be said about a subject but what subject matter can be raised at all. The misrepresentations, the implied silencing, and the insidious implications are not simply pernicious; they seem obviously designed to quash any criticism of Israeli policy. In short, such intervention has the effect of undercutting the very idea of the university.

Proposed Guidelines for Debating Israel/Palestine on Campus

Here, then, in the spirit of intellectual civility, are some guidelines that we believe will facilitate the discussion of Israel/Palestine on American college campuses. *These* are the criteria, we suggest, by which criticism – criticism of Israel *and* criticism of Israel's critics – should be assessed. We urge that when there are disagreements that interlocutors be judged by whether they:

- respond to arguments with counter-arguments, not ad hominem accusations;
- respond to evidence with counter-evidence, not mere assertions;
- focus on what is being said and on the extent to which what is being said is supported by evidence, instead of resorting to cries of "imbalance" and "one-sidedness";
- make every effort not to distort what someone else says: in particular, whether they reconstruct quotations out of context or quote only half-sentences;
- put words in other people's mouths, and try to portray someone who identifies herself as an advocate of peace and justice as in fact secretly – or is it obviously? – a monstrously racist advocate of violence;
- try to stifle dissent by threatening or jeopardizing the critic's career;
- discount the numbers of dead or injured or the innocence of the dead or injured among those regarded as "the enemy" while justifying the devastation produced by the action in question as "necessary" even if the effects were "unfortunate."

One other point. There have long been academic centers and teaching programs for Jewish Studies, as well as Middle Eastern, Near Eastern, Arab, and Islamic Studies. In the past, the best of those institutional formations have looked to engage – and to engage across personal and political divides, precisely – the complex relations marked by the segregating political conditions. More recently, as the separationist politics and their ideological rationalizations have hardened on the ground, academic programs have begun to mirror these isolating conditions. For instance, there have begun to emerge programs or research centers solely in Israel Studies, funded largely by private endowments, tending to ignore or lament or rationalize away the relation between conditions in Israel and those in the Occupied Territories. Such programs attempt to consider Israel as though it could be framed as an object of study in isolation from the Palestinians (who make up a fifth of its own population and half of the total population over which Israel rules) and the whole question of Palestine, to both of which Israel is in fact inexorably tied. Imagine trying to frame an American studies program today that consciously (or, worse, unconsciously) excludes any treatment of blacks or Hispanics.

Given the complex constitution of the region, accordingly, we consider it imperative that any teaching or research program about Israel-Palestine take seriously the complex and interacting ways that social, cultural, political, legal, and epistemological arrangements are deeply intertwined, that conditions of life and death for some turn relationally on those for others. This entails a different way of thinking not just about the region but also more about institutions of knowledge formation and their institutional arrangements than tends to be the dominant trend today.

To put off the table crucial counter-considerations is to unbalance consideration of the alternatives. A forum dominated by those who can shout loudest, have more access, have more resources, or feel more insulted is one-sided and, in the end, destructive. One-sided, self-regarding assertion is no exchange at all. In the final analysis it does no one any good, least of all the people suffering the consequences, on pretty much all sides of the divide.

We call, by contrast, for engaging the arguments, for respecting the right to say difficult things, countering without abuse, making criticisms and counter-criticisms without mischievous mischaracterization. Without *hasbara*. In calling for respectful exchange, for critical engagement, then, we are calling for respecting the positions taken by honest thinkers. In insisting on balance and recalibration, we are agreeing to balance in all the complexity, on all registers and dimensions. The lives at stake – all the lives – are owed nothing less.

Note

1. Editors' note: since the original publication of this article in 2009 there have been dozens of new cases, beyond the University of California, of highly publicized campaigns against academics, some of which are discussed in the testimonials in this anthology. The campaign against Professor Steven Salaita (Chapter 14) caused the University of Illinois Urbana-Champaign Chancellor Phyllis M. Wise to resign amidst public scandal over the corruption involved in his persecution, demonstrating the extent to which such campaigns can throw universities into crisis.

2

They Shoot Tenure, Don't They?: How I Crossed the Borders of Acceptable Academic Discourse on Holocaust Film and the Question of Palestine, and Never Came Back

Terri Ginsberg

Editors' note: Terri Ginsberg, a Jewish film studies professor, was forced to resign in 2008 from her post as curator of a Middle East film series, and then subsequently denied a tenure track position, at North Carolina State University, for having screened films critical of Israel. Professor Ginsberg subsequently brought a lawsuit against the University, but the North Carolina courts dismissed her charge of employment discrimination and violations of academic freedom. She appears to have since been blacklisted in the US academy, having applied between 2009 and 2012 to more than 150 jobs without receiving even one interview, despite her distinguished scholarship and eminent career record. Professor Ginsberg currently teaches at the American University in Cairo.

It all started in the early 1990s, when Ranjani Mazumdar suggested I write my dissertation on Holocaust film. Ranjani was an academic friend enrolled as was I at New York University, where we were both pursing doctorates in cinema studies. Prior to Ranjani's return to New York City from her native India in order to complete her graduate coursework, I had been preparing to write my dissertation on gay and lesbian avant-garde cinema. NYU seemed the perfect place at which to explore the topic. The Department of Cinema Studies had built its reputation around the study of the cinematic avant-gardes as celebrated famously by the formidable film critic Annette Michelson, one of the department's founders and, by the time of my enrollment, a longtime professor there, an intellectual patron of the historically important avant-garde film venue, Anthology Film Archives, and a fixture at the high cultural academic film/art journal, *October*, of which she was a chief editor. Michelson's published work on the great Soviet filmmakers Sergei Eisenstein and Dziga Vertov, among others, was renowned for its astute and perceptive integration of critical aesthetic philosophy with film theory.

At an earlier period Michelson had been drawn to Trotskyism, as were many art critics of her milieu caught up in the Abstract Expressionist movement and its various formalist offshoots often widely promoted by the Museum of Modern Art (MoMA) and funded covertly by the CIA and US State Department. Michelson, by some contrast to that anti-Communist tendency and its imperialist designs, which disingenuously upheld the impossible notion of structural neutrality as an ideal mode of resistance to the so-called excesses of both Western capitalism and Soviet socialism, developed, and was able to convey to her students, a profound, if often fraught, appreciation for the revolutionary materiality immanent to aesthetic occasioning. She thus came to influence many of us whose intellectual sensibilities were bound up with an affinity for the radical potentialities of cinematic form.

So when Ranjani suggested – insisted – that I change my dissertation topic from gay and lesbian avant-garde cinema to Holocaust film, I was initially taken aback at the prospect of alienating myself from the philosophical core of my training as a film theorist. True, European fascism, in particular German National Socialism, was a pervasive, at times central trope in my graduate writing. Ranjani had observed this phenomenon and was eager to help me locate a new dissertation topic after the department's then newest faculty member, representing probably the first "out" lesbian hire in the field of cinema studies, Chris Straayer, informed me she would not serve as my dissertation adviser on grounds of her disagreement with the leftist orientation of my proposed thesis, which was strongly informed by Marxism and Critical Theory and in that context aimed to critique the commercial cooptation of gay and lesbian aesthetic discourse and culture within the cinematic sphere.

Having read my developing scholarship, Ranjani did not believe that this proposed topic best represented the manifest "entry point" of my intellectual work, which in her view seemed instead to be engaged in a conceptual struggle to comprehend and interpret the latent fascism of capitalist socio-cultural relations as articulated to, and inscribed across, films regarding the Holocaust, the industrialized mass murder of millions of European and Asian people, a disproportionately large percentage of whom were Jews but which also victimized millions of others including hundreds of thousands of Nazism's political opponents, leftists in particular, as well as homosexuals, the mentally and physically disabled, Roma, Slavs, Soviet prisoners of war, and perceived social "misfits" and "undesirables" in veritable factories of death constructed and overseen by the Nazis. Ranjani's alternative vision for my project recognized and encouraged the possibility of a critical gay and lesbian perspective forming a layer or component of my dissertation, but in her view the political aesthetics of Holocaust film should best become the work's overriding focus.

My eventual dissertation adviser, William (Bill) G. Simon, then Chair of the department, welcomed this new topic with one caveat: I was not to share the work-in-progress with my prospective dissertation committee members until Bill gave me his approval. He did not give me an explanation, however, for this condition, which held even though one of those committee members was Robert Stam, whose partner, Mizrahi-Israeli Ella Shohat, an NYU PhD and now a full professor involved in program building at the NYU-Abu Dhabi campus, had written a dissertation advised by Stam at NYU that was later published to both critical acclaim and controversy for its groundbreaking focus on the racist politics of Israeli cinema. I should have known then that I was treading on thin ice with this topic, but I was in fact very naïve and did not realize just how much ire would be raised by my thesis, which was not simply an analysis of Holocaust cinematic representation but of the intellectual confinement of Holocaust film criticism – and the preponderant philosophical discourses on which it was based – to the problematics of representation and as such to the exclusion of political approaches that entailed sustained critique. In effect, I was concerned, in contrast to all other film scholars in this area, then as well as now, not with whether it is possible to recreate a credible semblance of holocaustal experience onscreen, ostensibly on account of the event's purportedly profound ontological and affective sublimity, but with the question of how critical obsession with that perceived sublimity has enabled Holocaust film scholars to ignore completely the question of Palestine.

Cinema studies was and is a field constructed upon the moving-image cooptation of the modernist avant-gardes in the context of the historical mainstreaming of Abstract Expressionism within the US art world. Throughout the field's institutional history, political aesthetics have been subordinated theoretically to formalist approaches emptied of much figurative and, by extension, social concern. The fact that I would stake my future academic career on the question not simply of whether the Holocaust may be represented adequately on film but of whether the very question of film's adequation to the "real" – the medium's capacity for verisimilitude – doesn't in fact serve to deflect the intellectually and politically far more interesting question of how Holocaust representation of any kind has been enjoined to dissimulate what Norman Finkelstein has called "the abuse of anti-Semitism" in the interests of facilitating Western (neo)colonial expansion in the Middle East and beyond, and by extension of erasing the question of why Holocaust film became so prolific – in the years leading up to and preceding the end of the Cold War – after several decades of relative cinematic silence regarding that horrific event; the fact that I would take this additional step, as it were, to try to resituate perspective on what I strongly believe is a matter fundamental to the sustained intellectual development of my field, in fact ran counter to the field's overriding apolitical character and thus presented itself as counter-intuitive to both the commonsense and career-mindedness not only of contemporary academia but of American culture in general.

* * *

When I was a very small child I used to sit awake at night in my bed lulling myself, through piqued attention to various odd sounds coming from outside and perhaps emanating from the settling foundations of our house, into a semi-conscious state of incessant rumination about mortality and the meaning of life. I was almost obsessively intrigued with the fact that so many things, for lack of a better description, lay beyond me. My father was a violinist who had insisted upon a musical education for me which evolved into an arts focus with theater at its center. Despite this performance background and eventual undergraduate degree in acting I could not shake my intellectual compulsions, and upon graduating from Syracuse University, where I'd been fortunate enough to study with radical leftist and anti-racist professors like Donald Morton, Mas'ud Zavarzadeh, and Leonard Dryansky, with feminist sociologist Judith Long(-Laws), and with numerous Marxist cultural workers during a study abroad in London, I found myself in New York City enrolling out of curiosity in cinema studies and screenwriting classes at NYU rather than auditioning for Broadway plays as originally planned. In little time I formed an opinion that cinema studies offered the perfect means by which to combine the apparently opposing elements of my peculiar range of interests, and that academia in general was ideally suited to their mutual articulation.

Upon receipt of my doctorate eleven years later I held a series of short-lived teaching positions at several institutions along the East Coast of the United States. Most of them were low-paying and lacking in benefits. Too often I was hired on the unspoken basis of my dissertation topic misrecognized by faculty search committees as Zionist. Neglecting to read my dissertation or published excerpts led to rude awakenings once I would arrive on campus and begin to express my views in the classroom and in conversation, on the part of colleagues shocked to discover my anti-Zionist position and as such to realize the uncommon fact that not all Jews favor the existence of a Jewish exclusivist state in historic Palestine (or elsewhere for that matter). This consistent sense of shock and in turn revulsion on the part of so many of these colleagues increased exponentially following the events of September 11, 2001, when the expressions of post-Cold War capitalist triumphalism which had been circulating with some difficulty in academic circles since the fall of the Berlin Wall found their ready justification and widespread prejudicial acceptance through the vehicle of anti-Arab and anti-Muslim racism and bellicosity. Teaching jobs during this initial period of fear-mongering and irrationality, since exacerbated, became scarcer, whereupon I found myself frequently un(der)employed and drawn increasingly to community organizing and political activism, not coincidentally around the Palestinian struggle. This political involvement supplied me with an on-the-ground education in dialectics, the mutual implication of apparently opposing tendencies, which I had understood previously merely in an idealist sense, as proffered within the walls of academe. This "people's" education would also inspire me to broaden the conceptual scope, while tightening the rhetorical expressiveness, of my scholarly writing. Between 2001 and 2012, I published three books (a prior first book, on German cinema, having been published while I was still in graduate school) and three special journal issues as well as numerous journal articles, book chapters, and the occasional blog entry. Not surprisingly, most of these works, in one way or another, concerned Palestine, Zionism, and US Middle East policy and articulated a left-oriented position. Ironically, although I could not forget how Bill Simon had once advised me to exercise caution with respect to with whom I might share my dissertation-in-progress, by the time I was interviewed for a full-time teaching position at North Carolina State University, the secret of my "controversial" views had become readily available to anyone with access to the Internet. And in the US academy, that meant just about everyone.

*   *   *

For better or worse, too many academic film scholars are oblivious to events recounted in the daily news. If questioned about this evident gap in their knowledge practice, these scholars will often argue that the detail and redundancy of the daily news distracts them from maintaining a degree of objectivity which they believe is necessary for maintaining critical perspective and foresight. The fact is, however, that the legacy of formalism is so strong within cinema studies that, notwithstanding significant turns in the field to cultural and postcolonial studies, including gender, sexuality, and critical race studies, which tended to focus as much on content as on form, political concerns retain the pedestrian connotation attributed to them during the heyday of the CIA-backed dominance of Abstract Expressionism. The notion that cinematic content may itself comprise a structural element of critical form is not deeply enough considered. The cinematic device becomes a "frame" emptied of political meaning, whereupon a film's narrative-compositional structure is misperceived as a transparent vehicle of manifest actuality, interpretable superficially in terms of easily recognizable generic conventions and the opacity of affect. Genuine politics is, in effect, anathema. Hence, when my potential employers would assume, in probable light of my Askhenazi surname, and surely for lack of serious attention to my written work, that my position on Holocaust film, and perhaps even on Palestinian/Israeli cinema, must be Zionist, their reactions, in light of correction, were not only swift but fairly vicious. These colleagues knew that their negative actions would be protected by the corporate veil most universities now wear in the wake of the government defunding and heightened privatization that has ensconced academic decision-making behind proverbial closed doors.

Indeed from 1998 to 2007, the mentioned series of short-lived teaching positions which I had held were not renewed, despite positive student and peer evaluations and a strong research and service portfolio, on inconsistent and dubious grounds. Explanations for these non-renewals were rarely forthcoming. When they were, reference was usually made to budgetary constraints and the ostensible fact that someone with my qualifications was simply too expensive in view of the fact that most departments now have access to large pools of albeit lesser advanced candidates, many of them graduate students or industry workers, who are willing to work for a pittance. In two instances my position was not renewed after my outspokenness against both Zionism and the US invasion and occupation of Iraq was received controversially on campus. In one such instance, Susannah Heschel, daughter of famed Jewish theologian Rabbi Abraham Joshua Heschel and at the time director of the interdisciplinary Jewish Studies Program at Dartmouth College, where I had been hired at the recommendation of another well-known scholar, Marianne Hirsch, to teach a writing course focusing on Jewish memoir and biography, threatened not to write letters of recommendation for me should I choose to continue pressuring her to allow me to screen *Peace, Propaganda and the Promised Land* on campus. *Peace, Propaganda and the Promised Land* is a relatively moderate documentary critical of US corporate media misrepresentation of the Palestinian–Israeli conflict. Two years later at Ithaca College, the Park School of Communications failed to rehire me after my decision to host a campus screening of the short Iraqi documentary, *Fallujah*, angered one student – an admitted and proven Defense Intelligence Agency (DIA) operative named Eric Webster – to such an extent that the college felt compelled to order a police escort to transport me to and from campus, and to guard my film theory classroom, lest Webster, perceived as mentally unstable by the Park School's assistant dean, become physically violent. In all of these instances I fought back as best I could, ultimately in vain, within the framework of the respective institutions.

This limitation of struggle to the institution was not self-imposed, however. To my chagrin and consternation, the majority of my activist friends and comrades, a significant percentage of whom at the time were young, educated, white, queer, and often of Jewish background – the "anti-occupation" left in New York City convening under the umbrella of the Palestine Activist Forum of New York (PAFNY) – were understandably committed to helping persons genuinely underprivileged in as direct a means as possible, and therefore were not as motivated to help someone like me who is by contrast part of the professional class and thus comparatively privileged. By the time I arrived at NCSU and started once again to experience the reactionary crunch, my frustration with this double-bind increased dramatically. At the same time, in view of the egregiousness of the negative actions taken against me by colleagues and administrators at NCSU, I also felt more than ever compelled – obligated – to fight back beyond the institution, both legally and politically.

Fortunately by then, my connections within the Palestine solidarity movement had become more solid in light of the increased involvement I had been able to sustain over my several years of un(der)employment, an involvement which, because of the limitations I had come to associate with "Jewish organizing," had shifted ground significantly in the direction of interacting and working directly with Palestinians, a number of whom were also academics. At Ithaca College I took an intensive Arabic course with a graduate student of Palestinian descent and Cornell Professor Munther Younes. I participated in a scholarly delegation to Palestine hosted by Faculty for Israeli-Palestinian Peace, where I met and listened to Palestinians living in both Israel proper and the Occupied Palestinian Territories hailing from a range of classes and social stations. Shortly before moving to Raleigh to take up the position at NCSU, I accepted an invitation to join the Board of Directors of the International Council for Middle East Studies (ICMES), whereby I came to work in various ways with Palestinian intellectuals Fouzi El-Asmar and Ghada Karmi, well-known Jewish anti-Zionist Norton Mezvinsky, Iraqi scholar Tareq Ismael, Syrian scholar Fuad Sha'ban, and, by way of introduction, Palestinian scholar and activist Mazin Qumsiyeh (not of ICMES). In fact it was in large part Palestinians and Arabs, both Muslim and Christian, who, when my experience at NCSU turned sour, came to the rescue with generous acts of assistance, from petitions, signatures and letters of protest to fundraising for what was to become a long, drawn out and very public lawsuit, to invitations to speak, write, and publish additionally on the general topic of Palestine and Zionism, to meaningful interpersonal engagement and support, to help with the job search that became necessary after my dismissal from NCSU, when my decision to sue the university sealed, for five years, the academic doors which had already been closing gradually on me for nearly a decade.

* * *

In 2006, NCSU advertised a one-year teaching position in film studies within the university's English Department. I applied for the job and was long-listed for preliminary interview at the annual Modern Language Association conference being held that year in Philadelphia. At the interview, Professors Marsha and Devin Orgeron and English Department Head Professor Anthony (Tony) Harrison asked me to hand over sample syllabi for courses I might teach should I be hired. Among those syllabi were outlines for courses on Holocaust film and on gay and lesbian cinema. The three interviewers also inquired about my current scholarly interests, to which I responded that I was co-editing an encyclopedia on Middle Eastern cinema, to which I was also contributing a significant number of entries, and that my primary focus within that context was cinema of the Palestinian–Israeli conflict. Harrison's face suddenly turned beet-red and fell nearly to his lap; I thought I'd lost my chances. Nonetheless, the Orgerons, a husband-wife team comprising two of four full-time film faculty at NCSU, seemed genuinely interested in my candidacy, as they concurred readily and eagerly with Harrison's subsequent statement that the position for which I was being considered, which would also entail co-curating a campus screening series with another NCSU program or department, could very well become permanent and tenure-track, and asked me directly if I would be interested in such a possibility. Of course I said yes.

Some weeks later I received an offer, which I accepted. Over the summer of 2007 I flew down from New York City to Raleigh at my own expense to seek an apartment near campus. During my three-day visit the Orgerons threw me a dinner party at their home, to which all of the film faculty were invited. There I met Maria Pramaggiore, then an associate professor in the Film Program, known widely in the field for a book she'd written on bisexuality in cinema; her partner Tom Wallis, a non-PhD lecturer in the Film Program; Andrea Mensch, also a non-PhD lecturer with whom I would later edit an anthology on German cinema;

and Joe Gomez, a full professor known mainly for a book he had written many years earlier on British director Peter Watkins and who was slated for retirement in one year. Gomez was very interested in Holocaust film. He had built a small video collection of pertinent films and on occasion taught the subject. Over dinner he was vocally critical of any attempt to raise the issue of Palestine in the context of teaching about the Holocaust, claiming that doing so would reinforce anti-Semitic tendencies amongst the primarily right-wing, conservative, white supremacist students he warned me I would encounter at NCSU. I listened politely and tried to assure Gomez that such tendencies could be mitigated by an intelligent, rational, and well-informed pedagogy.

Later that summer, Marsha Orgeron put me in touch, over e-mail, with Akram Khater, an associate professor in the History Department and head of the interdisciplinary Middle East Studies Program. After some discussion over e-mail, it was decided that Khater and I would co-curate the screening series referred to during my interview, that the two programs would co-sponsor it, that it would be held during the fall 2007 semester, and that it would ideally continue during spring 2008. Khater had been hosting a small-scale Middle East screening series on the NCSU campus for the past several years and seemed to welcome the interdepartmental collaboration insofar as it meant more money for film rentals and publicity (we would be able to afford to rent 16 mm prints and hold the series in a large auditorium, rather than using DVDs and screening the films in a more limited space, as Khater had done previously). He was, however, slow to respond to my e-mails and vague in the act of communication, but eventually, after some e-mail discussion, the desired films were selected, the schedule drafted, and the rental orders placed.

Although Khater, originally Lebanese, did show interest in speaking with me about Palestine once I had moved to Raleigh, he was likewise keen to inform me that he believed my pro-Palestinian position was imbalanced – a problem of "one-sidedness" he suggested I rectify by studying the Israeli position more carefully. Accordingly, he himself had participated in a scholarly delegation to Israel organized by a Zionist outfit and thought I might benefit from a similar experience. I later learned from Fuad Sha'ban, whom I would invite to NCSU to speak on the topic of American orientalism in the context of the screening series, that Khater was a Maronite Christian who had converted to Mormonism.

I learned subsequently through Khater's wife Jodi, a non-PhD instructor in Arabic with whom I had briefly resumed my formal study of the language, that the Khaters regularly performed missionary work in Egypt, and that many of her Arabic language students apparently accompanied them on the missionary tours.

The screening series ensued, as did the semester. Despite some reservations about Khater's disposition toward me and my unbalanced views, I was acclimating well to my new environs, having been born and raised in another Southern city, St. Louis, Missouri; and I anticipated applying for the tenure-track position once advertised, something all of the active film faculty as well as Tony Harrison strongly and repeatedly encouraged me to do. I was living a pleasant ten-minute walk from campus, in a 200 square foot, vintage studio apartment that cost a mere $400 per month, probably because of its close proximity to the state penitentiary visible from my window. My office belonged to another professor then on sabbatical leave. It was large, centrally located, and provided a panoramic view of one of several lush and leafy NCSU quads. I began meeting and befriending colleagues from the general area, known informally as the Research Triangle. These included Nadia Yaqub, an associate professor of Palestinian background at the University of North Carolina-Chapel Hill, whose work focused on Palestine and who held a strong interest in Middle Eastern cinema; and Andrea Mensch, whom I'd met originally at the Orgerons' gathering and whose German provenance and political interestedness, as well as her personal warmth and intellectual curiosity, became the source of our eventual book collaboration.

I was teaching an undergraduate survey course on post-war international film history and a Masters level course on Holocaust film. Both seemed to proceed smoothly, as did my editorial work on the Middle Eastern film encyclopedia then in process, and my ongoing research on Palestinian and Palestine solidarity cinema. Although I was busy, I found myself energized by the slower-paced Southern milieu, the relaxed character of the people, the generally warmer weather, the preponderance of greenery and animal life, the succulent local cuisine – and several colleagues' repeated insistence that I apply for the tenure-track position, that my candidacy was highly prized. That feeling of welcome and integration, however, was soon to end.

One of the films I had curated for the screening series was a Palestinian vehicle entitled *Ticket to Jerusalem*, directed by renowned Palestinian filmmaker Rashid Masharawi. Khater and Orgeron asked if I would introduce the film at the screening event, a reasonable request insofar as the film fell directly within one of my areas of expertise. I readily agreed. At the screening, I supplied information about Masharawi, a Gazan refugee who had mastered the art of filmmaking by hook and by crook and has since achieved international acclaim for several compelling narrative features. I discussed how Masharawi's films thematize cinematically the importance of producing and screening Palestinian cinema, especially to Palestinians – an aesthetic practice whose theoretical foundations are established knowledge within the cinema studies field. I concluded my introduction by thanking the audience for choosing to attend this free and open campus screening rather than purchasing a ticket for a commercial film somewhere else. I told them I believed their choice was commendable, that it evidenced support for the airing of Palestinian perspectives so often silenced within the United States, and thus challenged prevailing deployments and configurations of the cinematic apparatus partly responsible for such silencing. As I spoke these words, I saw out of the corner of my eye Akram and Jodi Khater standing, arms akimbo, at one of the entrances to the auditorium, their shadows stretching down the aisle to where I was positioned, microphone in hand, addressing the audience. The expressions on their faces evinced displeasure, an impression confirmed a few days later during a closed meeting to which I was called by Khater and Marsha Orgeron to discuss the future of the series. During that fateful meeting, Khater attacked me verbally for allegedly having told the audience it was "pro-Palestinian," and announced in front of Orgeron, who was by then chair of the faculty search committee to which I had just applied for the tenure-track position, that on account of my actions he would not continue to co-sponsor a screening series with the Film Program the following academic year, that I had ruined any chances for future interdisciplinary collaboration with my offensive, embarrassing politics and my poor choice of films and guest speakers. Khater deemed my introduction to *Ticket to Jerusalem* an inappropriate expression of "bias" that he believed was intended to "politicize" the campus in a purportedly undesirable direction, and which had offended anonymous audience members who, he claimed, had expressed to him privately their disagreement with my perspective. Orgeron, who is of Jewish background, additionally deemed my introduction "alienating" to NCSU students, despite having insisted on at least two occasions that she knows nothing about Middle Eastern cinema. This sentiment echoed her prior e-mail reference to Palestinian/Israeli film as "such an alien concept for many of our students that they don't really know what they'd be getting into."

During the meeting, Khater also censured me for having e-mailed him a strongly worded request for travel reimbursement for invited guest speaker Fuad Sha'ban, a Syrian and observant Muslim who at the time was completing a visiting lectureship at a university in a neighboring state, and who had given a well-attended campus presentation about orientalism in American culture in conjunction with our screening of *Al-'Ard* (*The Land*), directed by preeminent Egyptian filmmaker Youssef Chahine. Sha'ban's presentation offered scholarly criticism of Christian Zionism, the topic of his then most recent book, *For Zion's Sake*. Khater – who, almost immediately upon being introduced to Sha'ban, had revealed voluntarily and unexpectedly to him, in Arabic, that he (Khater) and his wife Jodi are members of the Mormon faith – had perfunctorily rejected my prior reimbursement requests on behalf of Sha'ban, on grounds which I subsequently learned, and explained in an ensuing e-mail, were unfounded. Khater angrily referred to that e-mail as uncollegial and belligerent and would not accept my corrective explanation of it.

Although I saw the writing on the wall, and for the first few minutes after Khater's tirade fell into a state of stunned silence, I proceeded to join Orgeron in making suggestions for the projected spring 2008 leg of the series. Khater, however, was not enthusiastic, and as the conversation was going nowhere, I excused myself and returned to my office, where I telephoned Tony Harrison to inform him of my resignation from the series. During our conversation Harrison expressed some frustration with Khater and offered me his sympathies. Unfortunately, the next several weeks would prove those sympathies cursory, as both Harrison and Marsha Orgeron began engaging in additional acts of bad behavior toward me. Orgeron, for instance, issued me an ambiguously worded teaching evaluation that implicitly emphasized my perceived radicalism and questioned its pedagogical appropriateness; and Harrison was finally unhelpful in mediating the ensuing tension between us. Orgeron then refused to purchase any of the "controversial," especially Palestinian, films necessary for my scheduled spring 2008 course on cinema of the Palestinian–Israel conflict. In the wake of these and other discriminatory actions, when some weeks later an announcement for a talk to be given by a short-listed candidate for the film studies tenure-track position appeared on a department bulletin board, my suspicions were confirmed that I was no longer being considered for the position. My colleagues began to shun me. I found solace in my ongoing scholarship and several new friends I had made, including at a local gay and lesbian nightspot, but I could not dispel the anger which Khater and Orgeron had provoked in me over the greater injustice their actions represented.

I decided, therefore, to contact a local Association of American University Professors (AAUP) representative, Cat Warren, a women's studies professor at NCSU, for advice. Warren had previously acknowledged the problematic language of Orgeron's evaluation of my teaching and directed me thoughtfully on how to proceed regarding it. She herself was experiencing run-ins with the NCSU administration, having reputedly resigned her position as Director of the Women's Studies Program in protest over the university's acceptance of an open-ended grant, totaling potentially in the billions of dollars, from far-right businessman and philanthropist Art Pope, who, as highlighted in an extensive *New Yorker* exposé in which Warren is interviewed, has been working hard to stock the North Carolina legislature with his cronies and in turn to re-segregate the North Carolina public school system, and whose various foundations support military-industrial development, among other things in cooperation with Israel. This time, however, Warren, who would oblige me to meet her Jewish husband during one of our scheduled appointments, was less sanguine. She put me in touch with a campus AAUP representative as well as a national AAUP representative, Robert Kreiser, then veritably recused herself, citing a conflict of interest. Kreiser talked me through the process of filing a grievance with the NCSU Faculty Senate, chaired at the time by a mild-mannered chemistry professor named James D. Martin. The process involved meeting with College of Humanities and Social Sciences Dean Toby Parcel, whose offer to investigate my allegations ended up delaying the process inordinately; and, under Martin's direction, revising the grievance seven times, whereupon its completion, too, was delayed, and whereupon the university was able subsequently to claim, falsely, that the submitted grievance was not timely filed. As a result, I was not granted a campus hearing. On top of that, Kreiser and the AAUP, then headed by outspoken Zionist Cary Nelson, were unwilling to represent me further.

At the end of May 2008 I moved back to New York City and began contacting Palestine solidarity activists about strategizing resistance. Petitions and articles were drafted and published throughout the summer of 2008, including two pieces in the NCSU student newspaper that were written by Palestinians, and a petition drafted by Mazin Qumsiyeh that was circulated initially via a listerv he established, Academics for Justice. Soon I was receiving offers of representation from civil rights attorneys who thought it behooved me to sue the university. After some careful thought, I decided to accept an offer from Rima Najjar Kapitan, a young, Chicago-based attorney of Palestinian background who was willing to fight NCSU on my behalf and to take the case as far as it could reasonably go. We did indeed take the case all the way from the NCSU Board of Trustees to the North Carolina Supreme Court until relinquishing in the face of persistent imperviousness on the part of the ultra-conservative North Carolina legal system, its refusal, on superficial grounds, to allow my case to proceed to a jury trial even though the facts, evidenced both directly and circumstantially, clearly warranted a trial. The faculty search committee files we subpoenaed, for example, explicitly stated that I had been bumped off the job candidates' list because of "too much focus on Jewish/Israel" and that therefore I was not qualified for the position, which called for expertise in one or more European cinemas, but encouraged additional expertise in other cinemas. Although Marsha Orgeron later tried to justify the bizarre claim that I am not a specialist in European cinema on the basis that the Holocaust is not necessarily a European concern, the fact that I had already published an anthology on German cinema and a second was in process (since published) was entirely ignored in the deliberations.

In the end, the search committee elected to hire one Ora Gelley, a young woman of Jewish background who, coincidentally, had taught as an adjunct in cinema studies at Dartmouth during the same semester in which I had also been employed there, and whose professional visibility Susannah Heschel had helped foster in the context of promoting a guest speaking event for Ella Shohat, whom the Cinema Studies Department, in conjunction with the Jewish Studies Program, had invited to campus to screen and discuss a film in which she appears, *Forget Baghdad*. *Forget Baghdad* concerns the Mizrahi ("Oriental") Jews in Israel while lending short shrift to the Palestinian situation. By the time my case against NCSU closed, I had published the equivalent of seven books. Since her hire by NCSU, Gelley has written one book – about movie star Ingrid Bergman.

*   *   *

The most important prayer in Judaism begins with the command form of the verb, "to hear." Over nearly three years of litigation, I received not a single formal hearing from any deliberative or juridical body, whether on campus or in the court system. This reality, much like hitting one's head repeatedly against an apartheid wall, was personally as well as professionally upsetting to me and at times physically sickening. Each time my case came before a judge, whose role it was to decide upon its worthiness, summary dismissal ensued, with meager explanation. In the formal sense, therefore, the legal effort led to a dead end. On the other hand, the wider community of Palestine solidarity workers and activists did eventually, with irrefutable commitment, rally collectively around my case, helping me publicize it both locally and (inter)nationally, thus strengthening its force and significance for the overall movement. As a result, my struggle against NCSU became a small but discernible catalyst in making campus discrimination against pro-Palestinian speech – teaching, scholarship, and student organizing—of greater concern to both the movement and the public at large. By extension, it facilitated broader attention to the academic and cultural boycott of Israel, now a key component of the Boycott, Divestment and Sanctions Movement (BDS) around which a good deal of Palestine solidarity work in North America and Europe has come to center. In due course I myself would become heavily involved in three organizations with missions pertinent to such efforts: New Yorkers Against the Cornell-Technion Partnership (NYACT); Committee for Open Discussion of Zionism (CODZ); and US Campaign for the Academic and Cultural Boycott of Israel (USACBI).

The Zionist war against Palestine now focuses a major part of its effort on what many of us call neo-McCarthyism: a concerted, well-funded attempt to squelch activism, scholarship, and other social, cultural, and educational expressions critical of Zionism and Israeli policy, of US Middle East policy respecting it, of anti-Arab/Muslim racism, and demonstrating unrelenting, well-reasoned support for Palestinian liberation and of anti-colonial/imperial struggles generally. Knowing what I now know, having experienced the Janus face of academia full force, I cannot overemphasize the importance of analyzing and exposing the disingenuousness of this Zionist onslaught against anyone who would criticize the ideology of so-called Jewish nationalism, as it purports academic excellence and prestige even while the state of Israel denies Palestinians from all walks of life equal educational and vocational opportunity, subjecting them instead to an ethnic cleansing that is ongoing, that is illegal, that is immoral, that should never have happened, and that must stop. My hope in having fought for the ability of scholars to bring discussions about Palestinian liberation into the academic sphere is that a just and lasting end to the Nakba and its global extenuations may be secured, based upon a genuine "hearing" of Palestinians, both individually and collectively, by their Jewish/Israeli exploiters and oppressors, one which leads finally to the formation of a regional entity in which Palestinian Arabs, the rightful owners of the land, will be permitted all the freedoms and privileges that Zionists have arrogated to Jews for over a century. Nothing less is acceptable; and I will not be silent until the day arrives.

3

My Ordeal with the Israel Lobby and the University of California

William I. Robinson[1]

Editors' note: William I. Robinson is Professor of Sociology, Global Studies, and Latin American Studies at the University of California at Santa Barbara. In January 2009, he sent to his students optional readings critical of the three-week 2008–09 Israeli military assault on Gaza, known as Operation Cast Lead. Over the following six months, he endured a public prosecution by the Israel lobby that stood out for the extent to which members of the University of California faculty and top-level administrators were complicit in the illegal campaign against him. As Professor Robinson points out in this chapter, his case had become, at the time, a "litmus test" for the Israel lobby to silence criticism of Israel.

The 2008–09 Israeli assault on Gaza, what the Israel military called Operation Cast Lead, could well be considered a turning point in the worldwide movement against Israeli apartheid and in support of Palestinian freedom. For three weeks, Israeli military forces pounded Palestinian communities in the densely populated territory with an arsenal that included white phosphorus munitions and cluster bombs, which are banned by international treaties. The carnage left 1,400 Palestinians dead, up to 80 percent of them civilians, including over 300 children, and 5,000 injured, along with 13 Israeli deaths, seven of them by friendly fire. The massacre provoked unprecedented worldwide condemnation of the Jewish state for its ongoing war crimes and its illegal occupation of Palestinian territories (subsequent international investigations would find Israel guilty, among other crimes, of "wanton destruction" in violation of the Fourth Geneva Convention).

In response to the international outcry, the Israeli state and its allies and agents stepped up campaigns of intimidation, silencing, and political repression against opponents of its policies. Israel may continue to win military battles – after all, it has the fifth most powerful military on the planet – but it has been losing the war for legitimacy. In the wake of the bloody 2008–09 attack on schools, hospitals, and United Nations refugee centers in Gaza, as well as periodic massacres and ongoing occupation, support has dramatically intensified around the world for the Boycott, Divestment, Sanctions (BDS) campaign. The BDS campaign in the United States has taken off since 2009, above all, on university campuses, which is why the Israel lobby is so intent on targeting academia.

I was attacked in the first half of 2009 by the Israel lobby in the United States, led by the Anti-Defamation League (ADL),[2] and nearly run from the University of California at Santa Barbara (UCSB), where I work as a professor of sociology, global, and Latin American studies. The campaign against me lasted some six months and garnered worldwide attention but I am hardly alone. Dozens, perhaps hundreds of professors and student groups have been harassed and persecuted for speaking out against Israeli occupation and apartheid and in support of the Palestinian struggle. The persecution to which I was subjected involved a litany of harassment, slander, defamation of character and all kinds of threats against the university by outside forces if I was not dismissed, as well as hate mail and death threats from unknown sources.

More insidiously, it involved a shameful collaboration between a number of university officials and outside forces from the Israel lobby as the university administration stood by silently, making a mockery of academic freedom. The disciplinary procedure initiated against me by UCSB officials involved a host of irregularities, violations of the university's own procedures, breaches of confidentiality, denial of due process, conflicts of interest, failure of disclosure, improper political surveillance, abuses of power and position, unwarranted interference in curriculum and teaching, and so on. As I would discover during the course of the ordeal, individuals inside the university and in positions of authority had linked up with agents of the lobby outside the university in setting out to prosecute me.

I may well have been run from the university if it were not for graduate and undergraduate students (together with a handful of committed colleagues), who early on in the persecution set up the Committee to

Defend Academic Freedom that launched a worldwide campaign in my defense. This in turn sparked a good portion of the faculty into action, several months into the campaign of persecution against me, to defend my academic freedom. This campaign also generated widespread support for me off campus, pressure that eventually forced the university to back down and the Israel lobby to give up and move on to targets of harassment elsewhere, thereby demonstrating that this lobby is not invincible, and indeed, is increasingly vulnerable. The entire story is documented on the Committee's website.[3] During the course of the six-month campaign, the Committee and I were able to piece together the events that are here reconstructed – in part and in brief – to the best of my knowledge.

Operation Cast Lead and the Israel Lobby's Inside-Outside Strategy

Operation Cast Lead ended on January 18, 2009. The following day, one week into our winter quarter classes, I forwarded to the listserv for my course on the sociology of globalization optional reading materials drawn from the international press for classroom discussion that evening on the Israel-Palestine conflict. The reading materials included among other items a *Reuters* news article reporting that a Jewish editor of the *Kansas City Jewish Chronicle* had been sacked for publishing an article by a Jewish-American journalist who visited the West Bank and denounced the occupation. They also included a photo-essay that had been circulating on the internet and that juxtaposed Israeli atrocities in Gaza and Nazi atrocities in Warsaw,[4] along with a commentary of my own, including this paragraph:

> The Israeli army is the fifth most potent military machine in the world and one that is backed by a propaganda machine that rivals and may well surpass that of the U.S., a machine that dares to make the ludicrous and obnoxious claim that opposition to the policies and practices of the Israeli state is anti-Semitism. It should be no surprise that a state founded on the negation of a people was one of the principal backers of the apartheid South African state not to mention of the Latin American military dictatorships until those regimes collapsed under mass protest, and today arms, trains, and advises military and

paramilitary forces in Colombia, one of the world's worst human rights violators.

My course on the sociology of globalization is offered every year. It takes up vital and controversial issues that impact global society and each class meeting starts with a discussion of some current affair, such as Operation Cast Lead. However, two students of the 80 enrolled in the course that I have never met and did not know[5] apparently did not feel that they should receive any course material that challenged their beliefs. Instead of attending class that evening they made contact with the Hillel organization on campus who then took them to meet with the ADL, the Simon Wiesenthal Center in Los Angeles, Stand With Us, and several other Jewish organizations affiliated with the Israel lobby and faculty members of campus. The ADL and these other organizations then went into action.

First, the Simon Wiesenthal Center, a Zionist organization in Los Angeles, sat down with one of the students to film her, with her face blotted out (the film stated the student "has asked to protect her identity for fear of reprisal"), as she claimed she was intimidated by my course material, and then posted the film on YouTube under the title "Jewish Students Shocked by UCSB Professor's Demonizing Email."[6] The Wiesenthal Center called for me to be punished and accused me of anti-Semitism until they learned that I am of Jewish background, and then charged instead that I was a "self-hating Jew."

Next, the students met with the local ADL chapter in Santa Barbara, and were apparently instructed by the ADL and its affiliated groups to contact the Charges Office at UCSB and lodge a grievance against me. The Charges Office is set up by the university to receive grievances over possible violation by faculty members of the Faculty Code of Conduct (e.g., sexual harassment, racial bias, etc.). The Charges Office is expected to investigate possible violations, and to dismiss frivolous charges, that is, charges that clearly do not involve a violation of the Code.

What I did not know at the time, but would soon learn, is that two of the three officers of the Charges Office belonged to the Zionist community in Santa Barbara that had already begun to conspire against me, and that at least one of them, Aaron Ettenberg, had already made contact with the outside groups working with the students. Ettenberg was a former president of the Santa Barbara B'nai B'rith, the parent organization of the ADL. Neither of these two revealed their affiliations or recused themselves due to the blatant conflict of interests. To the contrary, we would soon learn that Ettenberg met with Rabbi Arthur Gross-Schaeffer, director at the time of the Santa Barbara chapter of Hillel, a Jewish organization linked with the ADL, and an outspoken leader of the pro-Israeli Jewish community in Santa Barbara, to consult with him about my case prior to the university's decision to investigate me.

This explains why, on February 9, the director of the local ADL Chapter Cynthia Silverman sent me a letter protesting my course materials and accusing me of violating a number of items of the Faculty Code of Conduct. How did the ADL come into possession of my course material? Copies of this ADL letter were sent to my department chair, to UCSB Chancellor Henry Yang, and to then-UC President Mark Yudof (himself an outspoken Zionist). The campaign now picked up steam. Three days later Martin Scharlemann, who was the chair of the Charges Office, summoned me "urgently" to meet with him to discuss the complaint that the students had lodged with the Charges Office. I was told by Scharlemann's staff assistant, Stephanie Smagala, that it was "imperative" that I come down "that very afternoon" due to "an urgent situation." I did not understand at the time why such alarm, why Scharlemann was treating this as an emergency situation, whereas this was but a routine student grievance evidently not involving any urgent matter such as sexual assault, possible violence, or anything remotely of that nature, and strictly referred to two students' disagreement with the content of course material, a course that they had dropped.

At the same time as the university's Charges Office was organizing its prosecution, I was contacted through a mediator by Rabbi Gross-Schaeffer, who had previously met with Charges Office member Aaron Ettenberg. This mediator, a colleague of mine, then set up a confidential meeting between the two of us. "We [the Israel lobby] will pull back if you meet our conditions," he told me. You need to "ask for repentance, to apologize for what you have done." I told Gross-Schaeffer that I had done nothing morally objectionable and more so, I had not violated any rules, codes or procedures at the university and was acting fully within my rights of academic freedom. "Well apparently there are people at the university that disagree with you and are prepared to move forward against you if you do not repent," he replied.

Contriving Charges

The charges against me were *entirely* contrived. There is absolutely nothing in the Faculty Code of Conduct that even remotely suggests that my course material violated any item of the Code. In my February meeting with Scharlemann and his staff assistant Smagala, the two asked several questions entirely inappropriate and outside of their jurisdiction, including as to whether I had placed on the course syllabus the topic of the Israeli-Palestine conflict, which suggested that the two believed they were empowered as part of the complaint procedure to examine the content of my course and to determine what was and was not relevant to that content.

Such external monitoring and censorship of course conduct is a violation of faculty academic freedom and was not a legitimate part of the university's complaint procedure. Although the materials I distributed were relevant for my course, even if they had not been their inclusion in the course reading material would not have violated the Faculty Code of Conduct. Neither Scharlemann nor Smagala had any right to assess what was relevant for my courses on globalization (or indeed any other topics of sociology).

These gross violations by the Charges Office, as well as the contact between the Charges Office and outside pressure groups from the Israel lobby and other irregularities and violations of university rules and procedures as this persecution unfolded, were brought to the attention of university officials of the highest levels, right up to Chancellor Yang and Executive Vice Chancellor Gene Lucas, upon whom it was incumbent to defend my academic freedom and the integrity of the university. Yang chose, however, to ignore my insistence that he and the university defend my academic freedom and put an end to what was becoming a charade. In fact, he expressed more anxiety about the harassment campaign organized by Stand With Us and its members' threats to withdraw funding from the university if I were not fully prosecuted.

A week later Scharlemann notified me that the two students had filed formal written complaints and I was expected to reply and defend myself. The farcical and politicized nature of the attacks against me now became apparent. Here is an excerpt from one of the student complaints (the full complaints are posted on the Committee for Academic Freedom website).[7]

An important issue is the distinction between the legitimate criticism of policies and practices of the State of Israel, and commentary that assumes an anti-Semitic character. The demonization of Israel, or vilification of Israeli leaders sometimes through comparisons with Nazi leaders, and through the use of Nazi symbols to caricature them, indicates an anti-Semitic bias rather than a valid criticism of policy. I found these parallel images intimidating, disgusting, and beyond a teacher role as an educator in the university system. I feel that something must be done so other students don't have to go through the same intimidating disgust I went through … He has also violated the universities policies by participating in or deliberately abetting disruption, interference, or intimidation in the classroom (Part II, Section A, Number 5). Robinson has done so through this intimidating email which had pushed me to withdraw from this course and take another one … By Robinson using his university email account he attaches his thoughts with that of the university and they become a single entity sharing the same ideas.

The second letter repeats the accusation of anti-Semitism, a definition lifted verbatim from the US State Department and then continues:

In all the years of schooling and higher education I have never experienced an abuse of an educator position … To hide behind a computer and send this provocative email shows poor judgment and perhaps a warped personality. The classroom and the forum of which higher education is presented needs to be safe and guarded so the rights of individuals are respected. handle [sic] … The fact that the professor attached his views to the depiction of what my great grandparents and family experienced shows lack of sensitivity and awareness. What he did was criminal because he took my trust and invaded something that is very personal. I felt as if I have been violated by the professor. Yes I am aware of Anti-Semitism, but to abuse this position in an environment of higher education where I always thought it to be safe, until now, is intimidating. This professor should be stopped immediately from continuing to disseminate this information and be punished because his damage is irreversible.

The actual charges contained in the students' letters were simply absurd; they included a long list of charges copied straight from the Code of Conduct, including those against romantic relations with students, despite the fact that I had never met the students in question, and charges against the use of university property for commercial gain, which had no bearing whatsoever on the case. The letters of complaint, in fact, opened up with the bizarre charge that I actually violated *my own* right to present controversial material. They included the charge of discrimination, even though my only act for which the students submitted a grievance was to have sent reading material uniformly to the entire class, for which reason by definition discrimination was not involved. The litany of charges included also violations of the canons of intellectual honesty, speaking in private capacity while creating the impression that I represented the university, and so on. And all these accusations were generated by nothing more than an optional reading sent by internet to the entire course listserv and that represented some one-tenth of 1 percent of the assigned reading material for the course.

In matter of fact, the students' grievance was based strictly on their objection to the content of course material. This fact, indeed, is not in dispute, as is apparent from the text of their letters. According to the University of California procedures, a grievance procedure is available to students who feel that they may have been disadvantaged, graded unfairly, or otherwise discriminated against on account of disagreements with the professor's views, not when the students merely disagree with a professor's views, or with the views expressed in course readings. To the contrary, the very preamble to the university's Faculty Code of Conduct states that the primary purpose of the Code is to protect faculty's right to academic freedom, for example, to protect faculty from frivolous complaints by students.

I was bewildered at the time as to why Scharlemann refused to reject the claims as frivolous. Given that there was no substantiation of the students' long list of complaints and that the only basis for the students' complaint was an optional reading they received by email that criticized the Israeli government as part of a course on global affairs, what could Scharlemann possibly have found in these student letters to have led him *not* to inform the students that is was frivolous? I only learned subsequently that behind Scharlemann and several other university officials involved in my persecution was the malicious intent of a web of individuals outside the university representing the Israel lobby and coordinating with the students and university officials.

For much of March and into April Scharlemann ignored my request for him to substantiate the basis of his decision to press forward rather than dismiss the case. The university waited more than two months before actually informing me of exactly what was the charge against me, that is, exactly what aspect of the Code of Conduct I was alleged to have violated. On April 5, Scharlemann sent to me what is known as a "charges sheet," which accused me of distributing "highly partisan" material to my students "accompanied by lurid photographs" and "was unexpected and without educational context," that I had engaged in "coercion of conscience" as a result of which "two enrolled students were too distraught to continue with the course."

In fact, the university's Faculty Code of Conduct nowhere states that course material must not be "partisan" or that "lurid" images are violations of the Code. Indeed, *not a single one* of the charges against me are stipulated in the Code as violations. The charges amounted to a blatant attempt at political censorship and an illegitimate use of the university's grievance procedure. I asked Scharlemann for explanations, for example, what he meant by "lurid photos." In my letter[8] requesting further explanation I wrote:

"Lurid" is defined by Webster's as "vivid in a harsh or shocking way." In what way is the introduction of images vivid in a harsh or shocking way a violation of the Faculty Code of Conduct? Why would photos of military conflict not be "harsh and shocking"? And why would their presentation in a University course be a violation of the Faculty Code of Conduct? .... By suggesting that images that document shocking events and "partisan" material should not be introduced into a University course your charges sheet appears to advocate – beyond the suppression of academic freedom – outright political censorship. The Faculty Code of Conduct does not, in any way, proscribe "partisan" material or images that are vivid in a harsh and shocking way. To the contrary, the Code establishes as the right of faculty the "right to present controversial material relevant to a course of instruction" and its very Preamble states that the intent of the Code is to protect academic freedom.

Scharlemann ignored my letter, and more seriously, so did all of the university administrators to whom I wrote demanding an explanation for this political persecution and demanding that the university protect and defend my academic freedom. Instead, this Charges Office proceeded to establish a special investigative and prosecutorial committee (known on my campus as an Ad Hoc Committee) to further investigate my alleged violations and apply possible sanctions.

Enter the ADL's (and Mossad's) Abraham Foxman

The ADL, with 34 regional offices in North America, a staff of 400, and a \$32 million annual budget, is one of the core organizations of the Israel lobby in the United States, exposed by US political scientists John Mearsheimer and Stephen Walt in their study *The Israel Lobby and U.S. Foreign Policy*. The ADL has a long and sordid history of spying on, slandering, and vilifying critics of Israel[9] – victims of its infiltration have included the National Association for the Advancement of Colored People (NAACP), the American Civil Liberties Union (ACLU), Greenpeace, the Arab-American Anti-Discrimination League, and thousands of private citizens, among others – in cooperation with Israel's foreign intelligence service, Mossad. Then-ADL director Abraham Foxman (he stepped down in 2015) is an international lobbyist for Israel who has met frequently with national and world leaders, including all US presidents since Richard Nixon, and who brags that he has direct access to the Office of the Israeli Prime Minister.

On March 19, 2009, Foxman arrived at UCSB for a meeting hosted by Religious Studies professor Richard Hecht and attended by Deans David Marshall and Michael Young and several faculty members. Cynthia Silverman by his side, Foxman demanded that the university take action against me. Some of the meeting participants told me that Foxman requested the meeting at UCSB for the sole purpose of demanding that university officials investigate me for introducing course materials critical of Israeli state policies. In fact, the only agenda item of this meeting was my case. History professor Harold Marcuse, who attended the meeting, later stated: "When the meeting started, Foxman quickly launched into what I would call a rant about what he said was an anti-Semitic email that professor Robinson sent to his class. We then had an open discussion about Foxman's comments and the charges against

Robinson. In my recollection, that was the only thing we talked about at the meeting. Nothing else was discussed."[10]

Alongside the ADL, the organization Stand With Us (SWU) launched a nation-wide and worldwide campaign to pressure the university to fire me, including a petition drive and a letter-writing campaign. The founding mission of SWU is to counter criticism of Israel on university campuses worldwide, according to its website. Created in 2001, its site openly calls college campuses a "modern-day battlefront" for Israel. "Today Israel faces a new global threat, one that is fought in the media, on university campuses, and in the court of public opinion," reads the Stand With Us home page, while its Bay Area chapter is even more candid: "Our mission is to stand up to anti-Israel speech wherever it may surface," reads the site. "We are (unofficially) representing the state of Israel."

Stand With Us representatives threatened a campaign to have pro-Israel donors cut off financial donations to UCSB if I were not prosecuted. For instance, Stand With Us sent a letter to Vice Chancellor Gene Lucas dated March 16 and posted at www.standwithus.com. The letter states that Stand With Us board member Leah Yadegar was in contact with the two student complainants. It stated that Yadegar then "distributed the email widely to UCSB donors, media, and Jewish organizations, including Stand With US," and that Stand With US board member Howard Waldow, a UCSB donor, discussed my case with Chancellor Yang at a reception.

At the time, Roz Rothstein, international director for Stand With Us, told the UCSB student newspaper, *The Daily Nexus*, that the campaign against me could set a precedent for more action against Israel critics at other universities. My colleague Richard Falk, who was a visiting professor of global studies at UCSB and the United Nation's special rapporteur on human rights in the Palestinian territories, commented at the time that Rothstein's remarks indicated a "disturbing" escalation in pro-Israel pressure on college campuses in general, and at UCSB in particular. "Apparently, they have decided enough vulnerability exists in the university community for them to mobilize pressure campaigns," Falk said. "They're making this [the Robinson case] into a litmus test to silence criticism of Israel."

Falk was right; the Israel lobby had made my case a litmus test. On the other hand, I was carried away by support from around the world as international pressure mounted on the university to put an end to my persecution. The university received letters in support of me and demanding that the charges be dropped from dozens of professional associations and community organizations, among them, the National Lawyers Guild, California Scholars for Academic Freedom, the Middle Eastern Studies Association of North America, the editorial board of the UK-based scholarly journal *Race and Class*, the Global Studies Association, and the March 25 Coalition, an immigrant rights coalition in Southern California. It also received petitions signed by thousands of people from around the United States and the world, and countless letters from individuals from all five continents, a sampling of which has been posted at http://sb4af.wordpress.com/. The Committee to Defend Academic Freedom organized a teach-in on May 21 that left standing room only in the auditorium and media in attendance from around Southern California.

A Secret Absolution

The Ad Hoc Committee set up to investigate me in April concluded its investigation into me on May 15 and found that I was not in violation of the Faculty Code of Conduct. Yet Chancellor Yang kept these results secret from me and from the public for another six weeks, until June 24. Since Chancellor Yang and his immediate underlings, including Vice Chancellor Gene Lucas, ignored my correspondence with them, I do not know from the horse's mouth what their motives were for continuing to apply political pressure on me for another six weeks. Were they waiting for a major Jewish donation to the university to be consummated before publicly announcing their dismissal of the charges against me? Was the Israel lobby still conspiring on how to move forward in persecuting me?

On June 10 the Foundation for Individual Rights and Education (FIRE), a Pennsylvania-based non-profit, had come to my defense in the name of First Amendment rights and academic freedom.[11] One of their attorneys, Adam Kissel, wrote to the Chancellor warning him that if all charges against me were not dropped by 5:00 pm on June 24 his organization would launch a major media campaign and a lawsuit against the University of California. An hour or so before this deadline, the university chose to inform me of the decision, made six weeks earlier and kept secret, that the charges against me had already been dropped.

But the administration was also under mounting pressure from my colleagues. Spurred on by my students, whose mobilization in my defense included a sit-in at the Chancellor's office and threats of more sit-ins, an international petition drive, and other public protests, my colleagues mobilized against the improprieties. Some 100 faculty members and 20 heads of departments signed a petition protesting the university's handling of the accusations against me. And on June 8 some 80 faculty members filled a Senate meeting and passed a motion to investigate the irregularities surrounding my case. By this time my case had garnered worldwide media attention and the university was in the spotlight as public pressure mounted. Yet the university administration refused to put an end to the witch-hunt. Instead, Chancellor Yang sent me a message via an intermediary: "stop embarrassing the university."

Following the dismissal of charges against me I submitted a 40-page grievance to the UCSB Academic Senate. According to the Senate's bylaws, a committee should have investigated the litany of irregularities, violations of procedure, breaches of confidentiality, conflicts of interest, failure of disclosure, improper political surveillance, abuses of power and position, and other acts of misconduct against me as a faculty member, some of which has been discussed here and all of which can be found at the website http://sb4af.wordpress.com/, including original letters and documents pertaining to the case. Nonetheless, the Senate chose to investigate exactly one single violation – that of Ettenberg's undisclosed conflict of interest – and then exonerated him. How did they reach this decision to exonerate? According to the Senate's letter to me in response to my grievance, they simply asked him if he had a conflict of interest and he said he did not!

Whereas the allegations against me took just a few minutes to make, and the Senate investigation into breaches of my rights took but one word to dismiss, I had to suspend my research and professional activities and put on hold my personal life for the duration of the six months in which I had to defend myself against frivolous allegations. Indeed, across the country whenever such persecutions are launched the burden falls on those that are targeted to defend themselves, often tying up the individual's time and life for months and generating great emotional stress.

UCSB has yet to honor my demand that the institution apologize for the ordeal it put me through and the damage done to my professional reputation.

Nazi Propaganda Minister Goebbels' Tactics on US Campuses

Yet that ordeal is but a fly in the face of the horrific crimes to which the Palestinians are subjected on a daily basis by Israeli occupation, apartheid, and periodic massacres. It is in addition something faced by dozens, perhaps hundreds, of faculty and students who chose not to back down in the face of McCarthyist repression in their commitment to speaking truth to power. In late 2008, the American Israeli Public Affairs Committee (AIPAC) announced that it would target US universities, especially big state universities, starting with the University of California. AIPAC director Howard Kohr acknowledged at the 2009 annual convention the erosion of Israel's legitimacy, warning that there was a huge and growing international campaign against Israeli policies. "No longer is this campaign confined to the ravings of the political far left or far right," he said, "but increasingly it is entering the American mainstream."[12]

In their 2009 article in *Tikkun* and reprinted in this book, University of California at Irvine professor David Theo Goldberg and UCLA professor Saree Makdsisi noted that "no fewer than 33 distinct organizations – including AIPAC, the Zionist Organization of America, the American Jewish Congress, and the Jewish National Fund – are gathered together today as members or affiliates of the Israel on Campus Coalition," whose stated objective is to generate "a pro-active, pro-Israeli agenda on campus. There is accordingly, disproportionate and unbalanced intervention on campuses across the country by a coalition of well-funded organizations, who have no time for – and even less interest in – the niceties of intellectual exchange and academic process." They note that "scholars whose work is critical of Israeli policies have been denied jobs, denied tenure, and in general have their lives made difficult not because of academic criteria, but because of political interference."

They go on to observe how this apparatus systematically uses disinformation and misinformation, blatant fabrications, character assassination, and so on. The objective is not to engage in rational dialogue based on exchange of ideas in the search for truth, but "to create an environment of fear and intimidation on and off campuses, in which any criticism of Israeli policies is subject to sanctions and censorship." Then they note:

The *Hasbara Handbook: Promoting Israel on Campus*, which is distributed to campus activists by organizations like Stand With Us, explains that it is often better to score points than to engage in actual arguments, and offers an explanation for how, in its own words, "to score points whilst avoiding debate." Point-scoring, the *Hasbara Handbook* explains, "works because most audience members fail to analyze what they hear. Rather, they register only a key few points, and form a vague 'impression' of whose argument was stronger." Part of the strategy is to recycle the same claims over and again, in as many settings as possible. "If people hear something often enough," the document points out, "they come to believe it."

Needless to say, this was precisely the tactic developed by the Nazi Minister of Propaganda, Joseph Goebbels, which he called "the big lie."[13] Goldberg and Makdisi continue:

The *Hasbara Handbook* offers several other propaganda devices, all of which can be seen vividly at play in the coverage of the UCLA Gaza panel and other similar events, including again, the Robinson affair. "Creating negative connotations by name calling is done to try to get the audience to reject a person or idea on the basis of negative associations, *without allowing a real examination of that person or idea*," the handbook states with remarkable bluntness, in advocating this tactic. It also suggests using the opposite of name-calling, to defend Israel by what it calls the deployment of "glittering generalities" (words like "freedom," "civilization," "democracy") to describe the country, manipulating the audiences' fears, etc.

I can attest that these Goebbelsian tactics – when backed by the economic resources and political influence of the Israel lobby and in the context of US state support for, and sponsorship of, the Israeli Zionist project – are often effective. Such tactics cower many people, not just politicians but academics who become scared to even mention any criticism of Israel or support for Palestinians in their classrooms, their research, and their public appearances. I see this almost every day in my own professional work in academia, and of course in the media.

In my case, while some colleagues came out courageously and publicly in my defense (and many were aroused by the student mobilization to come out in support of academic freedom yet still kept themselves arms-length from me), many others, it seemed to me almost overnight, started to avoid me once the lobby placed a scarlet letter on my forehead. I became a pariah on campus. Some colleagues would literally turn the other way when they saw me; others would comment in hushed tones as I approached. Cowardly administrators avoided me like the plague, fearful of damaging their own status or security, principles-be-damned.

Political repression of the nature executed by the Israeli lobby and its agents and supporters can wreck lives and careers and leads to *self-censorship* among journalists, politicians, academics, and other public figures. It results in a kind of perverted hegemony in the Gramscian sense – the forging of a coerced consensus, or at least the appearance of one, imposed by intimidation and backed up by the threat of sanctions.

However, that hegemony has been eroding in the face of Israeli atrocities, defiant intellectuals committed to justice and the spread of the BDS campaign and other movements in support of Palestinian rights. My own case shows that the Israel lobby is not omnipotent; it does not enjoy uncontested power. To the contrary, those who choose to side with justice and are willing to speak truth to power may find that they are swept away by support from all corners of the globe.

Finally, a word on academic freedom. When academic freedom is suppressed the university becomes an indoctrination camp where truth is subordinated to ideology and power. Academic freedom is the life blood of the university. Any attack on such freedom exercises a chilling effect on the ability of the university community to engage in open debate and exchange of ideas on contemporary matters. Free speech and academic freedom are such threats to the Israel lobby, and indeed to all anti-democratic, authoritarian, or totalitarian projects, precisely because it proscribes censorship and prohibits any attempt to limit what is and is not acceptable to research, to teach, to question, and to debate, and precisely because academic freedom thrives on controversy and critical thinking.

It is no wonder academic freedom was suppressed in Nazi Germany, in apartheid South Africa, in military dictatorships in Latin America, in the former Soviet Union, in the United States – under McCarthyism and at many other times, such as the present moment – and elsewhere. Our mission as educators is to help develop citizens who can think critically and independently on the burning issues of our day, who can search out the truth without fear of what they will find. I believe this search for the truth inevitably leads us to a position of justice; silence in the face of social injustice is complicity in that injustice. We are morally compelled to speak out against injustice, in this case, against Israeli repression, colonialism, and apartheid, even when it means we run the risk of facing the wrath of the powerful, on our campuses and in the larger society.

Notes

1. The list would be very long of those I must thank for their principled support in 2009 for my right to academic freedom and free speech. I would like to acknowledge above all my sociology graduate students at UCSB, especially Yousef Baker (now Dr. Baker) and Maryam Griffin (now Dr. Griffin), as well as UCSB sociology professors Geoff Raymond and Verta Taylor, distinguished professor emeritus Richard Falk, and Kevin Robinson. The content of this chapter is my sole responsibility and acknowledgment of these individuals does not suggest in any way that they agree with the content herein or share my views.

2. The Anti-Defamation League is a national lobby organization that takes as its mission "to stop the defamation of the Jewish people and to secure justice and fair treatment to all." However, the group is at the forefront of efforts to characterize any and all criticism of the State of Israel, its policies and practices as *ipso facto* anti-Semitic.

3. The website can be found at http://sb4af.wordpress.com/. All websites last accessed November 20, 2015.

4. The editor in question was Debbie Ducro and the article she published was written in 2000 by Jewish-American journalist Judith Stone, reprinted at www.bintjbeil.com/E/occupation/001110_stone.html. The photo-essay was posted by Professor Norman Finkelstein on his website and is reproduced together with an interview with Professor Finkelstein on the photo essay at www.indymedia.org.uk/en/regions/world/2009/01/419392.html?c=on.

5. Their identities were later revealed as Rebecca Joseph and Tova Hausman. See http://notmytribe.com/2009/college-senior-rebecca-joseph-and-junior-tova-hausman-discredit-ucsb-87593.html.

6. As of January 26, 2016, just under seven years after its publication, the video can still be viewed at www.youtube.com/watch?v=yj0dWOOgOeQ.

7. The website features a summary of the case in which it provides links to a variety of relevant documents, including the students' complaints 1 and 2. See https://sb4af.wordpress.com/robinson-case/.

8. The full text of the letter is available online at http://sb4af.wordpress.com/robinson-case/charges-responses/third-robinson-response/.

9. Jeffrey Blankfort, "ADL Spies," *Counterpunch.org* (June 12, 2013), www.counterpunch.org/2013/06/12/adl-spies.

10. See the Committee to Defend Academic Freedom (CDAF) press release from May 2, 2009, available at http://sb4af.wordpress.com/2009/05/02/uc-santa-barbara-faculty-member-goes-public-about-adl-pressure-2/#more-474.

11. FIRE's letter is available at www.thefire.org/fire-letter-to-university-of-californiasanta-barbara-chancellor-henry-t-yang/.

12. The text of Kohr's address is available at www.aipac.org/~/media/Publications/Policy%20and%20Politics/Speeches%20and%20Interviews/Speeches%20by%20AIPAC%20Leadership/2009/05/HowardKohr.pdf.

13. For discussion, see, for example, Jeffrey Herf, *The Jewish Enemy: Nazi Propaganda During World War II and the Holocaust* (Cambridge, MA: Harvard University Press, 2006).

4

The Irvine 11: Power, Punishment, and Perseverance

Taher Herzallah with Osama Shabaik

Editors' note: In 2010, a group of undergraduate students from the University of California at Irvine and Riverside campuses staged a walkout during a speech given on the Irvine campus by Israeli Ambassador to the United States, Michael Oren. Born and raised in the United States, Oren, while serving as ambassador, was also an official with the Israeli army Spokesman's Office, a post from which he played a central role in legitimating the brutal 2008–09 Israeli military assault on Gaza. A worldwide public outcry over the violation of free speech ensued when 11 of the University of California students were arrested after their walkout and criminally charged in a case that became known as the "The Irvine 11." The case raised concern that racism and religious discrimination played a role in the repression, given that all 11 were students of color from the Muslim Student Union and that criminal charges for peaceful protest of this nature – it did not involve civil disobedience, and the students voluntarily exited the auditorium after their voices were heard – are almost unheard of. Local media in Orange County reported that Rabbi Aron Hier, an official from the Simon Wiesenthal Center, a key organization in the Zionist movement and the Israel lobby in the United States, met with the UC Irvine Chancellor before the university announced sanctions. According to these media reports, Aron, accompanied by the director of Hillel, another key organization in the Zionist movement and the lobby, also met with staff from the District Attorney's office before it filed charges in the case. Below, one of the 11, in consultation with another, recounts his experience in the protest and its aftermath.

It was about 5:30 pm on Monday, February 8, 2010. I was sitting anxiously in my seat in the back of the Pacific Ballroom at the University of California, Irvine campus alongside many friends and those in solidarity in a sea of nearly 700 spectators. We had all gathered for a speech that was to be delivered by the-then Israeli Ambassador to the United States, Michael Oren. I looked down at my index card and attempted to memorize my notes in preparation for my turn to protest. But my heart was beating too fast. I knew that when the time came I was going to say whatever came to mind. Two seats to my right was fellow protester Osama Shabaik and in between us was Mohamed Abdelgany. The Israeli Ambassador, Michael Oren, having been introduced by an admiring young fan, had just taken the podium with the Israeli and American flags prominently displayed in the background.

About 30 seconds into Oren's speech, Osama sprung up from his chair and shouted "Michael Oren, propagating murder is not an expression of free speech!" The crowd reacted to the interruption energetically. Some encouraged Osama and others shouted at him to be quiet and sit down. Oren, taken aback by the swift and loud voice of a young and passionate Muslim man, stood quietly on stage like a deer in headlights. Osama walked through the row of seats to the aisle where he was received by two police officers and escorted out of the room as the uproar continued among the crowd. So it began, the protest that would have a profound impact on my life and so many other friends, family, and colleagues.

In July 2009, Osama Shabaik and I met in Cairo, Egypt. We were there to take part in a humanitarian aid convoy to Gaza just six months after the devastating Operation Cast Lead, an assault during which Israel massacred 1,400 people in Gaza from late December 2008 to January 2009, including hundreds of children. We wanted to do our part to help the people of Gaza directly and to bear witness to the devastating destruction that Israel had inflicted upon the Palestinian population. We spent about two weeks in Egypt, shuttling between Cairo and Alexandria, collecting supplies, making contacts, and meeting with our convoy leaders to determine how to deal with the Egyptian authorities. At the time, the Mubarak regime [editors' note: the-then dictator of Egypt] imposed restrictions that made it nearly impossible for us to go to Gaza with any useful materials that the Gazans actually needed. As some in our convoy made their way to Al Arish, a town on the way to Gaza, the Egyptian authorities stopped them as they tried to cross the Mubarak

Peace Bridge over the Suez Canal. We learned later that an Israeli war submarine was passing in the canal, and our humanitarian aid convoy was deemed a security threat.

Finally, after two weeks of shuttling between Cairo and Alexandria, negotiations with the Egyptian government, and signing an affidavit absolving the US government of any responsibility for us once we crossed the border into Gaza, we were allowed to enter. The caveat was that we only had 24 hours in Gaza. We left Cairo in the early morning hours, and after six hours in which we were detained at the Rafah Crossing due to Egyptian security procedures, we finally arrived in Gaza after sunset. We were greeted by cheering crowds; everyone on our bus, Christian, Muslim, Jewish, Atheist, Arab, and Non-Arab was chanting one thing: *Allahu Akbar* (God is the Greatest). It was the best feeling I had ever felt in my life; I had never felt freer than at that moment. We had somewhat successfully broken the siege on Gaza and were now sitting with the bravest and most humble survivors of settler-colonial violence on the planet.

The Gaza authorities had prepared dinner for our entire convoy.

After a short nap I had the opportunity to visit with my relatives in Gaza. They took me on a tour of the city to show me buildings that had been destroyed by F-16s. The destruction was intense and frightening. Others in our convoy were able to visit damaged hospitals, such as Al Shifa, and visit with wounded patients in need of medical care. We also met the two young Samouni girls who had lost 21 members of their family in a single Israeli airstrike on their family home on January 4, 2009. The destruction we witnessed at the Jabaliya Refugee Camp was the most devastating scene I had ever witnessed in my life. Building after building – entire neighborhoods – were wiped out. Schools, United Nations food stock houses, homes, and farms were bombed to ashes. These were not "targeted" airstrikes on enemy combatants, as Israel claimed; rather, they were deliberately targeting civilian infrastructure. People with nowhere to go were living in the rubble of their destroyed homes, poking their heads out to look at our convoy as we absorbed the horrible sight with our tear-filled eyes. This was the journey that shaped my understanding of settler-colonialism and the Zionist project in Palestine.

So when a friend of mine at UC Irvine informed me in early February 2010 that Michael Oren, a man who played a key role in the Israeli government propaganda machinery during Operation Cast Lead, was coming to campus a week later, I knew I had to act. I began contacting everyone I knew at UC Riverside and beyond to inform them that we were planning to protest the Israeli Ambassador's visit. When the day of the ambassador's event finally came, the entire group of protestors, maybe one hundred in all, including the ten of us who were willing to risk arrest, gathered for a meeting under a giant tree in the middle of campus. Among those participating in the campus coalition were Chicana/o, Black, and Muslim student organizations, including the UC Irvine Muslim Student Union. Some of our sisters had put together a stack of index cards we were supposed to read during the protest. There was a long line to enter the event at the Pacific Ballroom in the Student Union building. A heavy police presence and metal detectors, not present at any other event I had ever seen on campus, gave us the impression that arrest was a distinct possibility.

The university had rolled out a red carpet for Oren. Zionist groups on and off campus as well as the Political Science department at UC Irvine had sponsored the event. Chancellor Michael Drake, the Vice Chancellor, and numerous senior faculty members were present. In addition, many of the university's major donors and Irvine community members were present since they had just participated in a private event with Oren before the lecture. We all felt that the university's treatment of Oren as a dignitary without questioning Israel's policies or allowing an opposing voice to challenge Oren was a tacit approval of Israel's genocidal policies.

The Muslim Student Union had organized many events around Palestine on campus before with national and international dignitaries such as former US Ambassador Edward Peck and former US Congress-woman Cynthia McKinney. Yet not once did the administration or the Political Science department offer to sponsor or give any assistance whatsoever to the events. The hypocrisy was plain to see. When the Muslim Student Union issued a statement a week prior to Oren's speech condemning the ambassador's presence on campus the university administration warned the group that it should remain "civil" and not dare to challenge Oren or the university administration on the matter. The Muslim Student Union responded that the organization itself was not planning to take any action but that it could not prevent its members acting on their own from protesting.

The Protest

Osama Shabaik was the first to get up and fire back at the ambassador. Oren, taken aback, stopped speaking as Mark Petracca, the head of the Political Science department, jumped on stage. "Having one person protest is fine," he declared. "Get it out of your system because we are going to be polite and courteous to our guest." Just as Oren resumed his composure, Joseph Haider, with a go-ahead text message from Mohamed Abdelgany, got up and interrupted Oren. Petracca again jumped on stage, lectured everyone to "be polite," and demanded that anyone who wanted their voice heard wait until the Q & A session. No sooner had Oren continued than Anas Qureishi interrupted him with a loud and thunderous rebuke of Israel and its actions.

By that point, Oren had had enough and walked off stage. Petracca jumped back on, livid. "Shame on all of you!" he exclaimed, threatening any further protesters with suspension and possibly arrest. We were pleased with the success of our protest, assuming that Oren was gone for good. But as we remained in our seats just in case he got back on stage, officials from the university administration and UC Irvine police apparently noticed that right before someone protested, Mohamed Abdelgany would text. They called Mohamed over to the side and demanded that he turn over his phone but he refused. If he were seen to be texting again, they warned him, his phone would be confiscated and he would suffer further unspecified consequences. Nonetheless, Mohamed came back to the row where we were sitting and handed me his cell phone. He told me to text the next person so it doesn't seem like he's the one coordinating the effort.

It was clear to us at this point that anyone else who chose to further the protest would likely be arrested. The seven of us slated to go next had to be willing to get arrested because we now knew that the administration had directed the police to do so. After a few minutes, Oren returned to the stage and resumed his speech. Nearly 20 seconds in, he was interrupted again, this time by Ali Saeed. Oren again went quiet but this time he decided to stay on stage. Finally, it was my turn on the list. I handed the phone back to Mohamed and upon his signal got up and exclaimed, "It is a shame that this university has sponsored a mass murderer like yourself!" With that, just as those who preceded me, I walked over to the police and was taken to the backroom where we were all being detained. I remember walking into that room and seeing my friends sitting on the floor with handcuffs on and their hands behind their backs. The police had tables full of riot gear, as if we were going to burn the place down. Two police officers put me against the wall and searched me while asking if I had anything on me. They took my wallet and my ID and placed handcuffs around my wrists and sat me down next to the rest of my friends.

Some of us were fasting for Ramadan and hadn't broken our fast yet. So one of the police officers got a cup of water and allowed us to drink. I remember her saying, "I agree with your position, just not fond of the way you went about this." A few moments after I was brought to the detention room, Shaheen Nassar was escorted in, then Khalid Akari, Asaad Traina, Mohamed Abdelgany, and Aslam Akhtar each arrived in turn. There were ten of us in the room when, all of a sudden, we see another brother come in escorted by the police. Unexpectedly, the police had arrested Hakim Kabir as he was walking out of the event with the rest of the group.

We were all cited that day for violating California Penal Code 626.2, which states,

> Every student or employee who, after a hearing, has been suspended or dismissed from a community college, a state university, the university, or a public or private school for disrupting the orderly operation of the campus or facility of the institution … and who willfully and knowingly enters upon the campus or facility of the institution to which he or she has been denied access, without the express written permission of the chief administrative officer of the campus or facility, is guilty of a misdemeanor and shall be punished …

As we sat in the room waiting for the event to finish and for the police to handle all the paperwork, we realized that there were some non-uniformed personnel in the room taking down all of our information. We asked who they were, but they didn't respond. The non-uniformed personnel then spoke to one of the officers, and, as he was speaking, we heard his unmistakable Israeli accent. It was clear that the person taking down our information was part of Oren's security detail and most likely an Israeli security agent of some sort. We protested with the officers that our information should not be given to that individual, but they ignored us. The chief of the UC Irvine police came into the room where we were being detained and lectured us on how disgraceful we all were and how our parents didn't discipline us properly. He then stated that he didn't have enough vehicles to take all of us to the police station to book us and put us in jail and that we were being released right then and there. The chief then stated that all students not from UC Irvine, which included myself, Shaheen, and Khalid, were banned from UC Irvine for a month. If we were to be seen on campus we would be arrested and subject to legal sanctions.

The Aftermath: Criminalizing the Protesters

The next morning, as the media was buzzing with the previous night's events, all of us involved in the protest began receiving emails from our respective administrations. All 11 of us were notified by our respective administrations that we were being summoned with the student conduct office to review alleged violations of campus policy. In my meeting with the student conduct officer, I confirmed that it was I in a video of the incident that she showed me. With my attorney Reem Salahi present, I asked the officer which administrator had asked her to call the meeting because the Vice Chancellor of Student Affairs on my campus at UC Riverside had previously attempted to censure our campus chapter of Students for Justice in Palestine for our activities. The student conduct officer refused to answer but from the look on her face it was clear to me who had put her up to the meeting. It was also clear that the student conduct office was less than enthusiastic about prosecuting us, as the office more typically deals with such cases as students who plagiarized or were involved in major offenses on campus.

A week or so later the university sent me and my two UC Riverside classmates another message informing us that we were all on academic probation for an entire academic quarter and that we would have to write a paper of considerable length about free speech and why what we had done was wrong. Academic probation meant that I could no longer be president of my Students for Justice in Palestine chapter and could hold no official role with any student organization on campus. It also meant I was not able to take any special independent study course or study abroad for those ten weeks. Our attorney advised us to write the paper as soon as possible and submit it to the student conduct office. So,

I did, but wrote it on why I thought our protest was a legitimate form of free expression and why the ambassador deserved to be the target of such peaceful protest. To my surprise, the essay was accepted and my academic probation was lifted ten weeks later.

At UC Irvine, the situation was different and far more repressive. The students there were dealing with severe punishments and the Muslim Student Union (MSU) was threatened with having its charter suspended. Somehow, an email discussion about the protest on an MSU-owned thread was leaked to the campus administration, which implicated the MSU as having coordinated the protest, despite our claims to the contrary. To this day, we have no idea how that email was leaked and who did it. That email would set in motion a set of sanctions against the individual students and the MSU. It would give the Orange County District Attorney a pretext to charge us with committing a crime and the conspiracy to commit a crime, which in the state of California can be charged as a felony.

Over the next year, from February 2010 to January 2011, the MSU and we protestors faced a campaign of academic repression and the violation of our rights to free speech. Most of us were placed on academic probation and a couple of us were entirely suspended from school. The university administration decided to take action against the MSU. The Muslim Student Union's charter was entirely suspended for an academic quarter. During this time our remarkable attorney, Reem Salahi, fought on our behalf. Throughout the year we heard from other members of the MSU that government investigators were knocking on their doors at 4 or 5 am to ask them questions about the protest and certain members of the organization. We learned that Orange County District Attorney, Anthony Rackaucus, was investigating the case. But the campaign to punish us was barely heating up. We learned that several students who were not part of the protest were being summoned for Grand Jury hearings to testify about the MSU and the Irvine 11 protest. Grand Jury hearings are usually used for major counter-terrorism and homicide cases, not for peaceful student protest. Jury members berated some of the Muslim sisters they summoned over their hijab and their spiritual rituals. None of this harassment had anything to do with the case, but our fellow Muslim students were made to feel extremely vulnerable, especially since one is not allowed an attorney during Grand Jury hearings.

Then, just days before the statute of limitations was to run out to charge us with misdemeanors, in early February 2011, we received notice that the District Attorney (DA) had filed criminal charges. We were being charged under California Penal Code 403 which states, "Every person who, without authority of law, willfully disturbs or breaks up any assembly or meeting that is not unlawful in its character, other than an assembly or meeting referred to in Section 302 of the Penal Code or Section 18340 of the Elections Code, is guilty of a misdemeanor." Attorney Reem Salahi put together a phenomenal team of attorneys from all over California and the United States, including Jacqueline Goodman, Dan Stormer, Dan Mayfield, Tarek Shawky, Lisa Holder, and for a limited time, the legendary Linda Moreno. All of them committed to this case *pro bono*. It was truly inspiring and empowering to have people like that on the front lines with us.

Soon after, we were asked to meet with the DA and others from his office to offer us a plea deal before trial. He offered to drop our charges if we agreed to make a public apology for our protest, pay the fines, and do some community service. All 11 of us felt that we had done nothing wrong and were proud of our protest. There was no way we were going to apologize. To whom were we to apologize? The university, which had just finished suspending and sanctioning us? The Zionist organizations on and off campus that had been trying to intimidate us and hinder our efforts to fight for justice in Palestine? No way. We rejected the deal. Pre-trial hearings opened and a seven-month criminal prosecution was set in motion.

The Trial

The day we were indicted, Rackaucus and his crony Susan Shroeder took to the media to smear us as much as possible. It was clear that the intentions of the DA were to use Islamophobia and other prejudicial public sentiments of the mostly conservative voter base of Orange County to win the case in the media. Shroeder was accusing us of interrupting Oren's speech because we "hate his religion," insinuating that our motives were inherently anti-Semitic. The DA himself made such statements as "we will not allow a small band of people to hijack our freedoms." In the midst of this inflammatory speech on the part of the state prosecution the judge decided to approve a motion by the defense attorneys to place a gag order on everyone involved in the case.

The DA's office was required during the pre-trial hearings to turn over all evidence it was going to use against us to our defense attorneys. At this point we became aware of the sheer magnitude of the emails subpoenaed by the DA: there were tens of thousands of documents! As Reem Salahi and her team were sifting through the evidence, they realized that the DA was using a single email sent by Hakim Kabir to claim that he was part of the conspiracy to join the protest. The problem was that email exchange occurred between Hakim and Reem herself, meaning that it was protected by the attorney-client privilege, and the DA was not supposed to have even looked at it. Once this revelation was made, the defense attorneys came together to file a motion to recuse the DA from the case because it was clear that his team had access to attorney-client privileged information. The judge refused to recuse the entire office but did recuse the lead investigator on the case as well as two others. Also, the charges against Hakim had to be dropped, and so the DA decided to allow him to walk with some community service.

From February to September 2011, we were dragged through the excruciatingly long pre-trial process, spending many hours in the courtroom. Shuttling back and forth to the courthouse was also taxing, since we had to be there early in the morning and most of us had a long drive. The trial date was finally set after much deliberation and after it became clear that neither side was going to capitulate. The DA deliberately wanted the trial date to coincide with the tenth anniversary of the September 11, 2001 attacks, and so our trial started a day after, on September 12. During jury selection a pool of more than 300 Orange County residents were brought in as potential jurors. One of our attorneys, Linda Moreno, created a questionnaire to ask the jurors basic questions so that she could identify who had a clear anti-Muslim bias. The answers to some of the questions were extraordinary – some people were openly racist. The jurors eventually selected comprised an all-white mixture of men and women. Our attorneys tried their best to include people of color but that was extremely difficult considering the pool we had to work with in Orange County.

The trial went on for two and a half weeks – unprecedented for a misdemeanor case. We knew going in that our chances of winning were slim, given that statistically Orange County jurors side with the prosecution more than 85 percent of the time. Moreover, the DA placed Dan Wagner, the head of his homicide division, on the case. Wagner was a UC Berkeley Law School alumnus who held a very successful record in prosecuting murder cases. That he was somehow assigned to a case involving student protesters demonstrates again just how important this case was for the state. The opening arguments in our case were something straight out of a counter-terrorism prosecution. Dan Wagner began by identifying Mohamed Abdelgany and me as leaders in the "Muslim student movement in California." He then claimed that our respective campuses' Muslim Students Associations were tied to the Muslim Brotherhood.

With this, Wagner set the tone for the rest of the trial. It was clear that Wagner's intent was not merely to convince the jury that we had substantially disrupted a public event. Rather, he aimed to tie us to something bigger, to something scarier, and to stoke fear among the jury and the public. Our trial was a unique mash-up of video presentations, witness testimonies, courtroom outbursts and high emotion among the public audience present and the court and in the larger US and world public. Our key witnesses were other student activists, community members, professors, and even the head of security for the Los Angeles Lakers basketball team! They testified to everything from previous campus protests to the history of the Palestinian-Israeli impasse to when the Israeli Ambassador had met with the Lakers player, Kobe Bryant.

Every single day of our trial, the courtroom was full of supporters. We had people coming from all over the country to attend our trial. The presence of all these people, among them family members, friends, and supporters along with a battery of reporters, made us feel empowered and raised our morale. It was truly inspiring to see that so many people cared about this trial and the precedent it would set. Our "Stand With the 11" campaign was receiving messages from all over the world expressing support for us. People from Palestine and students from Palestinian universities were thanking us for boldly challenging the Israeli government. International newspapers were covering the case and family members overseas were sending me pictures of newspaper clippings with my picture featured in them. The local and international support we received kept us going and helped us to stay strong throughout the entire ordeal.

After three days of deliberation, the jury came to a decision. The prosecution had successfully convinced the jury that we had "substantially disrupted" the Oren speech and had "conspired" to do so based on the email evidence. The 12 jurors unanimously found all ten of us guilty of *both* disrupting the public event *and* of conspiracy to commit a crime. Once the verdict was read, people in the audience, appalled by the injustice, began crying and yelling. Even one of the jurors started crying. The woman reading the verdict choked up and the bailiff gave us all big hugs. Some in the DA's office came to us and congratulated us on a well-fought battle. Apparently, a number of people in the DA's office had major disagreements with the DA. They tried to help us during the trial by leaking an internal email discussion about how the DA was framing our case as the "UCI Muslim Case."

After the conviction was read, the next step was the sentencing. The judge had to decide whether to give us jail time or community service with a fine. Since we were convicted of conspiracy it was possible that we would serve up to six months in prison. After a short break, the judge came back and stated: "the justice system is supposed to make people feel remorse for what they did," that we "were men of good moral standing in [our] communities and that [we] acted on principles [we] believed in." Jail time, he said, would only make us "political martyrs and empower [us] even more." He ordered us to complete 56 hours of community service and three years of informal probation and to pay a fine of several hundred dollars.

This was exactly what the DA had offered us in the plea deal. The DA was livid even though he had won the case! In a press conference immediately after the trial, he chided the judge for not punishing us more severely. Although we had lost the case, the media and community treated us as the victors. Our attorneys immediately began the process of filing an appeal with the help of a wonderful attorney named Lisa Jaskol and amici briefs written by supporting organizations. The appeal process would take several years and was eventually denied, in 2013, before a panel of three judges. A year later the appellate court denied our motion to transfer the case from the Appellate Division of the Superior Court to the Court of Appeal, effectively ending any chance of reversing the convictions.

I know that I speak on behalf of all of the Irvine 11 when I say that this ordeal has been life changing. For me, it was the fuel I needed to propel forward my activism for Palestine. I have since been hired by an organization dedicated to the cause of Palestine in the United States. My friends who were arrested with me remain strong supporters of the cause of Palestine and have never had an ounce of regret for standing against Oren and the State of Israel. As a matter of fact, some of them have joined me in other actions and demonstrations in the years since our ordeal. The District Attorney inadvertently ended up helping us to amplify our voices. The longer the trial went on, the more attention we received. This meant that we had more opportunity, in the national and international spotlight, to discuss the plight of the Palestinian people and to address activists around the world struggling for the noble cause of justice for Palestine. For those Zionists who believed that they were going to make us hide and disappear, their strategy clearly failed. The more they attacked us and put barriers in our path, the more we became seasoned soldiers. The only regret I have about that day is that I didn't protest longer.

5

A Problem Grows in Brooklyn

Kristofer J. Petersen-Overton

Editors' note: In January 2011, Brooklyn College rescinded the appointment of doctoral candidate Kristofer Petersen-Overton to teach a course on politics in the Middle East after New York State assembly member Dov Hikind complained about his criticism of Israel. Hikind wrote to the college after a student, who was planning to take the course, objected to Petersen-Overton's work with the Palestinian Center for Human Rights, one of the leading human rights organizations in the Middle East. Although Hikind accused Petersen-Overton of supporting suicide bombers in Israel, Hikind himself, ironically, is a former member of the Jewish Defense League, an organization described by the FBI as a "right-wing terrorist group." The college eventually reinstated Petersen-Overton after an outcry from faculty and community groups.

I came to Brooklyn College at an explosive time and, though I did not realize it then, the pushback against my arrival can be attributed to a number of factors that should have been obvious. In September 2010, exactly one semester before I was hired, Brooklyn College initiated a freshman outreach program in which students were asked to read English professor Moustafa Bayoumi's recently published book, *How Does It Feel to Be a Problem? Being Young and Arab in America*. The book's title is an explicit reference to W.E.B. Dubois' *The Souls of Black Folk*, and it probes anti-Muslim and anti-Arab sentiment in the post-9/11 United States. For one of New York City's most diverse institutions, it was a matter worthy of serious discussion, especially with undergraduates. Unfortunately, because the school aimed this particular initiative at the entire incoming class, some felt it was tantamount to an inappropriate endorsement of the views expounded in the book. Bruce Kesler, an alumnus of the college, posted a handful of angry and hyperbolic statements on his blog, charging the college with what he perceived as a campaign of political indoctrination. As Kesler described it, Brooklyn College was "quite liberal" when he graduated in the 1960s, but "there was no official policy to inculcate students with a political viewpoint." Now, he believed, there was.

Kesler focused his attention on several passages in the book he perceived as supportive of the Palestinian struggle against Israeli occupation and denounced Bayoumi as a "radical pro-Palestinian professor." With characteristic bravado, Kesler reported on his blog that he would be removing Brooklyn College as a beneficiary in his will. Though no amount of money was specified, Kesler's flair for melodrama was reproduced in the *New York Post* and *Daily News*. Even the more level-headed *New York Times* apparently felt the story justified a web-only article featuring quotes taken from Kesler's blog. Only after the media began to reprint Kesler's objections did anyone seem to care about the case. This kind of online bloviating would not typically have attracted any attention at all, but for one important factor that would play a role in my own case not long after: a media determined to depict any hint of Jewish-Muslim campus controversy as a microcosm of the Israeli-Palestinian conflict.

The City University of New York (CUNY) system has historically offered affordable education to the city's working class and immigrant populations. Located in one of New York's long-standing Jewish communities, Brooklyn College has until recently served a predominantly Jewish student body. When it was founded, CUNY also became a haven for Jewish professors, who were otherwise barred from employment at many universities like Yale. A number of world-renowned Jewish scholars have taught at Brooklyn College, including the great political philosopher Hannah Arendt among others. The simple point I wish to make here is that Brooklyn College has always occupied a special place in the imaginary of Jewish life and culture of New York City. But as the modern face of American multiculturalism has brought more Arab and Muslim students to the neighborhood, so Brooklyn College's majority Jewish student population has ebbed. The angle of demographic conflict and especially Jewish-Muslim relations has proved too appealing for the media. While many contemporary American university campuses – and certainly most other CUNY campuses – have a healthy range of student groups representing all positions on the Israeli-Palestinian conflict, the issues take on an importance at Brooklyn College out of all proportion to corresponding reality. Only by acknowledging this peculiar blend of factors is it at all comprehensible that an alumnus of unknown reputation was able to pique the interest of every major newspaper in the city armed only with his personal blog and an affinity for outrage expressed in caps-lock.

In this particular battle, the immediate precedent to my own case, Professor Bayoumi prevailed. The college cited their unfailing support for academic freedom, condemned the inappropriate intrusion of outside forces on academic curriculum, and went ahead with their initiative as originally planned. When I agreed to teach a graduate-level seminar on Middle East politics as an adjunct lecturer the following semester, I had never heard of Bruce Kesler and was unaware of all that I have just described.

Doctoral students at CUNY teach many courses at the two-dozen campuses that make up the nation's largest urban public university system. Yet by my second year in the political science program at the CUNY Graduate Center, I still had not landed a teaching gig and began to grow concerned about financing my degree. Fortunately, a Middle East scholar then based at the Graduate Center who was aware of my prior experience as a human rights activist in Gaza recommended me to the interim chair at Brooklyn College as an eligible instructor for a graduate seminar they were offering on Middle East politics in the spring of 2011. After drafting a syllabus and forwarding my CV to the Political Science department, I came to Brooklyn College in early December for an informal interview and to sign a contract. This all went swimmingly and resulted in my course being added to the catalog listing with my name attached. The first signs of trouble began not long after.

Shortly after my interview with the interim chair, he called to let me know about an online controversy brewing over my appointment. It was news to me at the time, but I was told not to worry. The department had weathered controversy before, he said, and they would support me all the way. When I got off the phone, a quick online search brought me to Bruce Kesler's blog for the first time and a post entitled "Gaza Defender Hired To Teach Middle East At Brooklyn College." Kesler's post mostly reproduces information sent to him from a student who had apparently registered for my course. Dina Kupfer – anonymous to me at the time – seems to have become concerned upon learning of my background as a human rights activist in Gaza. Culling information from my personal website about my past and present political commitments, Kupfer complained to the department that I was unfit to teach such a course. She dismissed me as an "active partisan of Palestinians in Gaza" and questioned my capacity for "wide scholarship, balance, and presentations that will bring credit to Brooklyn College." As evidence of my "chilling" politics and "personal support for Palestine and Palestinians only," Kupfer supplied a comprehensive point-by-point litany of sins, including virtually everything I had written online about the conflict up to that point, no matter how obscure. Her list included passages drawn from my scholarly work, some of which she felt "normalized" suicide bomb attacks, as well as many more casual comments left on blogs and other web-fora.

I learned later that her initial appeal to the department was duly rebuffed; the interim chair had suggested that she wait at least until classes began before pursuing a complaint. Kupfer did not wait. Instead, she passed along her letter to Bruce Kesler, who reproduced it on his blog with some added commentary. Kesler mocked my affiliation with a human rights group in Gaza; he questioned the academic worth of a book chapter I co-authored with two Danish scholars by insinuating that a prior publication with the socialist *Monthly Review* discredits their expertise; and he presented my personal correspondence with noted linguist and political activist Noam Chomsky as self-evidently damning. The right-wing Zionist blogosphere, notably Pamela Geller's Islamophobic *Atlas Shrugs* blog, was quick to run versions of the story as well. The descriptions of me in this otherwise bleak world were quite colorful, and I soon learned that apparently I was "pro-suicide bomber," "pro-Hamas," "pro-Muslim Brotherhood," "Islamist," a "terrorist lover," and advocate of "Jew hatred."

Like anyone who deals with the Israeli-Palestinian conflict in some capacity, I had expected this kind of nonsense sooner or later, though I was admittedly surprised to experience it so early. After all, I was an unknown graduate student with a lightweight publication record and no real influence to speak of. Why were they targeting me? It would be incorrect to suggest that I was concerned at this point, but the depth of vitriol did make me rather uneasy. I knew nothing in my record could be seriously construed as support for terrorism, but I nevertheless took steps to protect myself and removed any indication of my contact details from the internet. When the Political Science department at Brooklyn College reassured me again that everything would be all right, I tried to put the whole thing out of my mind and focus on my work. Unbeknownst to me, a local politician had just taken an interest in my case and was at that moment (again, thanks to my own website) thoroughly scouring everything I had ever written.

In Steps a Two-bit Local Politician with Powerful Lobby Connections

One afternoon several days later, I received an email from a journalist with the Orthodox Jewish newspaper *HaModia*. He asked if I had a response to a press release just issued by New York State Assemblyman Dov Hikind. I had not been aware of any such statement, so he forwarded me a copy. In the course of denouncing my appointment, Hikind had called me an "overt supporter of terrorism," drawing attention in particular to an unpublished seminar paper I had written on the conceptual role of martyrdom in Palestinian nationalism. To be clear, the notion of martyrdom – a term used in many societies for those who sacrifice their lives for a cause – is familiar to all forms of nationalism. It is also a volatile concept among polemicists and bigots, for whom it connotes Islamist terrorism alone and suicide bombings in particular. Though my paper barely mentioned suicide bombings, the Assemblyman crudely interpreted it as tacit approval of such attacks. He joked that I was "better suited for a teaching position at the Islamic University of Gaza" than at CUNY.

Unfortunately, I did not have the opportunity to teach at one of Gaza's largest institutions of higher learning before it was destroyed by Israeli missiles in 2014, but Hikind could not have known this. His comment was obviously intended to mock the notion that a university in Gaza could be anything other than a nursery for terrorism. So I made a statement, which, to its credit, *HaModia* published alongside the Assemblyman's unhinged charges. Hikind specializes in using his hard-line pro-Israel advocacy, notably as a former activist with the right-wing Jewish Defense League and as an owner of property in an illegal West Bank settlement, as a cypher for votes in his Jewish constituency – notwithstanding the formal purview of his office as having absolutely nothing to do with foreign policy. Still, I was an easy target and attacking me would boost his Zionist credentials, whatever the ultimate outcome. Things began to move quickly once he got involved. Local television news PIX-11 somehow found my number and called asking for an interview the next day.

I told the camera crew to meet me in the lobby of the Graduate Center in midtown Manhattan. Shortly before they arrived, the Brooklyn College Political Science department unexpectedly called with bad news. I was told the Provost had unilaterally and quite unexpectedly cancelled my appointment. Provost William Tramontano, a biologist by training, had concluded that my credentials did not justify teaching a graduate-level course. In principle, I would have to agree. By CUNY standards, however, where doctoral students regularly teach graduate seminars, it was not at all unusual for someone with my qualifications to teach such a class. Another doctoral student had taught the exact same course I was slated to teach previously. Indeed, I was probably *more* qualified than many of my peers, having already earned a Master's degree and published on the subject before arriving at CUNY. The chair apologized over the phone, stressed how unprecedented this kind of intervention was, and insisted the department would push to hire me in the future. I was utterly shocked. I had no doubts about the political motivation behind my firing but I simply could not believe that a two-bit local politician had actually succeeded in scuttling my appointment barely a week before classes were to begin.

It's important to mention that I was never once in contact with anyone from the administration before, during, or after the controversy. Instead, I culled the full extent of my knowledge about the reasoning behind their actions from press statements and from some of the more comprehensive journalistic accounts. From *Jewish Week*, for instance, I learned that a member of the Board of CUNY Trustees, Jeffrey Wiesenfeld, had complained about my appointment to the chancellor at the time, Matthew Goldstein. Wiesenfeld made no secret of his Zionist activism then or since. Before he got involved in my own case, he reportedly declared, "Every public and private campus has its share of 'revolutionaries' who think proselytization is synonymous with education. I've made it my business not to be silent when this phenomenon raises its ugly head at a CUNY campus."[1] Perhaps Wiesenfeld believed I fit this description and took measures to keep me out of the classroom. Certainly, after my case, he was more publically involved in a number of other controversies, including a failed attempt to prevent the playwright Tony Kushner from receiving an honorary degree because of comments he made about Israel and another failed attempt to scuttle a conference on Israeli "pinkwashing" at the Graduate Center.

On the day of my dismissal, the camera crew from PIX-11 arrived as scheduled, and their story quickly adapted to the circumstances, gleefully shifting from a story about the controversy to a story about my firing. I gave as level-headed an interview as I could muster and then raced home. There was no question about fighting for my job. It never once occurred to me not to, and I don't feel, as some told me later, that there was anything brave in doing so. Besides the principles I felt were at stake, it was my only source of income for the semester. Finding another position at such a late stage would have been extremely unlikely, and once the Graduate Center promised to fund me if Brooklyn College refused to budge, I had very little to lose by fighting back.

The first step was drafting a press release: "CUNY Provost Intervenes To Cancel Appointment of Controversial Brooklyn College Professor – Grave Implications For Academic Freedom." With the help of my then-wife, I began sending it to anyone I thought might be interested, including student mailing lists, activist networks, academic colleagues, and journalists. I got in touch with other victims of similar smear campaigns including Norman Finkelstein, Joseph Massad, Rashid Khalidi, and Moustafa Bayoumi, who all graciously offered their support in various ways. I sent copies of the press release to every major Middle East club or Palestinian student association in the country. Within hours, my inbox was overflowing with messages of support as well as copies of my own press release sent by mailing lists of which I happened to be a member. As we worked furiously into the night, it began to snow. The Northeastern blizzard of January–February 2011 had begun. It would shutter CUNY and give us time to consider our next move.

The days passed seamlessly, one into the next as we worked in sittings of 15 hours at a time, and still the snow fell, enveloping New York in a peaceful calm that contrasted sharply with the digital melee we were waging. For the next six days, I left the apartment only to give interviews with the independent news broadcast *Democracy Now!* and another community television program in Manhattan. The rest of my time was spent on the phone with journalists, activists, and colleagues. My inbox received so many messages; I could barely keep up with my determination to send a personal reply to each. A photo-journalist visited me at home to take my picture in what struck me as rather comical poses under the circumstances: first, sitting defiantly in my living room, then staring thoughtfully out the window. Versions of the story ran in the *New York Times*, *New York Post*, *Daily News*, *Chronicle of Higher Education*, *Inside Higher Ed*, *Salon*, *Jewish Week*, and countless blogs. The CUNY Graduate Center student newspaper began live-blogging the affair on their website, reproducing letters sent from academic heavyweights as they filtered in, including contributions from John Mearsheimer, Noam Chomsky, Rashid Khalidi, Susan Buck-Morss, Mahmood Mamdani, Neve Gordon, Joan Wallach Scott, and the former President of the American Association of University Professors (AAUP), Cary Nelson, among many, many others. An online petition calling for my immediate reinstatement produced 1,000 signatures within 48 hours and continued to grow. Student activists got in touch about having me speak at a protest rally they were planning to hold at Brooklyn College. The Political Science department at the Graduate Center considerably eased my lingering financial concerns by promising a small funding package if Brooklyn College failed to "come to their senses." Though I received several hate emails, the support was overwhelming and decisive.

When I wasn't speaking with journalists, I was on the phone with members of the Brooklyn College Political Science department. They perceived the administrative action as a violation of departmental autonomy, and nearly every member supported my reinstatement, though I later heard that a minority of faculty were not particularly eager to defend a mere adjunct against the full force of administrative will. More than anyone else involved, my discussions with the political theorist Corey Robin helped bolster my confidence and gave me the psychological boost I needed to pursue the fight. With his extensive contacts, he was able to marshal big names to my cause. In retrospect, Professor Robin's role in my case was something of a trial run for his later efforts to mobilize scholars in opposition to the University of Illinois Urbana-Champaign's firing of Steven Salaita. Without Robin's support and his tireless behind-the-scenes work on my case, it's impossible to know how things may have turned out.

CUNY Backs Down

When the snow finally stopped falling in early February, the roads were cleared, and CUNY's campuses reopened. In a meeting that was later described to me as their "most important ever," the Political science department voted unanimously to rehire me and effectively challenged the administration not to approve the decision this time around. The provost had received a deluge of letters, many from some of the most important scholars in their respective fields, on my behalf – indeed, on behalf of academic freedom; national organizations like the AAUP and Foundation for Individual Rights in Education (FIRE) condemned the college's actions; student groups were planning a demonstration to demand my reinstatement; and now the department that originally hired me was more or less daring them not to hire me. Under such pressure they crumbled. When the college announced my reappointment, they claimed that unspecified new information about my qualifications had come to light – presumably, at some point in the six-day period between my firing and rehiring and without speaking with me.

Whatever the precise confluence of forces initiated by the original student complaint, the administration came to view me as a liability. They consistently clung to their argument about my credentials, even when people stopped believing it and vehemently denied any suggestion that politics had influenced the provost's decision. Their press statements were contorted praises of academic freedom coupled with lamentations of regret over my supposed dearth of credentials. For anyone who has watched these battles unfold previously, my case adheres to some familiar contours.

Particularly since 9/11, professors with views perceived as anti-American or anti-Israeli have come under attack. For anyone who takes the autonomy of the university seriously, the involvement of public officials is cause for alarm. In the letter he sent to Brooklyn College President Karen Gould, Hikind invokes liberal language to justify suppressing my voice, apparently without a sense of irony. He writes of "the responsibility of a true academic," which, in his view, is "to remain objective in imparting information and to allow students to draw their own conclusions. Mr. Petersen-Overton's personal biases should not be allowed to pollute the academic realm, nor should taxpayer dollars be devoted to promoting his one-sided agenda." As a public servant, Hikind's involvement not only lent a degree of authority to the attacks against me but actually expanded upon them. Absent his involvement, the minor controversy over my appointment in some of the more fetid corners of the internet would surely have dissipated without wider acknowledgement.

One of the most disturbing elements of my case was the readiness with which Brooklyn College caved at the slightest whiff of controversy, effectively placing more faith in the ravings of an irresponsible politician than in the judgment of their own faculty who had hired me to begin with. The administration's lack of integrity can be linked to three general themes that appear not only in my own case but also in so many others involving the violation of academic freedom in the United States.

The first concerns my job title: I was an adjunct lecturer, one of many contingent instructors that today make up the proletarian backbone of the neoliberal university. As an adjunct lecturer,[2] my financial security was dependent on the goodwill of colleagues better placed than myself. From one semester to the next, my fate relied on their continued charity. It is rare for one to be fired exactly as an adjunct; instead, one's contract is not renewed. Those facing such a scenario are not typically even entitled to a reason – whether the unpredictable vagaries of a fickle job market or the tyranny of unsympathetic peers. In practice, non-renewal can occur for literally any reason at all. To avoid rustling feathers, I am personally aware of adjuncts teaching at CUNY today that refuse to engage on any controversial issue, whether in their classes with students or independently in their free time. Many go out of their way to avoid politics altogether. Even participation in faculty union activities could trigger punitive measures from a retaliatory department. A new chair who disapproves of this or that cause could spell economic disaster for an adjunct earning less than $3,000 a course.

A second theme that might help explain the college's pandering to extra-academic interests is related to the first: the adoption by university administrators of a boardroom mentality and especially the elimination of tenure. The corporatization of universities has caused administrators to become understandably more concerned with protecting carefully cultivated brands, in addition to a wide array of other consequences. Besides maintaining a reserve army of adjunct labor, corporatization has led to the erosion of tenure and the institutional protection it guarantees. The standards for tenure in the United States usually aspire to align with the AAUPs' "1940 Statement of Principles on Academic Freedom and Tenure." As the title indicates, the AAUP's statement draws a clear link between academic freedom – the ability to pursue research unfettered by political concerns – and tenure. The institutional defense of academic freedom goes to the very heart of the university's mission and the pursuit of knowledge for its own sake. Yet tenure has increasingly become the province of an elite few, rendering academic freedom meaningless in practice – certainly for anyone not admitted to the tenure club.

Finally, a third theme emerges from my case: the question of objectivity and scholarship. So much of the anger directed at my appointment seemed to contain a strange but common expectation of objectivity and a visceral distaste for its dreaded opposite: bias. What objectivity and bias mean when it comes to the academy evolves depending on the circumstances and the parties making the accusations, but the scholar is not a journalist, and a romanticized notion of objectivity is both unrealistic and undesirable. Scholarship is always embedded with normative concerns, intentional or not. As Corey Robin said to me in one of our many telephone conversations during my ordeal, "every syllabus is an argument." Why assign some books and not others? Why emphasize these themes and not others? The process of drafting a syllabus is as much defined by what is included as what is left out. No course can hope for the kind of breadth apparently advocated by those who challenged my appointment. As Lisa Anderson notes, "American universities don't teach pre-Copernican astronomy, phrenology, fascism, astrology, eugenics, and a host of other wrong-headed notions (except in courses on the history of ideas), precisely because debates about truth are at the essence of the university."[3]

Moreover, there is a massive literature on the subject of intellectual responsibility, and it offers a resounding consensus on the bankruptcy of detached scholarship and the importance of taking positions. As my detractors quickly discovered, I make no secret of my opposition to Israel's interminable occupation of the Palestinians. Indeed, I am deeply suspicious of anyone simultaneously writing on the subject and claiming objectivity, as they are either involved in a colossal effort at self-deception or simply lying. But eschewing objectivity as such is not sufficient to discredit the positions I have taken.

My case sends mixed messages about the future of academic freedom in the United States. I did not suffer the same fate as so many before me and since. Thanks to the enormous support I received, Brooklyn College was forced to back down. I won the privilege to teach my course, but I worry that the appearance of victory superficially conceals a deeper malaise. I fear my case indicates a new willingness on the part of anti-intellectual thugs to target scholars at the earliest stages of their careers.

These tactics encourage a chilling effect in the hiring of adjuncts whose political views upset those in power. How many departments draw from my case the conclusion that they must vet adjuncts more carefully before hiring them? Check their social media, their personal websites, and any trace of politics that might stir up an unwanted and inconvenient controversy. I cannot fault the Brooklyn College Political Science department for their handling of my case, and I am eternally grateful for the robust support they offered during the ordeal. Yet I was quite disappointed not to have been asked to teach the course when it was offered again several semesters later.

In reaction to my reappointment, CUNY trustee Jeffrey Wiesenfeld accused professors of running a "cabal that suppresses the very academic freedom they claim to represent,"[4] Assemblyman Hikind ominously declared, "We're going to monitor this particular professor."[5] The neo-conservative ideologue David Horowitz visited Brooklyn College to give an ill-informed talk about the Israeli-Palestinian conflict. The course itself, the very first teaching experience of my life, was a miserable one. Dina Kupfer, the student who made the initial complaint against me, remained for the duration of the semester and was no slouch in making it memorable for all the wrong reasons. After a brief but tense confrontation in which I rejected her inappropriate and presumptuous demands for a "syllabus review," she resorted to documenting anything and everything I said in the classroom, even publishing comments without my consent in *Jewish Press* under the pseudonym Yossi Cukier. During the session in which we discussed the development of Zionism and Palestinian nationalism, Dina stood up holding large and extremely graphic photographs of decapitated corpses she said depicted the victims of a multiple murder in the West Bank settlement of Itamar, a crime that had been in the news at the time. "This," she said confidently, "is the result of Palestinian nationalism." It was one of the more outrageous of her stunts, but one that seems to have alienated her from potential allies. A number of students complained that in addition to her classroom theatrics, she was sending them emails every week, documenting in excruciating detail the alleged falsehoods I had discussed in class. When a student forwarded a copy of one of her addenda to me, it didn't come as a surprise that most of it had been lifted verbatim from the website of the Committee for Accuracy in Middle East Reporting in America (CAMERA).[6]

In the end, I felt compelled to put aside my personal discomfort, and I taught the course on principle, but I would absolutely think twice before reliving such an unpleasant experience. A student who disagrees vehemently with my politics is one thing. A university system that underserves adjuncts by caving to any hint of controversy is another entirely. By far the most important lesson that can be dredged from the whole sordid affair has to do with the precariousness of academic freedom in the United States today. Were it not for the unusual support offered from scholars and activists around the world, the efforts to purge me would have succeeded, and I would have been just one more victim of the tectonic changes corporatization and adjunctification have brought to higher education. For those of us in the academy who would oppose these trends, we have our work cut out for us. If you'll excuse a slight twist on a common conservative axiom, my case indicates above all that academic freedom isn't free.

Notes

1. Jeffrey Wiesenfeld, "Letter to the Editor: Forum to Address Bias," *The Sun*, February 11, 2005, www.nysun.com/opinion/letters-to-the-editor-2005-02-11/9119/. All websites last accessed November 12, 2015.

2. Editors' note: An adjunct lecturer is a non-tenure track university teaching position in the United States and some other countries. The position is typically awarded on a course-by-course basis, and an adjunct teaching one course in a term is usually not considered full time for the purposes of receiving employment benefits. Some adjuncts hold full-time jobs in other professions, industries, or institutions, while others are doctoral students or recent PhD graduates scraping together work to make ends meet. As such, a subset of adjunct instructors represents a highly precarious class of workers. Moreover, part-time, non-tenured, and non-tenure-track faculty are the fastest growing group of university instructors and, in 2011, comprised over 60 percent of US college and university instructional staff. See J.W. Curtis, "The Employment Status of Instructional Staff Members in Higher Education, Fall 2011" (American Association of University Professors (AAUP), Washington, DC, April 2014).

3. Lisa Anderson, "Scholarship, Policy, Debate and Conflict: Why We Study the Middle East and Why It Matters," *Middle East Studies Association Bulletin*, 38, no. 1 (2004), p. 10.

4. Doug Chandler, "Academic Freedom Fight Heats Up At B'klyn College," *Jewish Press*, February 2 (2011), www.thejewishweek.com/news/new_york/academic_freedom_fight_heats_up_bklyn_college.

5. John Del Signore, "Pro-Palestine Brooklyn College Prof Rehired, Hikind Ashamed," *Gothamist*, February 1 (2011), http://gothamist.com/2011/02/01/ pro-palestine_brooklyn_college_prof.php.

6. Editors' note: CAMERA is a Zionist, non-profit organization dedicated to correcting what it perceives to be "anti-Israel bias" in the media. See "History of CAMERA" on their website, www.camera.org. According to Alex Beam of *The Boston Globe*, a senior member of CAMERA organized a campaign of more than 50 people to scour the popular website Wikipedia in order to "keep Israel-related entries ... from becoming tainted by anti-Israel editors." War of the virtual Wiki-worlds, *Boston.com*, May 3 (2008).

6

Speaking Truth to Power:
Advocating for Justice in/for Palestine

Rabab Ibrahim Abdulhadi

Editors' note: Upon her return from a research trip to Palestine and Jordan in early 2014, Professor Rabab Abdhulhadi, Associate Professor of Ethnic/Race and Resistance Studies and the senior scholar of the Arab and Muslim Ethnicities and Diasporas (AMED) Initiative at San Francisco State University (SFSU), faced a year-long campaign of harassment and intimidation by the Israel lobby. After she organized an event on campus to discuss her trip and research, the AMCHA Initiative, a California-based Zionist group led by its founding members, Tammi Rossman-Benjamin and Leila Beckwith, accused her of meeting with "known terrorists," threatening the safety of Jewish students and contributing to a "hostile environment." AMCHA demanded that SFSU and the California state government investigate her for abusing taxpayer funds – the public SFSU had awarded Professor Abdulhadi with a faculty research and travel grant, as it does for most faculty.

The administration reviewed the allegations and concluded that they had "no merit." However, pressure from the lobby continued despite a national and international outcry over the blatant harassment and the violation of Professor Abdulhadi's free speech and academic freedom. The university subsequently, in August 2014, took the unprecedented step of auditing Professor Abdulhadi's international travel for previous years all the way back to 2009. The audit absolved Professor Abdulhadi of any wrongdoing, but not before she was forced to put aside her scholarly research and public activities to defend her integrity. One of the intended effects of such campaigns of harassment and intimidation by the lobby, even when these campaigns do not result in official sanctions, is to subject those targeted to prolonged psychological stress, to undermining their professional and political activities, and to smearing their public reputations. Professor Abdulhadi reflects in her testimonial below on some of the harassment she faced in spring 2014.

Zionist attacks on academic freedom at San Francisco State University have a long history, as is the case with most centers of politically conscious intellectual work. As a Palestinian female faculty member, I have been on the front lines and in the crosshairs of these attacks because of my scholarly work and background. While it is not possible to chronicle every single way that Israel advocacy organizations have intervened to suppress conversations on campus in a short testimonial, I will here outline two specific controversies in recent years that expose the nefarious tactics and flawed logics of Zionist campaigns to silence criticism of Israel and support for justice in/for Palestine.

The locus of the first controversy I describe was a 2013 anniversary event commemorating six years of the Palestinian Cultural Mural on campus. The event drew the vitriol of Zionist organizations that fundamentally opposed the mural itself and so took the anniversary event as an opportunity to renew their silencing efforts. The Palestinian Cultural Mural honoring the late Professor Edward Said, inaugurated on November 2, 2007 around the birthday of Said, was the direct result of a long and difficult but successful campaign by a broad coalition of students, faculty, and staff at SFSU, working hand-in-hand with community members and organizations. The student coalition, led by the General Union of Palestinian Students (GUPS), included other student groups, such as the Student Kouncil for Intertribal Nations that was founded by Richard Oakes, the Indigenous student who in 1968 led the take-over of Alcatraz; Black Student Union that, along with the 3rd World Liberation Front, led the successful 1968 Student Strike for a College for Third World Studies at SFSU; as well as other student groups that have been part of the rich history of SFSU, such as the League of Filipino Students, La Raza Student Organization, and Movimiento Estudiantil Chicano De Aztlan.

The Deans of the College of Ethnic Studies, Ken Monteiro, and the College of Education, Jake Perea, were instrumental in the success of the mural. Activists and organizations in the Palestinian, Arab, and Muslim communities, Indigenous communities and communities of color, as well as anti-Zionist Jewish organizations, civil liberties organizations, trade unions, and feminist and queer groups, united around the principle of justice for Palestine as an integral and organic part of justice for all, came together to insist that the mural see the light. The battle lasted several years during which a strong campaign was unsuccessfully waged by the Israel lobby led by the Jewish Community Relations Council (JCRC) and other San Francisco Bay Area Zionist organizations against the mural and, for that matter, any campus presence of Palestine.

Having failed to block the creation of the mural, these same organizations have since sought to silence and intimidate students and faculty in any way connected to it. The most recent rendition of this harassment took place on November 18, 2013, when Tammi Rossman-Benjamin and Leila Beckwith, co-founders of the AMCHA Initiative,[1] sent an email to the SFSU president attacking AMED (Arab and Muslim Ethnicities and Diasporas Initiative) and the General Union of Palestinian Students. The email was copied to the Chancellor and Trustees of California State University to which SFSU belongs, SFSU Provost, Dean of the College of Ethnic Studies as well as members of the California legislature and the Board of Supervisors of San Francisco, heads of major California Jewish organizations that informally belong to Israel's lobby, and countless others.

In their email, AMCHA took aim at the November 2013 anniversary event commemorating the mural, "We Speak for Ourselves: Honoring our Forbearers." Benjamin framed the event as "an antisemitic [sic] on-campus activity that encourages students to glorify the murder of Jews ..."[2] To support these unfounded claims, Rossman-Benjamin and Beckwith referred to two stencils on a table in the Malcolm X Plaza during the afternoon of the event, one that AMCHA claimed was of Leila Khaled and the other inscribed with the statement, "My heroes have always killed colonizers." Aiming at invoking xenophobia and enlisting the "war on terror" in order to portray Palestinian campus activism as dangerous, illegal, and outside the bounds of acceptable discourse, Rossman-Benjamin and Beckwith refer to Khaled as "a member of the U.S. State Department-designated terrorist organization Popular Front for the Liberation of Palestine (PFLP) ... responsible for several plane hijackings, suicide bombings that killed several Jews, and the assassination of a Jewish member of the Israeli Knesset." Had they done a quick search as academics usually do, the AMCHA co-founders would have realized that the stencil was of a Palestinian woman wearing the hijab and not of Leila Khaled. Regardless, Khaled's image is frequently used by Palestinians and non-Palestinians alike to symbolize Palestinian women's roles in anti-colonial resistance and to counter Orientalist and racist portrayals of Arab (and Muslim) women as docile, oppressed, and unable to speak for themselves.

As for the second stencil, "My heroes have always killed colonizers," Rossman-Benjamin and Beckworth's objection is similarly uninformed. Contrary to their claim, Palestinian students were not calling for the murder of Jews or Israelis. In fact, the implication of AMCHA's argument – that all Jews have the same political stands vis-à-vis Israel or that all Jews are colonizing Palestinian lands – is itself anti-Semitic. And notwithstanding their simplistic linkage of Said's anti-colonial intellectual work, the Palestinian Mural anniversary, Palestinian students, and AMED, the stencil was not originally created to specifically target Israel. Instead, it was created with a more inclusive approach to the plight of Indigenous people and their historical resistance everywhere. The stencil was made a few weeks before the anniversary event by Indigenous activists for a different event marking the anniversary of genocide in the Americas on October 14, 2013. Announced on the Native American Indian Network as "The Second Annual 'My HEROES Have Always Killed Colonizers: Stories of Global Indigenous REZistance,'" the event aimed at countering the depiction of the "Indigenous warrior who has been labeled a terrorist, unpatriotic, and/or savage while defending the land, the people, and our traditional ways." The event included a variety of activities, including music, storytelling, poetry, and other performances aimed to "collectively Re-Indigenize our heroes, such as Leila Khaled, Boukman, Lapu-Lapu, Toy Purina and Geronimo so that they may claim their true role in history."

Finally, the November 2013 Palestinian Mural anniversary event was not solely sponsored by GUPS and AMED, as the AMCHA email had implied, with the evident objective of trying to isolate and target Palestinian activists. All the murals on the walls of the Cesar Chavez Student Center, including the murals of Cesar Chavez, Malcolm X, the Indian, Filipino and Native American struggles, belong to the center itself, and they all reflect student commitment to and activism on questions of justice relevant to struggles in their diverse communities.

The history of the Palestinian Mural at SFSU with its broad-based coalition of communal and campus alliances, on the one hand, and the multiple sites that clearly show that the stencil originated with Native American activism and spoke about colonized people everywhere, on the other, debunked the slander campaign. Why, then, would Rossman-Benjamin and Beckwith of AMCHA ignore all these facts and insist on smearing Palestinian activism?

As the movement for justice in/for Palestine gains grounds and grows broader beyond the Palestinian, Arab, and Muslim communities, the Israel lobby has escalated its campaign. Their goals are to arrive at an official position that equates criticism of Israel with anti-Semitism in order to discredit us and prevent us from speaking up. When they fail to do so, they try to manipulate the truth and exact statements of condemnation from university officials by making a lot of noise and mobilizing their listservs to create the impression that lack of statements amounts to acceptance of anti-Semitism. When all else fails, their last resort is to make enough noise to keep us occupied so we won't have the time or energy to speak up for the truth.

Personal Attacks on my Professional Endeavors

The second incident I describe involved a more personal smear campaign against me. This second attack was also mounted by AMCHA – with the full power of the other Israel lobby organizations behind it – but this time, Rossman-Benjamin and Beckwith took issue with a trip to Palestine by a group of academics and labor leaders that I organized and led in early 2014. The 2014 North American Academic and Labor Delegation to Palestine spent 14 days meeting with 198 individuals from 89 organizations, and visited 21 cities, towns, and refugee camps. We met with Palestinians from all walks of life: business people, social workers, legal experts, political prisoners, artists and cultural workers, feminists, trade unionists, LGBTQ youth groups, and members of the Palestinian Legislative Council from different political parties with a range of views regarding Palestinian anti-occupation liberation strategies, including Boycott, Divestment, Sanctions (BDS). The purpose of these meetings was to familiarize participants with the broadest spectrum of Palestinian politics, schools of thought, cultural production, socio-economic analyses, and social movements.

On the topic of this trip, the AMCHA co-founders wrote multiple letters to the SFSU administration and state officials between March and June 2014, alleging that the purpose and logistics of the trip were inappropriate and impermissible. They claimed that I should have only used the funding to attend a conference (which in fact I was unable to attend due to delays in receiving the travel and research grant) and that false pretenses were involved. The Dean of the SFSU College of Ethnic Studies, Ken Monteiro, reviewed and upheld my travel claim documents as completely correct and appropriate. The record, including documents that AMCHA cites, demonstrates that my application for travel authorization was transparent and accurate and had the stated purpose of attending an international conference, conducting research, networking, and collaborating with potential university partners toward a possible Memorandum of Understanding between SFSU and Palestinian universities. As Senior Scholar at AMED, it was part of my job duties to establish educational and research collaboration on Palestine and between Palestinians in the United States and elsewhere in the world.

Nonetheless, AMCHA put forward as evidence of wrongdoing that I "neglected to inform" the university of planned meetings with Leila Khaled and Shaikh Raed Salah. However, as the university administration itself would observe, I was under no obligation to inform the university of each and every person with whom I met. Furthermore, there is no law or university regulation that prohibits meeting and speaking with figures seen as "controversial" in US media and dominant discourses. Such activity is clearly protected under the First Amendment and is the very lifeblood of academia, journalism, and other fields of knowledge production. Additionally, as Dean Monteiro, College of Ethnic Studies, asserted in his May 2014 report, SFSU would not and cannot censor a scholar's communications with controversial figures.

AMCHA's intentionally misleading focus on our meetings with Sheikh Raed Salah and Leila Khaled aimed at insinuating that I support terrorism. While Salah is a respected leader of the Islamic Movement among Palestinians in Israel, Khaled is a member of the Political Bureau of the Popular Front for the Liberation of Palestine, a member group of the Palestine Liberation Organization (PLO). Our delegation also met with other Palestinians involved with political parties and groups who represent critical constituencies of Palestinian politics, among them Fatah, Popular Front for the Liberation of Palestine, Democratic Front for the Liberation of Palestine, FIDA, Palestinian People's Party, and Hamas in the West Bank and Israeli Communist Party, Abna el

Balad, Tajamou, and alad, and so on. But in AMCHA's racist estimation in which all Palestinians are viewed as terrorists, these distinctions are somehow rendered null. This type of racism is nothing but political bullying intended to stifle and criminalize any and all discussions of Palestine or Palestinians in order to shield Israel from accountability for its continued violations of Palestinian rights.

Because these racist and Zionist attacks against me focused a huge amount of attention on our meeting with Khaled, let me clarify the purpose of our delegation's meeting with her. Khaled is a Palestinian feminist icon. She is therefore relevant to my research and pedagogy, both of which aim to revise Palestinian women's studies by critiquing conventional wisdom within the feminist canon. In my courses, to provide a counter narrative to the Orientalist depictions of Palestinian and other Arab and Muslim women as weak and docile – and men as bloodthirsty and misogynist – I screen several films including *Leila Khaled: Hijacker?* and open these classes to the public. Meetings with Palestinian political prisoners were also directly related to my pedagogy, scholarship, and advocacy at AMED. For example, in May 2013 I initiated and co-organized a teach-in, "From Pelican Bay and Guantanamo to Palestine: Prisons, Repression, and Resistance," at SFSU that aimed at linking Palestinian prisoners' hunger strikes with two other struggles that were simultaneously taking place at Pelican Bay in California and Guantanamo Bay in Cuba. The meetings we arranged during our Palestine trip were crucial for us, as scholars and educators, to keep us connected to and educated about various transnational struggles.

I might add here that the Israel lobby has particularly sought to attack Palestinian universities, describing them as "well known for their virulent anti-Semitism and support of terror" in order to prevent communication and collaboration between the United States and Palestinian academies. During our visit, we met with representatives of An-Najah and Birzeit universities toward developing a Memorandum of Understanding and other collaborative relationships between SFSU and Palestinian universities. While I was still in Palestine, I emailed President Wong and Dean Monteiro, on January 23, 2014, to request a meeting for my colleague Joanne Barker and I to report on the exciting development regarding the Memorandum of Understanding with An-Najah University.

In March 2014, shortly after returning from Palestine, I organized a public forum on campus to report back on the results of the trip. It was at that point that the Israel lobby groups led by AMCHA moved into overdrive. They made the absurd claim that this public forum threatened the safety of Jewish students by contributing "to a hostile environment for Jewish students at SFSU." As a matter of fact, the event was a model of open, exciting, and timely public discussion on current events with urgent human rights and political implications and furthered the educational purpose of facilitating discussion about diverse Palestinian viewpoints. The standing room only audience included students of diverse backgrounds and from programs across the university, engaged in a healthy and vibrant discussion over the issues speakers raised. To facilitate discussion, all participants were able to raise their questions openly and respectfully. We addressed several questions and dissenting opinions in a collegial and respectful manner aimed at fostering critical thinking. Claims that "terrorism against the Jewish state was condoned by the speakers" at the event were craven distortions of opinions expressed by the speakers, as can be discerned from the public videos of the event.[3]

The lobby's call to investigate and punish my activities as well as those of other academics is aimed at suppressing the scholarship and speech of those who honestly discuss Israel's violation of Palestinian rights and express critical viewpoints, including our commitment to justice in and for Palestine as part of justice for all peoples. The Israel advocacy groups are committed to defending and promoting Israeli policies by stifling criticism of Israel in the United States through the misuse of legal instruments, and accusations that conflate criticism of Israel with anti-Semitism. Many groups have written about the serious consequences of this McCarthyist repression campaign on academic freedom and First Amendment rights to free speech.

While these accusations are typically demonstrated to be false, in my case, what the Israel advocacy groups were trying to achieve was to undermine the ability of scholars to use the resources of public universities to undertake research and academic networking just as all academics do who work at public universities or who apply for public funding for their research, teaching, and other professional activities. Specifically, such attacks seek to undermine critical analysis of Palestine/Israel, as many of the testimonials in this book demonstrate. The idea that state funding can or should be restricted for the study of a political conflict because those on one side of the conflict wish to suppress the critiques of the other is anathema to the most essential values of the academy.

Baseless accusations of anti-Semitism and support for terrorism have had devastating impacts on me and other members of the university community. Students and faculty have been consumed by defending our right to speak freely. These smear campaigns can affect our future and career opportunities and subject us to unwarranted government scrutiny of our speech activities.

Notes

1. Editors note: The AMCHA Initiative is a Zionist organization based in California that collaborates with other Zionist individuals and groups to suppress speech critical of Israel on university campuses across the United States. Its central tactic is to label any and all critical statements or questions about the Israeli state as "anti-Semitic."
2. This is a direct quote from the AMCHA email sent to the SFSU president and posted on the AMCHA site at www.amchainitiative.org/amcha-co-founders-challenge-san-francisco-state-university-president-about-campus-event-glorifying-the-murder-of-jews/. All websites last accessed February 1, 2016.
3. Video of the event may be viewed at the following links: Part 1: www.youtube.com/watch?v=r4u8GpC-AiQ; Part 2: www.youtube.com/watch?v=pQ_qVz1Rg0g; Part 3: www.youtube.com/watch?v=5HWjm0JYbyM.

7

Hanlon's Razor Cuts Both Ways

David Delgado Shorter

Editors' note: David Shorter, Professor and Vice Chair of the Department of World Arts and Cultures/Dance at the University of California at Los Angeles, taught a Tribal Worldviews course in 2012 that focused on indigenous peoples' use of the media to assert claims to sovereignty. For students' optional consideration toward completing their final projects, he included on his course website many resources, including the link to a webpage supporting the US Campaign for the Academic and Cultural Boycott of Israel (USACBI) together with several articles opposing the Boycott, Divestment, and Sanctions (BDS) movement. As Professor Shorter discusses in this testimony, for this "crime" he became the target of a sustained investigation by the university and public persecution in violation of the most elemental protocols of academic freedom and of UCLA's own internal policies.

At the University of California Los Angeles I teach a course called "Aliens, Psychics, and Ghosts" where we explore how the social sciences contribute to the study of the paranormal, or "perinormal" as Richard Dawkins has us consider. The course is quite popular for many reasons, though I want to believe the students are generally interested in a pedagogy that shows them that they should be critical of what they read, what they watch, and even of the professors standing in front of them, including my own course content and perspectives. The course covers alien abduction testimonies, scholarly studies of psychic abilities, and the possibility that consciousness continues after death. Because so much of the scientific method regards determining if evidence is valid, the students and I spend a lot of time discussing "Occam's Razor," the principle that among competing hypotheses we should choose the one with fewest assumptions. William of Occam's original statement was *non sunt multiplicanda entia sine necessitate*, essentially "let's not make things overly complex." In common usage, we could frame it as: among the multiple reasons for any phenomenon, go with the ones that are most reasonable. Such a means of weeding out improbable causes comes in handy when considering how "the paranormal" might be some combination of government conspiracies, human error in perception, as well as entertainment and marketing strategies.

I have also wrestled with Occam's Razor when attempting to understand the impulses, logic, and stratagems that have plagued me since my administration's 2012 conscious or unintended collusion with a right-wing, Zionist organization. A couple of administrators, maybe more (one never knows), conspired to appease this organization at the expense of my reputation and academic freedom. Using Occam's Razor, I would often conclude that as business-minded administrators, they simply thought the cost – academic freedom – was worth the benefit: financial support from pro-Israel donors, regents, and organizations. From a business perspective, such logic is not unimaginable. After all, the only thing hurt is one professor's reputation and name; the cost is perhaps some criticism from "the left."

But if their reasoning was simply about business, then Occam's Razor is less relevant here than an equally useful aphorism sometimes referred to as Hanlon's Razor: never attribute to malice what can be explained by stupidity. Three years of investigating by internal review committees have enabled me to perceive not so much a small group of administrators making simple-minded business decisions or even mean decisions, but actually stupid decisions because such decisions retard two core university functions: (1) faculty productivity and (2) the exercise and training of critical thought. Therefore, we can see how deciding to appease Zionists and other right-wing political groups affects the brand image of the university negatively and more importantly the quality of service provided to taxpayers. So instead of seeing my administration as making a business-wise decision, I started to see how their decision was a business-stupid decision. Which makes you wonder why they are being paid so much for doing such a poor job.

Administrators at my university, particularly the Executive Vice Chancellor and the Vice Chancellor of Academic Affairs, unfathomably thought that dozens of faculty should spend years investigating whether faculty in general should exercise academic freedom in the classroom. They thought that the reputation and labor of one professor, me, was less valuable than appeasing a right-wing political organization. They must have thought that academic freedom was slightly less important than Israeli nationalism. And if true, then they must have thought that the university itself should relinquish its teaching agenda to outside organizations. Hanlon's Razor helps us see not a group of people who are somehow evil or mean, but rather a group of people making stupid decisions, decisions that are not the best for the faculty, the students, the university as an institution of critical thought, or the university as a business. Their decisions soil the very core of the university's mission of pursuing thoughtful and open engagement of global issues.

The following is a brief account of lessons from my personal experience at the University of California Los Angeles. I refrain here from the tedium of all the attacks, all the committee meetings, and all the various decision processes since 2012. I obviously need to leave out much. But I provide here snippets, fragments of various moments. This first-hand report, then, is intended to give a glimpse into various perspectives and processes within my fight for academic freedom on my campus. I hope it helps us consider the true costs of poor university leadership, and the value of fighting for the mission of our universities and colleges.

I taught W33: "Tribal Worldviews" in the Department of World Arts and Cultures during the winter quarter of 2012, and I used a course website (CCLE) provided to professors for course materials. That course covered indigenous uses of media around the globe to assert their claims of sovereignty. My course website contained pages of source materials and URLS for struggles on multiple continents and includes United Nations documentation – 2000 and 2009 – on Palestinian people as "indigenous." That CCLE also contained a link to the USACBI website because students had the option of writing a final paper on how indigenous people were using media to gain political strength around the globe. I wanted them to see the USACBI website themselves. *I also included links for perspectives that were critical of boycott movements.* The students had four themes from which to choose for their final papers, and thus none were required to write about Palestine or BDS. And I did not lecture on any single day about Israel or Palestine. Because the course covered case studies on multiple continents, I was simply using the course content manager as a means to help them with their final paper research. There were links, for example, about natural resource extraction in Chile, another topic I never covered in classroom lectures. Though, to be clear, I signed a petition once about that Chilean damn project, similar to how I have put my name on many petitions or statements of support regarding a variety of my political leanings: Target, Chick-fil-A, and the USACBI. That college course ended in March, as did access to that site, which was only viewable to the enrolled students.

On April 4, 2012, about a month after the class ended, I was contacted by my departmental chair, Professor Angelia Leung, and was told that Andrew Leuchter, Chair of UCLA's Academic Senate, was reviewing my course site for inappropriate materials pertaining to the Academic and Cultural Boycott of Israel since he had received a letter of complaint from a student in that class. (We now know that no letter "from a student" had been received.) My chair, Leung, asked if I had any further information to provide. I emailed her my syllabus and a URL about organizations targeting US professors for their Palestine-related course materials. At the time, being a relatively new faculty member, I thought the review seemed oddly clandestine, but perhaps how things worked at UCLA. I was swamped teaching in spring quarter, but also running an open-rank, open department search on campus which led to me, in hindsight naively, thinking "this will prove to be nothing." Unfortunately, I was wrong.

On April 11, Professor Leung asked me to come to her office where she told me that after talking with Leuchter, she was responsible for conveying to me that I could either teach about a petition or be a signer of a petition, but that I could not do both. I expressed the myriad of problems with that decision and said that I would have to think about the implications of this supposed policy. I asked if I could defer the conversation until next year when I would teach W33 again. My chair asked if I understood what was being asked of me. I facetiously responded that I understood the larger situation, specifically that I understood the problematically political context of this entire review and the situations around the country where professors are being harassed for discussing Israel's policies. I remember rattling off some comment about how I had been critical of US policies toward American Indians for decades without a problem but Israel was somehow off limits, as I grumbled out of her office in stereotypical disgruntled professorial form. In hindsight, I was probably in sheer disbelief.

We now know that Leung reported back to Professor Leuchter as Chair of the Academic Senate, within the hour that same day, saying that David "expressed his understanding of the situation and said he will address this misstep in future course offerings." I did not phrase my actions as a "misstep." Professor Leung, as she later conveyed to me, thought it was best to appease Leuchter who had explicitly asked for an apology. (I would be remiss not to mention that Leung is a woman of color responding to a white male who is more senior to her in the university hierarchy.) Shockingly, we also now know that on April 12, Andrew Leuchter wrote to the complaining party (AMCHA[1]) and copied his email to everyone on their original complaint, including US Senators and University of California administrators (UCOP), saying that "posting of such materials is not appropriate. Professor Shorter's chair assures me that he understands his serious error in judgment and has said he will not make this mistake again." Following Leuchter's reporting to the complaining organization, AMCHA issued a press release about their victory over an anti-Semitic professor who was teaching anti-Israel materials at UCLA, quoting Professor Leuchter verbatim. They framed the issue to read as if UCLA, the institution, had officially issued a finding that my "actions were inappropriate." On April 13, the *Los Angeles Times*, the *Chronicle of Higher Education*, and *Inside Higher Education* contacted me, asking for a comment about my recent disciplinary action and my stances on Israel. *These calls from reporters were the first I had heard about anyone communicating to outsiders that I had even been talked to about this course.* Think of that: I heard from newspaper reporters about my "disciplinary action" before hearing from anyone on my campus about any final decisions or any "formal" review. When I called these reporters, they each responded that they had already spoken with Leuchter and confirmed with him, as the Chair of the Academic Senate, that I was disciplined. And as I now expect with press inquiries: they ran their stories whether they talked with me or not.

In my original June 2012 grievance letter to the Academic Senate Committee on Academic Freedom, I was very pointed about the cause of the problem (as I then knew it): Andrew Leuchter must have been to blame. After all, Leuchter single-handedly decided he would respond to this outside organization's complaint, but he never met with or talked with me during all of these exchanges and flows of information. Why did I think Leuchter did all of this on his own? First, because after hearing from reporters, my first call was to the Vice Chancellor of Academic Affairs, a woman I had previously considered a professional mentor. She expressed shock that any of this was happening, but also told me to just let it all blow over. (We now know she caused the entire matter to begin.) Second, I thought Andrew Leuchter was to blame because the Executive Vice Chancellor invited me to his office that summer to personally say that university administrators were not involved at all (a claim we now know to be a lie). He literally advised me to point my legal complaints toward Leuchter and not the university. I took the bait, hook, line, and sinker.

My questions in the 2013 grievance letter against Leuchter are still pertinent and bear repeating here in the case any reader finds themselves or their teaching "reviewed" by an administrator. What kind of "investigation" did he conduct? He did not speak with my teaching assistants who would have told him I never lectured about Israel or BDS, much less shared any personal opinion on the matter. He did not speak with my four students who wrote their final papers on Palestine and the BDS movement, three of whom are Jewish, and all four having received "A's" on their final papers. He did not speak with me, the person being investigated. Nor did he speak with my partner at the time, also Jewish, about my supposed anti-Semitism. Certainly, even if Leuchter had the authority to offer "due process," his actions did not constitute due process in any meaningful sense of the term, and, in fact, constituted a violation of the normal protocols of due process at the University of California or most other universities for that matter. To be very clear on this matter, the AMCHA Initiative, a non-university organization with a history of spurious claims wrote the university a threatening letter about trumped-up claims of my having criticized the state policies of Israel. Then, one professor, in his role as Chair of the Academic Senate, without any oversight at all, reviewed and judged me to be in error and then communicated his "opinion" to the press, my university administrators, and state representatives without ever having spoken directly with me. You could see why my anger rested with one person: Andrew Leuchter, the Chair of our campus's Academic Senate.

After the initial news reports, my life changed almost instantaneously. At the time, I was consulting for three entertainment studios on their representations of either indigenous peoples or the paranormal. One deal that was in the works would have contracted my labor for four months for approximately $17,000.00. I was in negotiations with other production teams, as well. The newspaper articles came out about my supposed character as an "anti-Semite," and I never heard from any of those industry agencies again. My relationship with a man from a prominent Jewish family then grew rocky and ended. I was removed from academic committees and advisory boards around campus and in the arts organizations around Los Angeles. I applied for four grants between 2012 and 2013 and did not receive any. I cannot be certain that I was unfairly prejudiced by what people perceived to be true based on national media coverage. But that's just one rub of such attacks: from now on, we simply do not know. AMCHA succeeded in having me labeled as an anti-Semite. My university administration played along.

On November 18, 2013, I walked to my car in its normal spot in an UCLA parking structure. Getting in, I noticed a slip of paper under my windshield wiper: "Expect to have an accident on the freeway, Israel hater!" (Department of Homeland Security Case Number: 43873924882). On December 5, 2013, I arrived at my home to find a note stuck in the door jam that read simply, "Jew Hater." On December 18, 2014, the online news source, *Times of Israel*, published a piece saying that I have hatred for Israel, that I advocate for the BDS in my classrooms, and that I am flagrantly abusing my faculty status and university resources. All three claims are untrue and lack a shred of evidence. If you were to do an internet search for my name, let's say that you were considering me for a TED Talk or a job or even a date: you would see among the results that I was embroiled in this issue pertaining to Israel and anti-Semitism. The internet does not forget things easily. These are but a very short list of the negative attacks against me.

To be sure, I also received meaningful signs of support. Colleagues, mostly privately, wrote emails of support. People from around the world, including many rabbis, wrote to me about the shame they felt toward organizations like AMCHA. Some important professional organizations came to my defense under the banner of academic freedom. I also received the support of students, including the students from that particular class, which struck a particularly reassuring chord. Glen Greenwald wrote a well-crafted piece in Salon about my case asking the obvious question: "what kind of person goes to college and demands to be shielded from political views that they dislike?"[2] Though, keep in mind that all I did was include a link to a website on a course content manager, without ever raising the discussion of the website in class besides saying it was there online for them if they wanted to write their final paper on the BDS movement. I was thankful for all the support, but it felt like they were supporting my right to do something I never did, such as speak out about Israel's subjugation of Palestinians, theft of Palestinian land, and apartheid policies.

And of course lawyers reached out, eager to take my case that seemed pretty obvious from one of the more balanced reports of my situation, an *Electronic Intifada* interview.[3] The legal teams that were offering their support in 2012 and 2013 were interested in the issue but were unsure as to the particular type of offense. Was this a case of freedom of speech, academic freedom, or employment discrimination? While they varied in their approaches, all agreed that I would need to pay for their work or ask the American Civil Liberties Union (ACLU) or the National Lawyers Guild to help support the suit financially. They also agreed on another aspect of the case that I found particularly troubling. Were I to sue UCLA, I would possibly win a million or so; but would probably not be a professor there when all was said and done. Either UCLA would require my leaving in the settlement terms or I would be incredibly uncomfortable working among colleagues and staff who would have spent years in depositions, submitting their emails for review and perhaps in the center of a media circus. I was faced with a difficult decision. I could seek legal redress against Andrew Leuchter (possibly a pawn himself, as the review teams were discovering) and my administration. But any "fight against Zionism," as it could be portrayed, would most likely become what I was known for professionally in my life, at the expense of the research programs I spent decades working toward and that I loved. Not to mention the money it would cost me, or the way an aggressive defense team might spin me more so as an Israel hater or anti-Semite. Would my colleagues be deposed? Would the university look tarnished as much by my actions as those by some idiotic administrators? If so, then I would be as idiotic as them to prioritize financial gain over what was best for the institution.

I decided to work with a law firm that had success in a previous suit against UCLA, because they seemed to believe we could gain some recourse without ever filing suit. They thought we could pressure the university to make financial amends for my professional losses as an industry consultant as well as get a statement clearing me of any accusations. Moreover, they felt we could get a statement from the administration affirming the importance of academic freedom. They also insisted that I continue going through the channels provided through the university itself for internal claims and grievances. These are the reviews to which I alluded in the introduction above. These committees require teams of faculty to research who did what and when. And these committees ran consecutively for three years. Is this what smart leadership wants its faculty working on, rather than their research?

Without going through the various processes of each review, by both the Academic Senate Committee for Academic Freedom as well as the Privilege and Tenure Committee (which investigates formal grievances), allow me to simply allude to the hours and hours of time these things take. Each review required my multiple statements, both written and taken at hearings. They also required statements, written and in person, by faculty and administration across campus who might provide helpful information. They required hours and hours of meeting times of the committee members themselves. Our administrators, supposedly business-wise, must think these are useful ways of spending our time and labor. In my case, the labor was valuable because they cleared my name across the board. While I did not receive any compensation, I have been vindicated in formal statements.

The first committee that reviewed my claims, the Committee on Academic Freedom, came to the following conclusions. First, the committee found that I violated no policy or procedure in my teaching of Palestinian rights, including providing the link to USACBI. Second, they reported that the Chair of the Academic Senate who reviewed my teaching at the behest of AMCHA acted outside his role as a faculty member. In other words, he did not represent the faculty or the administration. Third, they concluded that by handling the review with no committee oversight and by communicating directly to AMCHA, the chair threatened academic freedom of all faculty members. Their wording in the letter affirmed that faculty are not required to respond to outside political organizations and that a "review" should never have been started. Importantly, they also found that no student from the class ever actually complained, meaning the original complaint seemed to be wholly from a group external to the university.

And while these were great results for me personally, it was not within their purview as a committee on academic freedom to suggest any recourse. They could not ask that the administration do anything in particular. Leuchter would not be punished, and I would not be compensated for loss of consulting wages, nor provided any statement that I could publicly use for public relations purposes. That meant that organizations and media outlets could continually reprint AMCHA's claims, but I would lack any formal statement from the university to counter their false claims. For that reason, in 2014 I filed a formal grievance against the Chair of the Academic Senate, Andrew Leuchter. I would not have done so had any of the administrators empowered me with a letter from the university. I asked for such a letter from the Executive Vice Chancellor, Scott Waugh, as well as the Vice Chancellor of Academic Affairs, Carole Goldberg. Yet after this grievance investigation, we can see why these administrators did not want to support me: they were involved in covering up how the original AMCHA letter was handled.

Due to the interviews with my chair in 2014 by the Promotion and Tenure Committee that was investigating my charges against Leucther, we learned that Carole Goldberg personally asked Leuchter not only to review my teaching and respond to AMCHA, but also that she told him and my chair exactly what the results of such a review were to be: that I was sorry and that I stated I would not do it again. Goldberg, who was once a professional confidante, had personally decided that the university should appease AMCHA. Goldberg coincidentally also visits Israel regularly and was recognized in 2015 by Hillel for her contributions to the Jewish community.[4] She is one of my university's administrators that have been charged with making wise decisions for the future of our campus.

Thankfully, in the summer of 2015, three years after the original incident, the Privilege and Tenure Committee affirmed several core issues. First, they agreed that my rights and privileges were violated. Second, that no class member filed the original complaint. Third, that the Senate Chair (Leuchter) relayed erroneous information. As a form of mediation, this committee then worked with Andrew Leuchter to obtain a signed letter of admission and an apology. And importantly, for me at least, they obtained a signed statement from the Executive Vice Chancellor Scott Waugh heralding the importance of academic freedom at UCLA and admitting that any claims about my teaching were baseless.

> The Privilege and Tenure committee affirms that your rights and privileges as a member of the Senate were violated by a failure to follow established Senate procedures for responding to a complaint ... "no evidence was provided" that you violated the standards of scholarly inquiry and professional ethics.

I am not walking away from this matter unscathed, publicly or financially compensated from a lawsuit. I am, however, full professor in a profession I care about deeply. I am gifted with some of the best students a teacher could ever ask for. I have proven to my administration that I will not lightly be taken advantage of for their political and financial gain. And I have secured statements that should strengthen faculty resolve across this campus and others; particularly that academic freedom is central to the aims of any college worth its tuition. I have also become much more aware of the ways that right-wing organizations are attempting to silence the speech that they find disruptive to their colonial, imperial, and capitalist projects. One of the ways, clearly, is to write complaints that we teachers are using state (and thus taxpayer) funds to indoctrinate the youth to our devious leftist plots. And while I may expect certain groups to believe these claims, I expect more from the campus administrators who get paid quite well to make intelligent decisions shaping the direction of our universities.

I have written it in my grievance letters and have said it in my meetings with administrators: our time is one of our most precious resources as faculty members. As teachers, our time should be on teaching. As researchers, we have our positions to research. For many of us, we struggle to balance both of those and an ever-growing amount of service work to our departments, campuses, and professional organizations. The hours I spent collecting documents about my teaching, talking to reporters, responding to inaccurate news stories, essentially defending myself, these hours had to come out of some aspect of my primary work. Usually, I took it out of my weekend and sleep time, but of course it ultimately came out of my research and teaching time as well. We should be making the case clearly that organizations such as AMCHA wrote one ignorant letter about my teaching over three years ago. Not due to that letter, but due to what my campus administrators decided to do with it, countless hours have been lost by me, other faculty, students, committees, and administrators. And we all should heed the reminder by the investigating committees: universities are not required to respond to any piece of mail that lands on our desks. In this case, a couple of idiots at AMCHA convinced a couple of supposed "leaders" on my campus to leave Team Mean and join them on Team Stupid. Hanlon's Razor cuts deeper than Occam's Razor. It makes you wonder who the real idiots are when AMCHA's letter probably took ten minutes to write. If not for academic freedom, if not for critical thinking, if not for moral and just causes, then ignoring these Zionist organizations will at least serve our ability to work more effectively as teachers and researchers. But will our administrators be as wise?

Because we are inundated with so many cases across the country where universities throw intellectual integrity under the bus, this volume makes an important contribution to the redirecting of the slow, large vessels that are modern colleges. Our individual stories attest not only to the foibles of administrators, but to the persistence necessary to avoid the corporatization of our academic institutions. If I cannot be a signer of a petition or signer to a cause while also teaching topics related to those causes, then as a society we are asking some of the most informed voices not to speak on the issues within their areas of research. No biologist or environmental studies professor could support efforts to fight global warming. No zoologist could speak up against lab animal testing. No political science professor could speak about campaign finance reform. That a few of the administrators on my campus thought otherwise demonstrates not that they were mean, but that they were unreasonable, literally lacking reason/logic. Never assign to malice what is understandable as idiocy.

Notes

1. Editors' note: The AMCHA Initiative is a Zionist organization based in California that collaborates with other Zionist individuals and groups to suppress speech critical of Israel on university campuses across the United States. Its central tactic is to label any and all critical statements or questions about the Israeli state as "anti-Semitic."

2. G. Greenwald, "UCLA Professor Warned About Israel Views," *Salon.com*, April 24 (2012), www.salon.com/2012/04/24/ucla_professor_warned_about_israel_views/.

3. N. Barrows-Friedman, "LA Professor 'Wakes Up to Hate Mail' for Linking to Anti-Zionist Material," *ElectronicIntifada.net*, August 1 (2012), https://electronicintifada.net/content/la-professor-wakes-hate-mail-linking-anti-zionist-material/11547.

4. The video produced by Hillel to honor Goldberg is available on YouTube at https://www.youtube.com/watch?v=RtZYFlWmrK4.

8

The Intolerability of Intolerance

Persis Karim

Editors' note: Professor Persis Karim, an Iranian-American poet, essayist, and Professor of Comparative Literature at San Jose State University, organized a one-day workshop in 2013 for high school teachers and community college faculty on "Peacebuilding, Nonviolence, and Approaches to Teaching the Israeli-Palestinian Conflict" with a grant from the congressionally funded US Institute for Peace (USIP). Before the workshop could even get off the ground, Israel lobby groups went into action, charging that the workshop would be illegitimate and would violate USIP federal funding requirements under the Higher Education Act. The lobby launched a barrage of dirty tricks against Professor Karim, including the international circulation of a fabricated statement intended to damage her reputation, a public records request that she make available all documents and correspondence related to the workshop and its funding, and pressure on the university to cancel the workshop and sanction her. Although the university did not interfere with the workshop, the administration nonetheless chose not to publicly defend the event and Professor Karim's academic freedom.

When I was in graduate school in the Middle East Studies program at the University of Texas at Austin, I got a job as a student assistant to Professor Elizabeth Fernea, who was working on a film and book entitled, *The Struggle for Peace: Israelis and Palestinians.* I witnessed as Fernea came under repeated attacks for simply representing the suffering of Palestinians in her film, let alone daring to show the efforts of Palestinians and Israelis to sit together and speak of their mutual frustration, hopelessness, and suffering, as well as their desire to work for a genuine and lasting peace. I was deeply touched by the human stories contained in both the movie and the book, and I knew that I would some day want to go and see this place for myself.

While completing my PhD, I focused on the story of Iranians and diaspora narratives – stories of those who fled Iran's tumultuous Iranian revolution, the Iran-Iraq War, and the backlash against more secular-minded folks who had sought to change the repressive conditions of their country. But when I began teaching at San Jose State University (SJSU), I felt the pull back to read and study the stories of Israelis and Palestinians and their "struggle for peace." I wanted not just to have a political position, but to know the human stories of those who were often rendered invisible in the US media; I wanted to learn both about those who were motivated by the traumas of European anti-Semitism, as well as those Palestinians who were deeply traumatized by the arrival of Europeans on their land in the nineteenth and twentieth centuries.

In 2009, my teenage stepson Kyle began to speak of going to Israel and joining the Israel Defense Forces (IDF). At age fifteen, he was entertaining the thoughts of joining a foreign army, and I grew concerned and afraid. In my heart of hearts, I knew Kyle was a teenager, fishing around for identity, connection, and for a way to connect to his Jewish heritage. While I wanted to protect our son from war and all the damage I saw inflicted on young people who served in the military, I knew that I had a limited ability as a stepparent to influence or change his mind. I was experiencing what I believe many who live close to the politics of the Israeli-Palestinian conflict feel as the deep political and emotional divisions that can come between family members.

Although I wanted Kyle to like me, love me even, I didn't want to alienate him with my point of view. But because I had read extensively and taught about the Israeli-Palestinian conflict and had a deep sense of the injustices of the occupation, I also felt I could not skirt this issue. My own mother had seen the effects of the Holocaust up close, working for an agency in France to help Jewish orphans relocate after being separated from their parents, and so I understood the depth of my stepson's youthful convictions about anti-Semitism and the need for Jewish people to feel safe. But I hated the thought of anyone serving in any army, let alone one that was engaged in a long-standing military occupation of another people, another land, whose lives and livelihoods were marked by daily indignities and violence that reminded me of the ugliness that Jews experienced in places like the Warsaw Ghetto.

In 2010, feeling the need to learn more about the situation in order to better communicate with our son, I decided to apply for an academic tour that would take me and ten other academics on a tour of the West Bank universities inside the occupied Palestinian territories. Sadly, that trip did not take place. Kyle died in a car accident on March 31, 2010, a month and a half before I was to travel to Israel/Palestine. In the aftermath of his death, my husband and I were reeling with the shock and agony of losing a child on the cusp of his own adulthood. In an effort to pay tribute to his interest in Israel, my husband organized a trip with some of Kyle's classmates from Berkeley High to Israel/Palestine the following year on the one-year anniversary of Kyle's death. The trip was a tribute to Kyle's growing interest in Israel as well as his curiosity about the conflict between Israel and Palestine. In addition to visiting Yad Vashem museum and taking a tour of Jerusalem, they also met with the Bereaved Family Forum and "Breaking the Silence," a group of Israeli soldiers who had served in the South Hebron hills and have come to oppose the occupation. The trip was an incredible experience for the young people who were friends with Kyle, and for some of them the trip brought the painful truth of the occupation closer to home. They came back with a powerful sense of what Kyle was drawn to – as well as an awareness of the pain and suffering that was visited upon both Israelis and Palestinians.

Almost a month later, I would take a similar trip, this one with the Palestinian American Research Center (PARC), where much more of my time was spent visiting communities and universities in the West Bank and seeing up close the conditions of the occupation. We traveled throughout the West Bank, met with university professors, and experienced the separation wall, the checkpoints, the absolute poverty, and psychological and physical abuses of the occupation in a very immediate way. I saw with my own eyes the indignities of the occupation and came home knowing I would not forget what I witnessed. After returning home, I replayed in my mind the daily harassment of Palestinian colleagues as they struggled to get to work, the denial of their students' opportunity to learn about their own history, the intentional deprivation of resources to the entire Palestinian population, and the regular attacks by Israeli settlers. The trip left a deep and painful impression on me, and I have, ever since, advocated the need to tell the story of what is not available in the US media – the story of Palestinians living under occupation and the necessity of teaching the conflict as a very real and relevant part of our American involvement there.

Once I had returned to the United States, I decided to make my own small contribution to challenging this terrible situation by teaching about the occupation, the separation wall, the checkpoints, and the efforts of Palestinians inside Israel to inform people about the history of their displacement from their homeland. My goal was to bring tools to teachers to help them present the conflict from multiple perspectives. In early 2013, I received a small grant from USIP to facilitate a one-day workshop for high school teachers and college faculty on teaching the Israeli-Palestinian conflict.

Almost immediately, one of my colleagues at SJSU, history professor Jonathan Roth, called into question the validity of the workshop and the fact that he was not one of the invited speakers – even though he has never invited me to speak at his pro-Israel events, nor have I protested them. With support from my dean and his, I stood by my right to organize the workshop with speakers who met the academic and philosophical criteria of the grant: namely, that they operated from the framework that understanding both sides of the conflict is an important step on the path to peace.

I received a flood of emails from Professor Roth, questioning the "balance" of the workshop, offering a veiled insinuation that I was "anti-Semitic" and questioning, ultimately, my leadership of the Middle East Studies program on campus. This was not the first time I and other colleagues had been intimidated by Professor Roth's emails and efforts to silence criticism, but it was certainly the most vociferous of his efforts to dissuade me from organizing a public forum.

When I held my ground, Professor Roth clearly involved others, including the AMCHA Initiative.[1] AMCHA, along with several other Zionist organizations, has regularly equated criticism of Israeli policies and teaching or speech about Israel's occupation of Palestinian lands with anti-Semitism. Their attacks against those Jewish scholars they deem "self-hating Jews," because they hold positions that are anti-Zionist or anti-occupation, are particularly ugly and painful. They are also prone to targeting anyone with a Middle Eastern (i.e., Arab, Iranian, or Muslim) sounding last name and labeling them (without any evidence) anti-Semitic.

As the USIP-funded workshop drew near in May 2014, Tammi Rossman-Benjamin, the founder of the AMCHA Initiative, wrote to the president of my university and suggested he "look into the workshop," stating that they "believe that none of the six workshop speakers will present the Israeli narrative, and that some may even make presentations which demonize and delegitimize Israel." She also claimed that the workshop would violate federal funding guidelines by focusing on advocacy rather than education.[2] Her comments were picked up and reprinted by other organizations such as Campus Watch and *Commentary Magazine*.[3] The point of the workshop, of course, was never to debate the conflict, but rather to offer tools that teachers could use to share both Israeli and Palestinian perspectives, notwithstanding these types of concerted attacks against anyone that tries to do so.

Rossman-Benjamin seemed to have particular antipathy toward me. She predicted that my workshop would be "a forum for promoting hatred" of Israel, and she accused me of "supporting the elimination of the Jewish state." Unaware that I'm married to a Jewish man who does not see a contradiction between being "pro-Israel" and "anti-occupation," she assumed by my last name that I am Muslim, and therefore anti-Jewish and anti-Israel.

Organizations like Campus Watch and AMCHA Initiative attempt to intimidate faculty, students, and campus administrators, who will feel stung by accusations of anti-Semitism, bias, improper use of federal funds, or abridgement of freedom of speech. But they do more than intimidate. The groups also file lawsuits, such as a recent case against the University of California, Berkeley, that accuse universities of creating a climate that is unsafe for Jewish students any time they merely allow criticism of Israeli policies on campus.[4] Even when the accusations and lawsuits fail, they can make it uncomfortable and costly to speak about the Israeli-Palestinian conflict. Campus Watch recently threatened to instigate a campaign to withdraw private funding from campuses where criticism of Israel's occupation is discussed.

My workshop, entitled, "Peacebuilding, Nonviolence, and Approaches to Teaching the Israeli-Palestinian Conflict," went forward with the backing of my campus administration. The president of the university even visited to show his support. The workshop featured educators engaged with teaching the conflict in a variety of contexts and disciplines, including Dr. Samia Shoman, a high school teacher from Hillsdale

High School, Dr. Phil Metres, a poet and scholar of literature at John Carroll University, Dr. Kathryn Davis, Professor of Global Studies and Geography at SJSU, Dr. Diana Stover, Journalism and Mass Communications, and Rabbi Michael Lerner, a Bay Area peace activist and founding rabbi of Beyt-Tikkun, "Synagogue without Walls," and founding editor of *Tikkun* magazine. Rabbi Lerner has taken a principled stance against the Israeli occupation, and his book, *Embracing Israel/Palestine*, had recently been published and featured as part of the reading materials for the workshop. All of the speakers called the workshop a success.

Several days afterward, however, I received an email from campus Special Projects saying that an anonymous public records request had been made asking me to turn over all the documents (grant proposal, award letter, etc.), and all my emails and planning materials related to the workshop, including correspondence with the five workshop speakers. Although I had nothing to hide, this was deeply disturbing. I felt intimidated, as if I was being accused of doing something wrong.

Several weeks after the records request, I received an email from an undergraduate student at Stanford University, asking if I had seen the press release circulating with my name on it. When he sent it to me, I was aghast. It was a complete fake. It said that I was a founder, with several others, of an organization calling for a boycott of Arab, Syrian, and Iranian goods.[5] The goal of this press release was to generate mistrust and suspicion of me among Arab or pro-Palestinian groups. It was also aimed at putting a spin on the word "boycott" by impugning my character as someone using the strategy of boycott in an anti-Arab context. I had never heard of the organization, much less founded it. This outrageous tactic not only disgusted me, but it also hurt me exactly because I have, since my son's death, dedicated myself to addressing the injustices of the Israeli occupation and the need for peace-building.

Even though the press release was fake, once it was posted on the Internet, the damage to my reputation was done. A Palestinian website found and immediately published the press release, removing it only when a *Chronicle of Higher Education* reporter informed them it was fake.[6] The Stanford student also shared with me a second press release he had received in an email, from a fictional Bangladeshi cleric calling for a *fatwa* against him for his Students for Justice in Palestine activities. Although these press releases are ridiculous and full of farcical statements, as they circulate around the Internet, they can have dangerous and terrifying repercussions.

I contacted the Middle East Studies Association (MESA) Committee on Academic Freedom about the fake press releases, and without hesitation they issued a letter asking that my university defend my right to academic freedom and ensure that the campus remains a place where diverse political opinions can be expressed, taught, and understood.[7] However, my previously supportive university told the *Chronicle of Higher Education* that it would not issue a letter in support of me, as "no matter what we put in the letter," it would be perceived as "taking a political position." The president and his staff refused at every turn to publicly support my academic freedom and distanced themselves from this incident.

Since the passage in December 2013 of the American Studies Association (ASA) resolution endorsing an academic boycott of Israel,[8] many professors and institutions have experienced a campaign of harassment, public attacks, and renewed efforts to silence criticism of the Israeli occupation of the West Bank.[9] The New York State legislature went as far as passing a resolution threatening to punish universities and individual faculty members that receive public funding if they belong to organizations such as the ASA that support the boycott.[10] Although the resolution itself failed, the result is a chilling effect on speech and political discourse, and the undermining of scholars' rights to teach and research in an atmosphere of academic freedom.

Efforts to silence people like me who discuss the occupation and the US role in sustaining it harken back to McCarthyism. As is apparent across the chapters in this book and many other cases around the country, organizations like the AMCHA Initiative and Campus Watch threaten our basic freedom to think, speak, and teach our students.[11] We must defend our rights not just to raise a wide spectrum of issues and perspectives, but also to teach in an atmosphere free of hostile personal or political attacks.

After this ordeal, I have become disgusted by the ugly, cheap tactics of people who cannot tolerate any point of view other than their own. At the USIP workshop I organized, a young woman who was then an Israel fellow at Hillel, objected to the idea that Samia Shoman, the Palestinian-American teacher on the panel, should use even a clip of the video *Occupation 101* in a syllabus that includes teaching the narratives of Israelis and Palestinians side by side. When I spoke with this young woman during the break, she told me that she would not use the word "occupation" to describe the conditions under which Palestinians live. I probed her further and asked, "what would you say to a young Jewish college student who came into Hillel asking about the Palestinians?" She very smugly answered, "What do you mean what would I say about the Palestinians? – that's like saying what about the Greeks, it would take all day."

I had no words for her. I turned instead to the memory of my own trip to Palestine, where I witnessed the resilience of Palestinians who, despite the very degradation of their conditions, sustain a dignity and humanity that I can never forget. In the end, I know that what I have dealt with is only a fraction of the pain, the ugliness, and the indecency that shadows the lives of Palestinian people every day. While I rarely speak of my son Kyle and the tremendous grief of losing him in a public way, I know that one day we would have had the important conversations about the Palestinian struggle that I always hoped we would. Perhaps it is naive, perhaps it is wishful thinking, but I'd like to believe that we might have even traveled a similar road and found a way to work together to liberate not only the Palestinian people, but also the forces of denial that ultimately do harm to Israel as well.

Notes

1. Editors' note: The AMCHA Initiative is a Zionist organization based in California that collaborates with other Zionist individuals and groups to suppress speech critical of Israel on university campuses across the United States. Its central tactic is to label any and all critical statements or questions about the Israeli state as "anti-Semitic."
2. The full text of Rossman-Benjamin's letter to SJSU President Qayoumi is posted on the AMCHA website at www.amchainitiative.org/2027-2/. All websites last accessed February 22, 2016.
3. The links to their reprints are, respectively, www.campus-watch.org/article/id/12989 and www.commentarymagazine.com/2013/04/17/can-the-left-stand-up-against-anti-semites/.
4. Peter Schmidt, "U. of California Settles Lawsuit Alleging Anti-Semitism at Berkeley," *Chronicle of Higher Education*, July 11 (2012), http://chronicle.com/article/U-of-California-Settles/132827/.
5. The text of the fake press release has since been posted online by my colleague Philip Metres to explain that it is a fabrication. Available at http://

behindthelinespoetry.blogspot.com/2013/05/the-attack-upon-persis-karim.html.

6. Peter Schmidt, "Fake News Release Targets Scholars and Students Critical of Israel," *Chronicle of Higher Education*, May 20 (2013), http://chronicle.com/article/Fake-News-Release-Targets/139397/.

7. A PDF of the letter is available on the MESA website at http://mesana.org/pdf/US20130516.pdf.

8. The explanation of the ASA resolution is available on the Association's website at www.theasa.net/what_does_the_academic_boycott_mean_for_the_asa/.

9. Peter Schmidt, "Backlash Against Israel Boycott Throws Academic Association on Defensive," *Chronicle of Higher Education*, January 5 (2014), available on the *New York Times* website, www.nytimes.com/2014/01/06/us/backlash-against-israel-boycott-throws-academic-association-on-defensive.html.

10. Alex Kane, "New York Senate Passes Bill Punishing ASA over Israel Boycott," *Mondoweiss.net*, January 18 (2014), http://mondoweiss.net/2014/01/punishing-israel-boycott/.

11. See, for example, Asa Winstanley and Nora Barrows-Friedman, "Documents Reveal Zionist Group Spied on US Student Delegation to Palestine," *Electronic Intifada*, January 29 (2014), https://electronicintifada.net/content/documents-reveal-zionist-group-spied-us-student-delegation-palestine/13130.

9

Responding to Columbia University's McCarthyism: Excerpts of Statement on March 14, 2005 to Columbia University Ad Hoc Grievance Committee

Joseph Massad

Editors' note: In the first years of the twenty-first century, Columbia University in New York was the target of ongoing attacks by the Israel lobby against several faculty members from its Middle Eastern studies program. Professors Joseph Massad, Rashid Khalidi, and Edward Said, all leading international scholars on Middle East history and contemporary affairs – and all Palestinian – faced sustained harassment, as did a few years later Professor Nadia Abu El-Haj (see her testimonial in this collection). Perhaps the most egregious persecution was that suffered by Professor Massad. In January 2005, the University's Vice President, Nicholas Dirks, set up a McCarthyist prosecutorial "ad hoc" committee at the instigation of President Lee Bollinger to investigate complaints against Professor Massad and other faculty members of the Department of Middle East and Asian Languages and Cultures (MEALAC). The justification for this prosecution was the release by the David Project, a well-funded pro-Israel activist organization based in Boston, of a video that contained interviews of Columbia University students who complained that they felt uncomfortable with the course lectures of several professors, among them Massad. At the time, right-wing publicist Charles Jacobs, a prominent public figure in the Israel lobby, headed the David Project. The video, *Columbia Unbecoming*, was shown privately, including to Columbia University top brass and to several officials from the Israeli government, but remarkably has never been released to the public. Reproduced below are major excerpts from the testimony that Professor Massad gave to the ad hoc committee in March 2005. Massad's testimony is remarkable for the level of detail in which he chronicles the extent to which the Israel lobby was willing to conspire and deceive, as well as the complicity of high-level Columbia University administrators and several media outlets.

I appear before you today because of a campaign of intimidation to which I have been subjected for over three years. While this campaign was started by certain members of the Columbia faculty, and by outside forces using some of my students as conduits, it soon expanded to include members of the Columbia administration, the rightwing tabloid press, the Israeli press, and more locally the *Columbia Daily Spectator*. Much of this preceded the David Project film *Columbia Unbecoming*, and the ensuing controversy. In the following statement, I will provide you with the history of this coordinated campaign, including the facts pertaining to the intimidation to which I am being subjected by the Columbia University administration, most manifestly through the convening of your own committee before which I appear today out of a combined sense of intimidation and obligation and not because I recognize its legitimacy.

I started teaching at Columbia in the fall of 1999. At the conclusion of my first academic year, during which I taught my class on Palestinian and Israeli Politics and Societies, I received a Certificate of Appreciation for teaching presented by "The Students of Columbia College, Class of 2000," and was nominated and was one of the two finalists for the Van Doren teaching award which went that year to Professor Michael Stanislawski.

In my second year, I began to be told of whispers about my class on Palestinian and Israeli politics and societies. Jewish students in my class in the Spring 2001 would tell me that I was the main topic of discussion at the Jewish Theological Seminary and at Hillel and that my class is making the Zionists on campus angry. I took such reports lightly, as the class had doubled in size from the first year. I did notice however that the class included some cantankerous students who insisted on scoring political points during the lectures. I would always defuse the situation by allowing all questions to be asked and by attempting to answer them informatively. I would do so in class and during office hours. I had strong positive evaluations from most of my students with some complaining that the class was biased. The point of the class description [included in my syllabus] was to make sure the students understood that no side was being presented, neither the Palestinian nor the Zionist side, but rather that this was a course that was critical of both Zionism and Palestinian nationalism.

It was with this as background that I started my Spring 2002 semester. My Palestinian and Israeli course seemed to have a more cantankerous crowd that year than before. Even though this year, the class had two discussion sections to accommodate the number of students, a group of students insisted on having discussions during the lecture. Some would bring with them a pro-Israel lobby propaganda book from which they would insist on reading in class. I would let them.

One student in particular stood out. A smart older student in General Studies [Columbia's version of Continuing Education], who identified herself as having a South African Jewish background, would insist on asking many questions every lecture, most of which were about scoring political points. The class had over 80 students and therefore it was difficult to accommodate such a large number of questions from students. No matter, I decided to let her ask all her questions in every lecture in order to make her feel comfortable and that the class is a space where she could express herself freely. She would e-mail me asking for exact sources for information that I would give in class. I would e-mail her back what she needed … I later found out from other students that she was circulating a petition in the class to have me fired from Columbia.

I saw her on college walk one day after Spring break. She came up to me and told me that she had just been to Israel and the Occupied Territories and expressed how bad she felt about the situation there. She apologized about the petition and told me that she had been approached "from the outside" to do it, but she had dropped the matter. She spoke of people at the medical school and others from outside the university who were behind the idea but did not provide details. I did not inquire.

"Surreptitious" and "Conspiratorial" Meetings

Another student of mine who self-identified as a "Likudnik" [in reference to Israel's right-wing ruling Likud party] also approached me on campus one day during the Spring 2002 semester, telling me that he and a few other students had been invited to see a female professor at the medical school. He described the meeting as so "surreptitious" and "conspiratorial," that it felt that they were planning on having me "murdered." In fact, the plan was to strategize how to get me fired. The student told me that they discussed the option of meeting with a female administrator who worked at the time at the Middle East Institute, to coordinate the plan with her. ...

The female student who initiated the petition against me was not the only student in class who consistently posed hostile questions. Three or four other students would do so intermittently. One of them insisted on reading out loud in class paragraphs from a propaganda book issued by a pro-Israel lobbying organization. The book is "Myths and Facts: A Guide to the Arab-Israeli Conflict" written by one Mitchell Bard and published by the American-Israeli Cooperative Enterprise. It states on its website that, "We are committed to arming students with the information they need to respond to the very difficult issues raised on the campus" through the publication of Bard's book. Many students complained that these few students were disruptive of class, especially as there are discussion sections for them to raise their concerns. I allayed their anxiety by explaining that there is something to learn from some of the students' politically-motivated questions, namely that all students would learn the political arguments of proponents and opponents of certain scholarly analyses of the conflict, and that students who had political queries would also learn that there are indeed persuasive answers to the queries they raise from a critical and scholarly angle. For me, allowing these students to disrupt my lecture was of pedagogical benefit to them and to the rest of the class.

During the same semester, in April 2002, I was attacked and misquoted by the *Spectator* after attending an on-campus rally in support of Palestinians under Israeli military attack in the West Bank and Gaza, and an op-ed piece and letters were published in the *Spectator* accusing me of "anti-Semitism" for a lecture I had given at the Middle East Institute at Columbia University in February 2002. The op-ed piece by a third-year undergraduate student at Barnard named Daphna Berman, who was not my student, drew parallels between a swastika found in a law school bathroom and my lecture and rebuked the university for allowing me to speak out.

As for the political rally, I was one of countless speakers. I spoke out and asserted the following: "Like white South Africans who felt threatened under apartheid and who only felt safe when they gave up their commitment to white supremacy, Israeli Jews will continue to feel threatened if they persist in supporting Jewish supremacy. Israeli Jews will only feel safe in a democratic Israeli state where all Jews and Arabs are treated equally. No state has the right to be a racist state." The *Spectator* misquoted me as saying that Israel is "a Jewish supremacist and racist state," and that "every racist state should be threatened." When I protested the misquotation, the *Spectator* journalist who wrote the story apologized and informed me via e-mail that she did not even attend the rally and got the quotes from another reporter. After a back and forth for almost a week on e-mail, the *Spectator* ran the correction on April 24, 2002.

However, two major pro-Israeli propagandists, namely Martin Kramer and Daniel Pipes, would insist on reproducing the misquotation in articles that they wrote to newspapers and that they posted on their websites. On June 20, 2002, Kramer, an Israeli academic who teaches at Tel Aviv University, posted an article on the Middle East Forum website titled "Arab Panic," in which he attacked a number of Columbia professors, myself included. He argued that "Massad's views are not all that unusual in Middle Eastern studies, and he has every right to express them on Columbia's Low Plaza, in public lectures, and in print. But should someone who is busy propagandizing against the existence of Israel be employed by Columbia to teach the introductory course on the Arab-Israeli conflict? ... Suffice it to say that this column has received a surfeit of student complaints about the course, suggesting that there is no difference between what Massad teaches and what he preaches." Kramer also included the misquotation from the *Columbia Spectator*, despite the paper's retraction that had already been published.

Prior to Kramer's column, a website for an organization called "The Columbia Conservative Alumni Association" listed me among the six "worst faculty" at Columbia, a list that also included Edward Said, who was identified as a "homosexual" who supports Hamas. Martin Kramer was only too happy to quote from that website in his article, as would other columnists writing for the *New York Sun*. On June 25, 2002, Daniel Pipes and one Jonathan Schanzer published an article in *The New York Post* titled "Extremists on Campus," in which they listed me as one such extremist and complained that I use my class as a "soapbox for anti-Israeli polemics." The *Wall Street Journal* published on September 18, 2002 an article about a pro-Israel website calling itself CampusWatch being launched by Daniel Pipes, stating that the website listed 8 professors (including me) with our own public dossiers as enemies of America and Israel and called on our students to monitor us in class.

Following the launch of CampusWatch, my e-mail was spammed for months with over 4,000 e-mails daily, which I had to sift through until finally Columbia was able to install an anti-spamming program. Moreover, I was subjected to identity theft when thousands of racist e-mails would be sent in my name to individuals and listservs, including a few to the White House and Congressmen threatening them with terrorist action. Moreover, thousands of other e-mails would be sent to people with requests of notes of receipt being sent back to my e-mail account, which clogged it further with thousands of such e-mail receipts. I also received tens of racist e-mails and phone messages including death threats directed at me. In the meantime, Pipes's website called on our own students to spy on us in the classroom and report to him, and Kramer called for my dismissal from Columbia University. ...

In late January 2003, I began to write a column to the Egyptian Weekly *Al-Ahram*, which deals mostly with Palestinian-Israeli affairs and with the Arab World more generally. Every time I published an article, Kramer and Pipes would write about it, as would new student recruits that they had on campuses. One such ideological recruit was a first year student in General Studies whom I had never met called Ariel Beery. Beery would become one of the main people defending the claims of the David Project in whose film he appeared [*Columbia Unbecoming*] and called me "one of the most dangerous intellectuals ... on campus." Beery has never taken a class with me and never met me. Beery, who claims to have served in the Israeli army in Lebanon, had his own *Spectator* column and a personal blog. Beery arrived on the Columbia campus when I was on sabbatical, yet surprisingly he chose to write about me in his column.

Basing his arguments on one of my newspaper columns, Beery added the following:

If anything, Massad's claim [in his column] that there is no anti-Semitism in the Arab world should disqualify him from setting foot in a Columbia University classroom as a professor of Modern Arab

Politics. Just as you would not trust a surgeon with shaky knowledge of the human anatomy, Columbia should not trust the minds of its charges to a professor with a limited knowledge of the body politic of the region he supposedly is an expert in. [Massad also] says that the claim that Israel is democratic is no more than a "propagandistic image"... th[is] ... charge on Israel should again disqualify Massad from teaching at Columbia.

In April 2003, I decided to respond to Kramer and Pipes in an article titled, "Policing the Academy," in which I fleshed out their agenda and their plans. I concluded by stating that,

Kramer, Pipes, and co. are angry that the academy still allows democratic procedure in the expression of political views and has an institutionalized meritocratic system of judgment ... to evaluate its members. Their goal is to destroy any semblance of either in favor of subjecting democracy and academic life to an incendiary jingoism and to the exigencies of the national security state with the express aim of imploding freedom. Their larger success, however, has been in discrediting themselves and in reminding all of us that we should never take the freedoms that we have for granted, as the likes of Kramer and Pipes are working to take them away.

...

Upon returning to Columbia in the fall of 2003, I gave a lecture at the Society of Fellows at the Heyman Center. The lecture was attended by a large number of people including many faculty members. Professor Nicholas Dirks, who had not yet become Vice President, was among them. After the lecture, I was asked a number of hostile questions from young students and from one Rabbi Charles Sheer, about whom I had heard the previous year when he railed against MEALAC professors in the context of the pro-Palestinian rally that took place on campus in April 2002. I had never met him before. I answered all the questions put before me.

On January 6, 2004, Rabbi Sheer posted a letter on the Hillel website addressed to Columbia and Barnard students, in which he discussed my lecture and made a startling announcement. Sheer declared that "the principal anti-Israel voices [on Columbia's campus] are not pro-Palestinian student leaders and groups, but Columbia faculty and academic departments ... [These] faculty members whose teaching style is called 'advocacy education' espouse a consistent anti-Israel and pro-Palestinian bias. Their personal politics pervade the classroom and academic forums. The record is public: search under 'Columbia University' at websites such as www.campuswatch.org and www.martinkramer.org. Be prepared; it is not a pleasant read."

Sheer proceeded to mention that he had attended my lecture at the Heyman Center and then summarized it by making outrageous claims that were never made in the lecture

Professor Massad has reversed the roles of all the players and redefined many of the historic events: the Zionists are the new Nazis; the Palestinians are oppressed victims and therefore the new Jews ... From a distance, this diatribe may sound ludicrous. However, its impact on campus is serious. MEALAC should enable our students to explore issues vital to their understanding of the modern Middle East in a balanced way ...

We will see how the false claim attributed to me by Rabbi Sheer that I said that "the Zionists are the new Nazis," a claim I never made, would find its way to Ariel Beery who would make the same claim in the video *Columbia Unbecoming* – a false claim that would be repeated *ad absurdum* in the media. Sheer concluded with two interesting claims, one which effectively called on students not to take my class, and another announcing the filming of *Columbia Unbecoming*:

Of course, academic freedom is a cornerstone of our University. However, students are understandably reluctant to take courses from faculty who impose their biases in their teaching. A student group is currently working on a video that records how intimidated students feel by advocacy teaching, and how some are discouraged from taking MEALAC courses or majoring in Middle East studies.

Suffice it to say that my class had over fifty students for the Spring 2004 and students did not heed the call made by Sheer. The class did however include a number of auditors (I found out they were unregistered during the last week of class) who would consistently harass me with hostile ideological questions that ignored all the readings. Students complained about the disruption this caused the class. I tried to emphasize to the auditors that their questions must be relevant to the subject at hand and that they must do the readings. They never did and I continued to answer their questions until the end of the semester to avoid creating a tense atmosphere in the classroom.

During this period, the *New York Sun* and Kramer and Pipes continued to attack me in their columns and on their websites. On May 4, 2004, the *Sun* ran another article about me by one Jonathan Calt Harris, identified as an associate of Daniel Pipes at CampusWatch, titled "Tenured Extremism." After a litany of misquotes, half quotes, and outright fabrications, Calt Harris, who referred to my views as akin to those of "Nazis," concluded by stating: "Mr. Massad is soon up for tenure review. Should this once distinguished university stoop to provide a permanent forum for his views, it would signify a truly stunning oversight ... He knows no distinction between a classroom lecture and advocacy at a public demonstration."

Based on this repeated call to deny me tenure at Columbia, which had already been expressed by Kramer, I met with Provost [Alan] Brinkley. I sought his help and the help of the university's legal services to fight this defamation of character. I provided copies of my written work for the Provost and told him of the campaigns to which I had been subjected in the previous years. I asked him if he could arrange for me to meet with legal services to which he reluctantly agreed. I had to remind him by e-mail to set up a meeting for me. After he put me in touch with legal services, my e-mails to them went unanswered. I asked the provost to intervene which he did. His intervention produced a response from their office asking me about my available times to set up an appointment. I sent it to them and never heard back. I dropped the matter after I left in mid-summer for vacation abroad.

In the meantime however, I received a letter from Joel J. Levy, director of the New York chapter of the Anti-Defamation League [ADL], copies of which had been sent to President Bollinger and Provost Brinkley. The letter was significantly dated on May 6, 2004, two days after Calt Harris published his article in the *Sun*. The letter [writer] complained to me that, according to one report [he] received from one student who attended a lecture that I had given at the University of Pennsylvania on March 24, 2004 (which incidentally was the same lecture I gave at Columbia's Society of Fellows the previous October), ideas expressed in my lecture are "anti-Semitic." The letter made false claims about what my lecture said and asked that I retract them and issue an apology for my allegedly anti-Semitic remarks. I wrote Mr. Levy back and copied President Bollinger and Provost Brinkley. I stated in my letter that:

> My principled stance against anti-Semitism and all kinds of racism is a matter of public record and cannot be assailed by defamatory "reports" or by letters from the ADL that consider them credible sources. Indeed I have condemned anti-Semitism in my Arabic and English writings, regardless of whether the person expressing it was pro-Israel or anti-Israel, an Arab, an American Christian, or an Israeli Jew ... I therefore expect a prompt correction of the errors contained in your letter and demand an immediate apology, a copy of which should be sent to President Bollinger.

I never heard back from the ADL or from the provost.

It was with this as background that news about the David Project film *Columbia Unbecoming* surfaced on October 20, 2004 in a *New York Sun* article.

The Aftermath of *Columbia Unbecoming*

I was horrified by the media campaign against me and the calls for my dismissal from Columbia that were issued by Congressman [Anthony] Weiner and by the editors of the *Daily News* and the *New York Sun*, as well as calls by Jewish members of the New York City Council to investigate the matter. These calls were issued as declarations about the controversy by the national head of the ADL and Mayor Bloomberg and were also made to the press. In addition, the film was suddenly being shown in Israel before a government minister at an anti-Semitism conference. I had requested a meeting with Provost Brinkley who did not contact me once during the early days of the controversy during which President Bollinger was making all kinds of statements to the press.

My request to meet with the Provost was made through the chair of my department, Marc van de Mieroop, who attended our meeting in the Provost's office on the 27th of October. I inquired of the provost as to why he would sit down secretly to watch a propaganda film produced by a lobbying group and why he would remain silent about it after he had seen it. The provost apologized and admitted that these were mistakes but that now we needed to contain the problem. He assured me that he had received countless letters in my support and few against me. When I spoke with Vice President Dirks later, he also informed me that he had received "hundreds" of letters in my support and "three or four" against me.

I subsequently corresponded briefly on e-mail with Provost Brinkley, mainly about my concerns regarding statements made by President Bollinger, which the Provost would challenge and represent as the media's inaccurate rendering. Soon there would be no further communication with him. President Bollinger to this day has not contacted me ...

Let me [respond] to the claims put forward in *Columbia Unbecoming*, based on press reports and on the recent transcript of the film made available on the web. I still have not seen the film. Let me reiterate what I said in my statement regarding the claims put forward by the students in the film:

> I am now being targeted because of my public writings and statements through the charge that I am allegedly intolerant in the classroom, a charge based on statements made by people who were never my students, except in one case. In fact, Tomy Schoenfeld, the Israeli soldier who appears in the film and is cited by the *New York Sun*, has never been my student and has never taken a class with me, as he himself informed *The Jewish Week*. I have never met him. As for Noah Liben, who appears in the film, he was indeed a student in my Palestinian and Israeli Politics and Societies course in spring 2001. Noah seems to have forgotten the incident he cites. During a lecture about Israeli state racism against Asian and African Jews, Noah defended these practices on the basis that Asian and African Jews were underdeveloped and lacked Jewish culture, which the Ashkenazi State operatives were teaching them. When I explained to him that, as the assigned readings clarified, these were racist policies, he insisted that these Jews needed to be modernized and the Ashkenazim were helping them by civilizing them. Many students gasped ... Moreover, the lie that the film propagates claiming that I would equate Israel with

Nazi Germany is abhorrent. I have never made such a reprehensible equation.

As for the claim made by Ariel Beery, whom I have never met and who has never been my student, that my "favorite description is the Palestinian as the new Jew and the Jew as the new Nazi," such a statement is an outright lie. Beery gets this quote not from anything I said or wrote, but from the fabrication made up by Rabbi Sheer on his Hillel web posting of 4 January 2004.

....

In the aftermath of the film, I have received, and still receive, a barrage of hate mail and racist e-mails and voicemail messages. The first such e-mail message was from a medical school professor called Moshe Rubin. Professor Rubin wrote me on October 20th, the same day as the first report was published in the *Sun*. Under the subject heading "Anti-Semite," he wrote:

> Go back to Arab land where Jew hating is condoned get the hell out of America you are a disgrace and a pathetic typical arab liar
> Moshe Rubin

Many more such e-mails would follow. The campaign would quickly expand and include medical school professor Judith Jacobson. Such threatening e-mails have also targeted others in my department. A recent e-mail was sent last week to all the Jewish students and faculty at MEALAC from an Israeli group calling itself "United Trial Group – Peoples Rights International," informing them that:

> We advise you to immediately dismiss/kick ass of Joseph Goebbels, a Joseph Massed, based on the President Bush Bill against anti-Semitism and according with the US anti-terrorism law, proscribing Nazi propaganda and incitement to terror. If you and the administration won't immediately dismiss that fascist bastard, you and the administration will be personally liable and accountable for aiding, abetting and harboring this Muslim criminal, and subject to criminal prosecution and multimillion compensations in damages … You have 30 days to comply and inform us.

I should state that I have received immense support from across the world, through countless letters and thousands of signatures on an online petition. These include hundreds of individual letters from academics, students, and supporters, and tens of letters from my own students, especially my Jewish students. All these letters were sent to President Bollinger, Provost Brinkley, and Vice President Dirks. Copies of many of these letters were sent to me. In addition, a colleague at the University of Texas at Austin, Professor Neville Hoad, circulated a letter within a few days of the controversy and obtained 828 signatures of major scholars and academics around the United States and the world, which he also submitted to the President, the Provost, and the Vice President. An on-line petition obtained upwards of 3,000 signatures, a copy of which was also sent to Bollinger. Hooligans attempted to undermine the petition by signing names like "Adolf Hitler" and 'Osama Ben Laden," but they were not able to shut the petition down.

In addition, two letters were sent to the President, the Provost, and the Vice President, one by 24 graduate students at MEALAC, and another by 52 graduate students from other departments at Columbia. The Middle East Studies Association's Academic Freedom Committee issued a letter defending my academic freedom, as did the American Association of University Professors (AAUP), the New York chapter of the American Civil Liberties Union (ACLU), and the American-Arab Anti-Discrimination Committee. Thirty professors from the American University in Cairo also sent a letter defending me. President Bollinger has as of yet not responded to any of these individuals or organizations with the notable exception of the ACLU. A response was also sent by the Provost to the AAUP.

President Bollinger's Failure to Defend the Faculty

The response of the Columbia University administration to the David Project was swift. In statement and action, Columbia's President Bollinger prejudged the accused faculty, and failed to defend us or the MEALAC department, and he refused to defend Columbia's own record of pluralism and tolerance, the variety of courses the university offers on the Middle East, or Columbia's established commitment to promote Jewish and Israel Studies. Instead President Bollinger and his administration gave legitimacy to the film *Columbia Unbecoming*, referred to its claims as facts, and promised an "investigation." His subsequent statements and actions have emboldened those engaged in the campaign to intimidate me and would confirm to the public that the allegations against me are in fact true, at least, as far as he was concerned. Let me illustrate how this transpired.

Columbia's first response to the allegations contained in the film, *Columbia Unbecoming*, was a statement released by the President himself. This statement was released after Congressman Anthony Wiener called on Columbia to fire me in a letter to Bollinger, and after two newspapers (the *New York Sun* and the *Daily News*) added their voices to Wiener's and asked that I be fired, and after a medical school faculty member, Moshe Rubin, sent me a racist e-mail which I had immediately forwarded to Provost Brinkley.

In his statement, Bollinger referred to the "disturbing and offensive nature of incidents described in the film" without using the word "alleged" before incidents. This was certainly not an oversight, especially coming from a lawyer. He further added that academic freedom "does not, for example, extend to protecting behavior in the classroom that threatens or intimidates students who express their viewpoints." Bollinger failed to make any reference as to whether academic freedom extends to protecting students engaged in intimidating professors by raising a media campaign against them. Nor did the statement address whether the intimidation of the faculty and the Columbia administration by outside pressure groups, the press, and government officials would be tolerated. In his statement, instead, Bollinger announced that he had asked the Provost to "look into" the students' claims, which in subsequent press reports quoting him, he referred to as an "investigation."

The next day, Bollinger met with the national director of the Anti-Defamation League, Abraham Foxman. According to press accounts, Bollinger sought to meet with Foxman and other leaders of Jewish organizations. On November 11th, after delivering a lecture at the University Club on Fifth Avenue, Mr. Bollinger was asked about the student accusations against Columbia faculty members, "according to an audience member who did not wish to disclose his identity ... Mr. Bollinger ... said he was committed to academic freedom but wouldn't condone 'stupid' behavior by faculty members." Such a biased and disrespectful choice of words would continue in Bollinger's press declarations. ...

Bollinger never contacted me to check whether [the litany of allegations against me] was true. Indeed, Bollinger now speaks of these allegations as outright facts. Witness what he told students over dinner a few days ago as reported by the *Columbia Spectator*: "I'm not going to talk about whether the accusations are true or not. Let's just assume they're true." The *Spectator* reporter adds the following:

> The second claim made by the film, according to Bollinger, was that some professors did not permit students to voice their own opinions about matters of discussion in the classroom. He identified this action as a clear violation of academic freedom ... The third claim was that some MEALAC courses are blatantly biased, presenting only one side of the spectrum of opinions on contentious subjects. Bollinger said that the warnings professors gave ahead of time about the one-sidedness of their courses were "unacceptable."

Not only did Bollinger or Provost Brinkley never contact me about my course, neither of them responded to my announcement that I had cancelled it, which I made in my publicized statement in response to the intimidation to which I was being subjected. I had indeed sent a copy of my statement to Provost Brinkley before posting it. He wrote me back counseling me not to release it. However neither he nor Bollinger, nor even Vice President Dirks, expressed any discomfort that I, a Columbia faculty member, was canceling one of my courses because of intimidation. None of them informed me that I would be protected by the University were I to teach it again and that the University would ensure my rights and defend me against intimidation. Indeed, what I was subjected to is not more protection by my own university but more intimidation, the most concrete manifestation of which was the formation of your committee.

The Ad Hoc Committee

The step taken by the administration to establish a committee to investigate professors based on student grievances that were not lodged with any university body but rather aired through an off-campus lobbying group sets a dangerous precedent of violating the academic freedom of professors. The establishment of the committee coupled with the statements by Bollinger to the press have given the clear impression that the David Project had legitimate issues to raise with Columbia, and that even though Bollinger himself had assured everyone that there were no registered complaints against any of the accused professors through any Columbia channel, and that he had already convened a secret committee to investigate similar allegations the previous semester, the so-called Blasi committee, which found no evidence of bias, he still saw a need for a second special committee to address such complaints.

The matter of the committee charge is of grave importance. I requested and had a meeting with Vice President Dirks in his office on December 9th to discuss this particular matter. I told him then that I would not consider the ad hoc committee a legitimate body unless it included in its charge the investigation of claims of intimidation of faculty by students, by administrators, and by off-campus pressure groups.

He responded positively to my concerns by asking me for my telephone number in Amman, Jordan, as I was traveling the next day on December 10th. He said that I needed to be next to a phone and fax in the next day or two so that he could call me and fax me a draft of the charge to approve so that he could release it then to the public. I was satisfied with this arrangement. Vice President Dirks however never contacted me. I e-mailed him on December 14th to inquire about the charge. He wrote back on December 19th informing me that he had not "yet been able to come up with a statement about the committee. I'll send you something as soon as it is ready." I never heard back from him.

Upon returning to Columbia in mid-January 2005, my students forwarded to me a mass e-mail that Vice President Dirks had sent out inviting students to appear before the committee. I was taken aback by such a step, as I still did not know what the committee's charge was. I wrote to the Vice President to inquire on January 20th as to what had transpired. He wrote me back clarifying that he had not promised to share with me the circular he had sent out to the students. As for the charge, he explained that he still had not finalized it and would do so in a couple of days. I heard again from him a week later asking me to pick up a copy of the charge from his office. I did and was shocked to find that it did not include the investigation of faculty intimidation by students and administrators. I never heard back from Vice President Dirks, who never offered an explanation or an apology for his disrespectful conduct, having failed to inform me of the change of plans and then offering me the charge as a fait accompli.

I am very concerned about the choice of Floyd Abrams as your advisor, a position whose mandate has not been made public. Mr. Abrams is publicly identified with pro-Israeli politics and activism. He has spoken at fund raisers for causes in Israel, has worked and consulted with the Anti-Defamation League, one of the parties campaigning against me, and received a major award from it in 2003, the Hubert H. Humphrey Award, and has endorsed the book *The Case for Israel* by Alan Dershowitz, who has been speaking publicly in lectures and to the media against me, in the context of the ongoing witch-hunt, alleging that I support terrorism. [Given these facts] the decision to appoint Mr. Abrams as advisor to this committee conveys at the least the appearance of partiality.

On the question of my scholarship and my integrity as a teacher, Bollinger's statements sadly suggest that he has taken sides against the faculty and the university in this controversy. Compare his recent declarations with those of Martin Kramer, one of the main people behind this witch-hunt. Kramer wrote on November 5, 2002 in a web posting:

> The other issue of overriding concern here is the apparent absence of any effort by the Columbia administration to promote diversity. Here I don't mean the false diversity of academic mafias. They think it's crucial to assemble people of different ethnic, national, religious, racial, gender, and disciplinary backgrounds – provided they say the same thing. I'm talking about intellectual diversity, which used to be a value at Columbia. The only historian of the modern Middle East at Columbia [besides the possible employment of Rashid Khalidi] is another Palestinian, Joseph Massad, who is a militant follower of Edward Said. (He's now up for tenure.) Imagine that Khalidi were added, and Massad were tenured, both to teach history. They work in the same area, and their politics, while not identical, are very similar. The whole thing begins to look like a cozy club of like-minded pals, who peer at the Middle East through exactly the same telescope, from exactly the same vantage point.

Compare Kramer's statement with Bollinger's. With regard to this alleged lack of intellectual diversity at Columbia and in Middle East Studies more generally, *New York Magazine* reported that: "today, [Bollinger] says he's equally committed to intellectual diversity" which "may not augur well for professor Massad's longevity at Columbia, no matter how favorably disposed the provost's committee may be to him." Bollinger went on to declare to *Jewish Week* that "the Israeli-Palestinian conflict is not being taught in a balanced way that reflects the complexity of the region." [According to this *Jewish Week* report] Bollinger recommended that MEALAC be "expanded" and that it continue to teach the Palestinian-Israeli conflict but not as it has done so far:

"I happen to think that the Israeli-Palestinian conflict is of central importance in the modern world," he said, "and we want to be able to think about that in its full complexities. That's going to mean that there will be thoughts some people will find difficult, or even offensive, and yet we must be able to explore given our belief in academic freedom. However, it is our obligation to do that with full respect to the complexity, and if we don't do that, we have failed ourselves, we have failed our own principles."

The implication being that those of us, and the reference is clearly to me, who teach the Palestinian-Israeli conflict at MEALAC do not teach it with its "full complexity" or that I do not "respect" such complexity.

I derive my authority as a scholar of the Middle East from my doctoral training here at Columbia's Political Science Department, which granted me my PhD with distinction, a rare honor that was further certified by the Middle East Studies Association, which granted me its most prestigious award for a social science dissertation for 1998, the Malcolm Kerr Award. My book [*Colonial Effects: The Making of a National Identity in Jordan*], which was based on my dissertation, was published by Columbia University Press, and has been endorsed and reviewed favorably by the most prominent Middle East scholars in the academy. My book and my articles on the Palestinian-Israeli conflict are used as standard texts for courses on nationalism and on Palestine and Israel across the United States and Europe. My recent work on sexuality and queer theory is also taught across the country, and a book length study on the subject is forthcoming. An attack on my scholarship therefore is not only an attack on me and on MEALAC but on Columbia's political science department, on prestigious academic presses, including Columbia University Press, and on the Middle East Studies Association (MESA),

I should affirm here that President Bollinger is under the impression that he can set the research agenda for Middle East scholarship at

Columbia much better than Columbia's Middle East faculty. He told the *Jewish Week* that "we need to integrate better than we have other fields that have knowledge relevant to the work being done in MEALAC. What is the relationship, for example, between the environmental facts of life in the Middle East and Asia, or its diseases, and the culture there?" This retreat to 19th century climatology and medical anthropology is disturbing. Would President Bollinger also think that there is a relationship between "environmental facts, its diseases and the culture" of African Americans or of American Jews?

I am concerned that Bollinger may well be making an academic judgment about me that is based not on my scholarship or pedagogy but on my politics and even my nationality ... When a number of faculty members [including Edward Said] and I signed a petition in 2002 calling on Columbia to divest from companies that sell weapons to Israel, a country guilty of human rights abuses, Bollinger's response betrayed a strong emotional reaction and a stronger political bias: "The petition alleges human rights abuses and compares Israel to South Africa at the time of apartheid, an analogy I believe is both grotesque and offensive."

While the off-campus campaigners against me do not have the direct power to influence my future employment at Columbia, Bollinger clearly does, and therefore his failure to defend academic freedom is detrimental to my career and my job. I am further chilled in this regard by reports that at the recent general meeting of the Faculty of Arts and Sciences, Bollinger sought to change the fifty-year tradition regarding how tenure cases are decided at Columbia when he stated that he and the trustees, in accordance with the statutes but in contravention of established tradition, would want to have the final say in tenure cases in the future.

In conclusion, the foregoing has given you [the ad hoc committee] the minimum of details and historical narrative regarding this coordinated campaign from inside and outside the university targeting me, my job, and my chances for tenure, based on my political views, my political writings, and my nationality. That the Columbia University administration acted as a collaborator with the witch-hunters instead of defending me and offering itself as a refuge from right-wing McCarthyism has been a cause of grave personal and professional disappointment to me ... The major goal of the witch-hunters is to destroy the institution of the university in general. I am merely the entry point for their political project. As the university is the last bastion of free-thinking that has not yet fallen under the authority of extreme right-wing forces, it has become their main target. The challenge before us is therefore to be steadfast in fighting for academic freedom.

Editors' note: The 2005 testimony ends here. Professor Massad wrote the following epilogue to his testimony for this book.

Looking Back from 2016

The McCarthyist attack on me which started in the Fall of 2004 would be finally defeated in the Spring of 2009 when I was granted tenure at Columbia University. The five years during which the battle was waged were a very difficult period and the outcome was not always certain. But I pressed on, fighting back on every front while continuing to produce scholarly work, which, after all, was what the McCarthyist attack was hoping to halt. In the meantime, I received huge support from my students, from numerous colleagues at Columbia and beyond the university, in the United States and internationally, and especially from the American Civil Liberties Union, New York Chapter, which provided me with crucial legal counsel throughout the ordeal. I also received support from the American Association of University Professors, which continued to monitor the situation, and from academic associations. Despite the persistent public and open closeness of university administrators with the McCarthyist organizations and media arms that fought against academic freedom, the battle was finally won when academic freedom and scholarly merit defeated these repressive forces. I hope and expect that my victory will inspire a new generation of scholars to continue the fight against threats to the university and to academic scholarship with the foreknowledge that these forces can indeed be defeated.

10

A Multiyear Zionist
Censorship Campaign

David Klein

Editors' note: David Klein is Professor of Mathematics at California State University in Northridge (CSUN) and the former director of the CSUN Climate Program. A prominent public figure in his field, Professor Klein is also a founding member of the US Campaign for the Academic and Cultural Boycott of Israel (USACBI). As he explains in the following testimony, in the wake of Israel's 2008/9 massacre in Gaza he "violated the '11th Commandment,' never to criticize the State of Israel," in response to which some of the organizations and personalities that comprise the Israel lobby launched a months-long campaign of threats and harrassment. The lobby eventually backed off when, unlike the experience of many other scholars and students, the CSUN administration came out in defense of Professor Klein's rights to free speech and academic freedom.

My story begins in January 2009 during Operation Cast Lead, Israel's three-week assault of Gaza. Between December 27, 2008 and January 18, 2009, Israel closed off all means of escape from the Gaza Strip and proceeded to slaughter some 1,400 people while destroying as much infrastructure as it could. Half of Gaza's hospitals were bombed along with ambulances and refugee centers. Dozens of mosques and schools were obliterated, and even kindergartens were not spared. Farms, food centers, water systems, and homes by the thousands were destroyed while Israeli soldiers used Palestinian children as human shields.

A month before the massacre, I had joined California Scholars for Academic Freedom (CSAF), a group of faculty from California's universities. CSAF operates through its listserv and has a history of defending scholars under attack for criticizing Israel's policies or advocating for Palestinian human rights. In the midst of Operation Cast Lead, CSAF struggled to find ways to oppose the ongoing slaughter. Exchanges on the listserv resulted in 14 members of CSAF, including myself, creating a separate organization, the US Campaign for the Academic and Cultural Boycott of Israel (USACBI). During the course of these events, I created a website dedicated to Boycott, Divestment, and Sanctions, or BDS, on the server of California State University Northridge (CSUN), where I am a Professor of Mathematics, and I linked it from my faculty webpage.[1]

Boycott Israel Webpage

My "Boycott Israel Resource Page" criticizes segregated roads and buses, racist marriage laws, and institutional de-Arabization programs in Israel. It is unrelated to my mathematical research and teaching – I've never mentioned it in my classes – but it supports other duties. These include serving as faculty advisor for Students for Justice in Palestine (SJP) and the CSUN Greens, whose national organization endorsed BDS. The page is also a resource for other faculty members who, through faculty governance, would support academic boycott or a call for divestment of the CSU system from corporations that bolster Israel's ethnic cleansing and apartheid system.

In the immediate aftermath of Operation Cast Lead, I wrote an op-ed piece entitled "Support for Israel Must Stop" for the *Daily Sundial*, CSUN's school newspaper. I recounted the loss of life and destruction, and I quoted "The Six Months of the Lull Arrangement," an Israeli government intelligence document that revealed that it was Israel, not Hamas, which broke the ceasefire and initiated the carnage.[2] I also referred readers to my boycott webpage.

In publishing my letter and posting the webpage, I had violated the "11th Commandment," never to criticize the State of Israel. Two colleagues immediately took it upon themselves to denounce me in letters to the editor. Political Science professor James Mitchell described my piece as "unvarnished, uncompromising, and decidedly myopic," leaving "little room for any possibility of reasoned dialogue on the matter." He went on to repeat standard propaganda and ignored the internal Israeli document that I cited, falsely declaring in his letter, "The fact is, this most recent salvo began with the Dec. 19 breach of a cease-fire by the

Hamas side."[3] Sociology professor Harvey Rich's letter praised Mitchell's, described my piece as "vitriolic and ideological," and then chided the *Sundial* for its decision to "even print such a piece without a counter piece alongside it," evidently finding his and Mitchell's letters, along with a myriad of *Sundial* blog attacks against me, inadequate to the task.[4]

Mitchell and Rich were not alone, but neither was I. Outraged by Israel's brutality, some colleagues added their names to USACBI's growing list of US academics in support of the academic and cultural boycott of Israel.[5] I also invited faculty both on and off campus to link my boycott webpage to their faculty pages, or create their own versions. A handful did link my page to theirs, but subsequent pressure in the form of scary legalistic sounding letters from Zionist organizations caused all but one to unlink it. This was part of a general tactic of Zionist censors: first isolate critics of Israel from supporters, then go after the critics.

Later that semester, a colleague and two student clubs, the CSUN Greens and the Muslim Student Association, proposed a debate, "Palestine & Israel: What is Next?" The organizers first invited CSUN Jewish Studies professor Jody Meyers to debate me, an appropriate choice. Back in 2008, she had vehemently opposed my speaking invitation to Norman Finkelstein. Echoing other Zionists who had blocked Finkelstein's tenure at DePaul University in 2007, Meyers repeated the absurd claim that he was academically unqualified to lecture at CSUN. Finkelstein nevertheless did come to CSUN and gave three well-attended lectures across a one-week visit.[6]

Meyers, however, declined the invitation. Instead, CSUN librarian Wayne Cohen debated me on April 16, 2009 and brought with him a dozen or so militant supporters. At the end of the debate, one of them informed me that he had been an Israeli soldier. He accused me of being a liar, without identifying any lies, and said, "I hope God kills you." Hate mail arrived in the form of email and postal letters, but most attacks came later.

AMCHA

In 2011, the California State University system began a process to reinstate its Israel Study Abroad Program, previously suspended due to costs and a US State Department travel warning. With two colleagues from other CSU campuses, I wrote an open letter to the CSU Chancellor,

Charles Reed, in opposition to reinstatement. The letter cited examples of Israeli soldiers injuring or killing US citizens including students, and argued that CSU students in the program "could face discriminatory treatment, based on race and ethnicity." The open letter was signed by 52 CSU students and alumni, and 85 CSU faculty and administrators, including department chairs, several deans, and the provost of CSUN, Harry Hellenbrand. I posted the letter on the CSUN server and linked it to my faculty webpage.[7]

Press coverage and the solicitation of signatures throughout the 23-campus CSU system publicized the open letter, which was what we wanted, but the publicity also brought a backlash. Hate mail poured in laden with obscenities, accusing me of being a kapo, anti-Semite, Nazi, self-hating, violating state law, putting Jewish students in danger, and much more. I posted them on a "hate mail webpage" linked to my boycott page in order to reveal how Zionist censorship operates, and have continued to do so.[8] Many of the senders signed off with impressive titles including, professor, PhD, MD, and law degrees. The hate mail at first focused on the open letter, but soon shifted to my boycott webpage. They were sent not only to me, but in some cases to the chair of my department, the provost and president of CSUN, the chancellor of the CSU system, state senators, the governor, reporters, and Zionist organizations.

The most persistent attacks came from the AMCHA Initiative, a California Zionist group that collaborates with other Zionist organizations to suppress speech critical of Israel on university campuses. Tammi Rossman-Benjamin and Leila Beckwith, the founding members of AMCHA, took the lead in pressuring the CSUN administration to remove my webpage.

Rossman-Benjamin, a lecturer at UC Santa Cruz, is an anti-Palestinian activist with a history of racist accusations against students and litigious threats against faculty.[9] According to Rossman-Benjamin, "I don't separate my Zionism from my Judaism. What it means to be a Jew is to have a love and a connection for Israel."[10] By conflating Judaism with Zionism, Rossman-Benjamin implicitly denies that the ultra-orthodox Jewish sect, Neturei Karta, is even Jewish (because it is anti-Zionist on religious grounds), and her conflation associates to Judaism an unending list of racist crimes objectively documented by human rights organizations. In this way, AMCHA's extreme Zionist ideology is ironically anti-Semitic.

AMCHA's two founders sent an email letter in November 2011 to then CSUN president Jolene Koester accusing my webpage of containing a "litany of false and inflammatory statements and photographs intended to incite hatred and promote political activism against the Jewish state," and demanded that it be taken down. As usual, they could find no actual "false statements" to quote, but that did not stop them.

In response to the flood of Zionist accusations, President Koester ordered a formal review of my webpage and issued a December 5, 2011 public statement in which she acknowledged "a personal discomfort with some of the material on Professor Klein's web pages" but also wrote,

> the review considered whether the web content is in violation of California State University (CSU) or Cal State Northridge web use policies. While the review raised many difficult issues, it found no such violations. This conclusion was affirmed by CSU legal counsel.[11]

A later, more detailed administrative report was posted which found that

> Professor Klein has every right to express his opinions about the treatment of the Palestinian people at the hands of the government of Israel. Furthermore, based upon his thoughts and feelings about the issue, he has every right to call for a boycott of the country. Neither action is anti-Semitic.

In early December 2011, I received an anonymous recorded phone message that said, "Be afraid, Mr. Klein, be very afraid." Also about that time, a Christian Zionist, Steve Klein (no relationship), showed up at my office. I believe he is the same Steve Klein who consulted for the anti-Muslim film, *The Innocence of Muslims*, which triggered violent protests in the Middle East. Steve Klein was upset by the open letter about the Israel Study Abroad program. Following his half hour visit, he sent his own letter to each of the roughly 140 signers of the open letter, and to the *Los Angeles Times* (which did not publish it). His letter began,

> The blind-with-hate enemies of the Jews really don't need help – or encouragement from CSU Northridge math professor David Klein or from you ... Klein has a long record of sympathy for Palestinian baby-killers and cowardly kindergarten bombers ... I think he would

probably feel fine if those bothersome, embarrassing Jews simply and quietly walked themselves back into the German ovens. Klein comes off just slightly less smug than Jon Stewart ...

He then gave his own peculiar history of the Middle East, vilifying Nelson Mandela and Desmond Tutu in the process, both opponents of Zionism and supporters of Palestinian rights. I was alarmed by his libel, but relieved to be placed (undeservedly) alongside such honorable company since that weakened his attack.

Outraged by the CSUN administration's refusal to remove my webpage, legalistic letters from Zionist organizations poured in to the administration. One dated December 7, 2011 from AMCHA repeated earlier arguments but with sharper demands, including:

> We demand that you exercise your responsibility and declare to the University community that Professor Klein's views are deeply offensive and violate the University's policy of tolerance and inclusiveness.

It concluded with a warning: "Please understand that the Jewish community will not remain silent while anti-Semitism goes unchecked on your campus."[12] That same day, another letter to the CSUN president arrived from the Zionist Organization of America's (ZOA) president Morton Klein and ZOA legal director Susan Tuchman in which they said,

> Recently, the ZOA was contacted about the bigoted and repulsive content on the Web pages of one of your professors, Professor of Mathematics, David Klein, who has made no bones about his hatred for Israel. For instance, we understand that Professor Klein was behind an "open letter" sent last week to Charles Reed, the Chancellor of California State University (CSU), opposing the reinstatement of the CSU study abroad program in Israel. Outrageously and absurdly, the letter contends that "participating CSU students could face discriminatory treatment, based on race and ethnicity," in Israel – the only functioning democracy in the Middle East ...

The ZOA leaders also urged President Koester "to investigate whether Professor Klein's hateful conduct is creating a hostile environment for Jewish and pro-Israel students on your campus." Copied recipients included the CSU Board of Trustees, both US Senators from California, and Congressman Brad Sherman. AMCHA supporters also sent emails, some calling for President Koester's resignation.[13]

Koester finished her presidency amidst this chaos, and when Provost Harry Hellenbrand stepped in as CSUN's interim president on January 1, 2012, he immediately became a target of Zionist attacks. AMCHA informed its followers that,

> Surprisingly, Harold Hellenbrand, the new interim President of CSUN, is publicly listed as a signatory to a letter that demonizes Israel and seeks to prevent students from studying there, which was authored by Professor Klein and posted on Klein's CSUN-hosted web page.[14]

An email from Gary Gerofsky of "The Never Again Group Canada" accused Hellenbrand of being an "interim President who counts himself among the haters of Jews and Israel and I advise Dr. Hillenbrand [sic] to step down now due to his conflict of interest with Jewish staff and students at Cal State."[15]

In December and January, CSAF and USACBI each posted open letters, and USACBI launched an online petition to the CSU chancellor defending me. The petition garnered nearly a thousand signatures with many supportive statements, including from Holocaust survivors, Palestinians, and Israeli Jews.

Zionist pressure continued unabated through the winter break. On January 4, 2012, the CSUN History Department (with which I have no affiliation) received two angry diatribes against me as recorded phone messages. The pressure was taking a toll. In early February, CSUN's Dean of Humanities, Elizabeth Say, asked via email to have her signature removed from the Israel Study Abroad Letter she had signed.

Censoring Ilan Pappé

In coordination with faculty from UCLA and two other CSU campuses, I helped arrange a speaking tour for famed Israeli historian Ilan Pappé, with a February 20, 2012 visit to CSUN. The event was co-sponsored by the CSUN Students for Justice in Palestine, CSUN Greens, Muslim Student Association, South Asia Club, and CSUN Communications Association, with CSUN funding. Sherna Berger-Gluck, a community activist, and Estee Chandler, the organizer of the Los Angeles Chapter of Jewish Voice for Peace (of which I am a member) helped to advertise Pappé's visit.

Flyers for the event were posted around campus, and predictably torn down or marred by Zionist graffiti. In particular, a flyer on my office door was replaced by an unsigned note with the sarcastic threat, "I do hope you are ok and don't have cancer or something. Be seeing you." I requested and was granted campus police patrols near my office.

AMCHA pulled out all stops to try to prevent Pappé from speaking at CSUN and the other campuses. It circulated a YouTube video vilifying him, his other CSU hosts and myself as anti-Semitic. In addition, Rossman-Benjamin and Beckwith sent a letter to the CSU chancellor and the presidents of CSUN, Cal Poly, and CSU Fresno, expressing concern for the safety of Jewish students and urging the campus leaders to "revoke sponsorship of Ilan Pappé's tour." AMCHA claimed that lectures by Pappé would violate CSU policies and state law.

With remarkable integrity, perhaps unprecedented in the United States, Hellenbrand and the two other CSU presidents issued their own open letter, dated February 16, 2012, in which they shattered Zionist hopes for censorship of Ilan Pappé. In it they wrote:

> We are writing in response to concerns that have been raised about the appearance on our respective campuses of Ilan Pappé ... The individuals who invited Professor Pappé to our respective campuses have acted within their rights to invite speakers they feel bring a perspective to an issue ... There is no danger to a free society in allowing opposing views to be heard. The danger, instead, is in censoring them.[16]

Months later, in May 2012, the three presidents' joint statement was brought before the CSU Statewide Academic Senate. Following lengthy debate, the Senate endorsed the letter, made it one of their official documents, and reaffirmed the Senate's commitment to academic freedom.[17]

Some 300 people attended Pappé's February lecture, with perhaps a fourth of them hostile. In violation of campus rules, members of the Zionist group, Stand With Us, set up a video camera on a tripod at the front of the auditorium near the stage. But the camera was aimed at the audience, not the speaker, as a form of intimidation. Because of Zionist threats, Pappé had to be accompanied by campus police as he visited CSUN classes and student groups.

Despite the powerful statement from the three campus presidents, Zionist censors scarcely missed a beat. In March 2012, California Assemblyman Bob Blumenthal, a committed Zionist (now on the Los Angeles City Council), demanded information from the CSUN administration on Ilan Pappé's visit. Blumenthal was not satisfied with the campus response and communicated that he did not believe academic freedom was the issue. Siding with AMCHA, he felt there was a misuse of the CSU/CSUN names and a violation of policies related to the use of state and university resources.

The first of four Public Records Act (PRA) requests that I would receive arrived in early April 2012. The PRA is a law passed in California in 1968 that requires inspection and/or disclosure of governmental records to the public upon request. The campus, including myself, was required to provide to a "Shira Gold," all email correspondences, with on- or off-campus recipients related to Ilan Pappé's visit, all financial documents, room reservations, and receipts. My wife, Edie Pistolesi who is a CSUN Art professor, was also served notice to provide correspondences. And there was more to come. A second PRA request came for analogous information regarding Norman Finkelstein's much earlier campus visit in 2008 (see above).

The third PRA request, arriving in May, demanded all correspondences between "Dr. Koester, Dr. Hellenbrand and Dr. Klein regarding Dr. Klein's website." A fourth PRA request from a "Mitt Riggins" arrived in October 2013 and cast a much wider net. It demanded records related to a 2011 CSUN symposia, "The Middle East Across the Curriculum," with which, except for my attendance, I had nothing to do.

California Attorney General

Having failed to pressure the CSUN administration to remove my boycott webpage, and then failing to persuade the CSU chancellor, AMCHA and its allies turned to California Attorney General Kamala Harris. In a letter dated April 2, 2012, Kenneth Leitner, the director of the Global Frontier Justice Center (GFJC), and his counsel, Mier Katz, urged Attorney General Harris to prosecute me and any CSUN administrator who permitted me to maintain my boycott webpage. They cited numerous statutes and focused on the word "csun" in the web address of my boycott page, arguing that the URL associates CSUN with the content of the webpage (in spite of disclaimers on the page).

According to Ali Abunimah, the GFJC has little real-world existence. It is apparently a front for Shurat Hadin, a well-funded far-right Israeli lawfare group also known as the Israel Law Center. And "according to Max Blumenthal, Shurat Hadin is partly funded by John Hagee, the Islamophobic, anti-Semitic and homophobic radical Christianist founder of Christians United For Israel."[18]

Absent from the GFJC legal analysis was any mention of the fact that CSUN Hillel also included "csun," not only in its web address but in its very name, that it had pro-Israel political links, and that it openly recruited students for two of the most racist political organizations in America: Stand With Us and the ZOA. CSUN Hillel even recruited students for internships with the Israeli government. Whatever legal arguments against associating CSUN's name with political positions that could possibly have applied to my case would have applied to theirs with greater force. As of this writing, the website for "Hillel 818" is titled, "Hillel at California State University, Northridge, Pierce College, and Los Angeles Valley College," and it includes a link entitled, "Site Launched to Counter Boycotts of Israeli Goods."

The response from the Attorney General's office to the call for my prosecution arrived in my mailbox in late May 2012, and it was a major disappointment to Zionists. The key sentence read, "Because we conclude upon review that the evidence ... provided does not support a finding of misuse of such name and resources, we find no basis for any action on our part." The Attorney General declined to prosecute me.

Undeterred, Mier Katz shot off another letter dated June 5, 2012 to the Los Angeles City Attorney, Carmen Trutanich, accusing Harris "of abdicating her responsibilities as Attorney General of the State of California," and asked Trutanich to take up the cause. In opposition to Katz's letter, CSAF immediately sent a letter to Trutanich defending my free speech rights. I don't know whether the City Attorney replied to the GFJC, but no action was taken by the City Attorney's office.

Meanwhile, partly in response to AMCHA's attempts at censorship, the CSU Academic Senate passed a resolution to strengthen its constitutional commitment to academic freedom. In preparation for its adoption by the CSU Board of Trustees, each of the individual faculties of the CSU campuses had to vote on the proposed change. Of the 23 campuses, 22 voted in favor, with CSUN in sole opposition, voting against it by a narrow margin. I was informed that some of the opposition came from liberal Zionist faculty.[19]

My personal standing on campus was mixed. Some colleagues turned away when they saw me, and others cheered me on. I never knew the proportions of the split, but there must have been quite a bit of opposition to my boycott website because on April 27, 2012, President Hellenbrand sent out an email, with no advance warning to me, to all CSUN faculty. In his piece, "J'accuse! The New Anti-Anti-Semitism," he wrote,

> Many of Klein's critics implicitly fuse the elected policy of the Israeli government with God's covenant with the Jews as a spiritual people and/or ethnic tribe. This consolidation empowers them to denounce, with the fury of Jeremiah, dissent to policy as if it were apostasy ...

> AMCHA charges, too, that Klein is guilty of misusing state resources – the CSUN web – for political ends, citing state code. But AMCHA conducts some of its political work through UC email accounts, while [Scholars for Peace in the Middle East (SPME)] has solicited sponsorships for its lectures from UC departments. There is nothing fundamentally wrong with SPME and AMCHA's political advocacy in an educational context. The context presents advocacy as a contestable proposition.

Congressman Brad Sherman

Hellenbrand returned to his position as provost when Dianne Harrison was appointed CSUN's president in June 2012. One of Harrison's first meetings was with Brad Sherman, the local congressman, for the purpose of discussing opportunities for him to address the student body. However, Sherman turned the meeting into a rant about my boycott webpage, demanding that it be removed, or at least a letter sent out denouncing it.

Brad Sherman is arguably the most fanatically Zionist member of the US Congress. He publicly called for the arrest and prosecution of any US citizen involved with the 2010 Gaza Freedom Flotilla, in which nine aid workers, including a US citizen, were killed in international waters by Israeli commandos. Sherman announced that he planned to work with Homeland Security to make sure that all non-US citizens aboard the Aid Flotilla would be permanently barred from entering the United States. That would include Nobel Peace laureate Mairead Maguire, former United Nations Assistant Secretary General Denis Halliday, and government officials from nearly a dozen countries.

President Harrison's very first letter to the CSUN community, dated July 9, 2012, was indeed about my webpage. She reaffirmed earlier findings "that the website was not in violation of any CSU or CSUN policies and there was no evidence that the safety or well being of students was compromised as a result of the statements on the website." She added, however, "Let me state in no uncertain terms that I do not agree with Dr. Klein's positions and, particularly, the manner in which he has chosen to present them." I asked her which of my positions she disagreed with, but, as is typical, I never received an answer.

Continuing Censorship Campaign

Petitions, testimony, and letters from Zionists calling for the removal of my webpage continued without pause. AMCHA's Rossman-Benjamin and Roberta Seid of Stand With Us testified before the CSU Board of Trustees on September 25, 2013, calling again for the removal of my webpage, but they faced opposition. Testimony in defense of my academic freedom came from supporters including Estee Chandler, who also wrote about it in San Diego Jewish World.[20] Chandler herself was no stranger to Zionist threats. Shortly after forming the Los Angeles Chapter of Jewish Voice for Peace, she came home to a "Wanted Poster" with her photograph, charging her with "anti-Jewish activity" and even targeting children in her extended family.[21]

When the American Studies Association and several other academic organizations endorsed the academic boycott of Israel in 2013, CSUN President Harrison joined the CSU chancellor and hundreds of university presidents rushing to the defense of the apartheid regime and denounced the boycott. In response, I published another opinion piece in the school newspaper, asking why she and other CSU leaders, while waxing poetic over principles of academic freedom for complicit Israeli institutions, had nothing to say about the denial of academic freedom to Palestinians caused by Israel's bombing of schools, arrest and torture of students and faculty, and closing down of universities. My challenge elicited nothing but yawns.

AMCHA continued sending letters in 2013 and 2014 to the California Attorney General and CSU administrators calling for censorship of my webpage, but I was defended in numerous ways by attorneys from the National Lawyers Guild, the Center for Constitutional Rights, and Palestine Legal, including Carol Smith, Liz Jackson, Jim Lafferty, David Mandel, Dan Segal, and Mark Kleiman, all of whom selflessly gave time and energy in support of principles of free speech. Activists from various groups including CSAF, USACBI, Independent Jewish Voices Canada, Jewish Voice for Peace, and others also wrote on my behalf. I could not have resisted the attempts at suppression for so long without the help of all these amazing people.

The conclusion, however, is unresolved. In 2015, some 24 Zionist organizations signed a letter to Attorney General Harris calling for the removal of my webpage, hoping for a different decision after she announced her candidacy for the US Senate. Unable to deny the facts of Israel's ethnic cleansing and apartheid regime, they have no better options than intimidation, character assassination, and censorship.

Notes

1. Boycott Israel Resource Page: www.csun.edu/~vcmth00m/boycott.html. All websites last accessed June 15, 2015.
2. David Klein, "Support for Israel Must Stop", *Daily Sundial*, February 6 (2009), http://sundial.csun.edu/2009/02/supportforisraelmuststop/.
3. James A. Mitchell, Letter to the Editor, *Sundial*, February 11 (2009), http://sundial.csun.edu/2009/02/lettertotheeditorfeb-2/.
4. Harvey Rich, Letter to the Editor, *Sundial*, February 12 (2009), http://sundial.csun.edu/2009/02/commentsfromtheweb/.
5. US Campaign for the Academic and Cultural Boycott of Israel (USACBI).
6. "Why is Norman Finkelstein Not Allowed to Teach?" *Works and Days, Special Issue: Academic Freedom and Intellectual Activism in the Post-9/11 University*, 26–27 (2009), pp. 307–22, www.csun.edu/~vcmth00m/finkelstein.html.
7. Open Letter to CSU Chancellor Reed, December 2011, www.csun.edu/~vcmth00m/studyabroad.html.
8. Hate mail webapge: www.csun.edu/~vcmth00m/hatemail.html.
9. See, for example, Ali Abunimah, "Zionist Group Publishes Target List of anti-Israel US Professors," *Electronic Intifada*, 14 September (2014), and links therein, http://electronicintifada.net/blogs/ali-abunimah/zionist-group-publishes-target-list-anti-israel-us-professors.

10. Ben Harris, "Waving the Zionist Flag at Santa Cruz (on Tammi Rossman-Benjamin)," *The Jewish Journal of Greater Los Angeles*, November 16 (2011), www.jewishjournal.com/los_angeles/article/waving_the_zionist_flag_at_santa_cruz_20111116/.

11. Boycott Israel Resource Page: www.csun.edu/~vcmth00m/boycott.html.

12. Hate mail webapge: www.csun.edu/~vcmth00m/hatemail.html.

13. Ibid.

14. Ibid.

15. Ibid.

16. Nora Barrows-Friedman, "Zionist Group Fails to Disrupt Ilan Pappe's Tour at California State Universities," *Electronic Intifada*, February 18 (2012), http://electronicintifada.net/blogs/nora/zionist-group-fails-disrupt-ilan-pappes-tour-california-state-universities.

17. Endorsing the Joint Statement on Academic Freedom by California State University (CSU) Presidents Armstrong, Hellenbrand, and Welty, AS-3061-12/FA (Rev), Approved May 3–4 (2012), www.calstate.edu/acadsen/Records/Resolutions/2011-2012/3061.shtml.

18. Ali Abunimah, "In Blow to Zionist Censors, California Backs Professor's Right to Call for Israel Boycott on State University Website," *Electronic Intifada*, June 5 (2012), http://electronicintifada.net/blogs/ali-abunimah/blow-zionist-censors-california-backs-professors-right-call-israel-boycott-state.

19. By "liberal Zionist" I mean someone opposed to racism except in Israel.

20. Estee Chandler, "Jewish Voice for Peace Answers SWU Critics," *San Diego Jewish World*, February 24 (2013), www.sdjewishworld.com/2014/02/24/jewish-voice-peace-answers-swu-critics/.

21. "Los Angeles Jewish Voice for Peace Activist Targeted at Home," Jewish Voice for Peace Press Release, February 4 (2011), https://jewishvoiceforpeace.org/blog/los-angeles-jewish-voice-peace-activist-targeted-home.

11

Some Thoughts on Facts, Politics, and Tenure[1]

Nadia Abu El-Haj

Editors' note: Nadia Abu El-Haj, a Palestinian-American anthropologist, joined the faculty at Columbia University/Barnard College in 2002. Her widely acclaimed and award-winning 2001 book, *Facts on the Ground: Archaeological Practice and Territorial Self-fashioning in Israeli Society*,[2] traced the rise of archaeology and archaeological discourse in Israel as a key component of the Zionist narrative legitimating the relationship between settler colonialism and the production of historical knowledge. The book sparked a firestorm of condemnation from Zionist intellectuals and the Israel lobby. The attacks against Professor El-Haj reached a crescendo in the two years leading up to and during her tenure review (2006–07). Three out of four academic committees had already approved her tenure file when, in 2007, a Barnard alumna, Paula Stern, who was living on an illegal Israeli settlement, started a petition against her tenure case on grounds of faulty scholarship, a charge later shown to be misleading and inaccurate. At the same time, as she discusses in the following testimony, Israel advocacy organizations blasted their websites with reviews of her work. The intention was to attack her scholarship with the effect that her case generated a flurry of public and media attention. The university eventually granted Professor El-Haj tenure but not before a lengthy campaign that significantly affected her personal life; for instance, after receiving threats, she was forced to remove her office contact information from the school directory out of concern for her own safety.

In September 2015, Palestine Legal and the Center for Constitutional Rights published a report, *The Palestine Exception to Free Speech: A*

Movement Under Attack in the U.S. As they document in great detail, faculty and students who speak critically about the Israeli state face anti-discrimination legal suits, punitive measures, and a plethora of bureaucratic obstacles: jobs being withdrawn; administrative sanctions against Students for Justice in Palestine groups; public calls for "civility" and accusations of anti-Semitism. In some ways, this story is nothing new. Beginning in the 1980s, the American Israel Public Affairs Committee (AIPAC) and the Anti-Defamation League (ADL) collected and circulated materials that accused scholars of being "anti-Israel propagandists and pro-Arab apologists," they created "blacklists" of scholars and worked to block their appointments to academic positions.[3] In other ways, however, the Palestine Legal report recounts something that isn't simply just more of the same: ever more ubiquitous and proliferating political strategies born of a neo-conservative Zionist politic that took form and gained steam in the post-September 11, 2001 era in the United States.

The renewed assault on scholars who write and speak critically about Israel and Zionism began the year before the September 11 attacks. With the start of the second intifada in September 2000, the illusion that a two-state solution was just around the corner imploded before the world's eyes. And with that implosion came the further constriction of the possibility for critical speech on Israel in the US academy and within American society more generally. Suicide bombers targeting Tel Aviv, Haifa, and other cities and towns brought Israeli society and many of its supporters in the United States to the point of near hysteria: *Oslo offered the Palestinians peace – a state – and look what we get in return*, they said over and over again. Trying to explain suicide bombings in Israeli cities was virtually impossible. The knee-jerk reaction was that to explain was to condone and to condone was to promote a politics well beyond the pale.

If the second intifada was one crucial turning point in the development of new political strategies and reenergized pro-Israel campaigns, September 11 sealed the deal: following the Al-Qaeda attacks, American politics shifted radically to the right and neo-conservative Jewish-Zionist pundits and activists entered the political mainstream. Through the figure of the suicide bomber, the Israeli state and its supporters in the United States equated the US fight against "Muslim terrorists" with their struggle against Palestinians. Douglas Feith, Richard Perle, and Paul

Wolfowitz, neo-conservative Jewish thinkers and policy-makers who wanted to align US interests ever more tightly to the defense of Israel, were powerful figures in framing US policy on the Middle East within the Bush Administration.[4] And new neo-conservative Zionist groups launched vociferous public campaigns to monitor and censor public debate on the question of Israel and Palestine in particular, and on US policy in the Middle East more generally. They specifically focused on the academy where they believed that anti-Israel speech and sentiment had taken hold.

The year 2002 saw the founding of both Campus Watch and the David Project, groups central to attacks on Middle East Studies scholars in the early-to-mid 2000s (see also contribution by Joseph Massad in this anthology). Campus Watch, an arm of the Middle East Forum – a neo-conservative Zionist think-tank founded by Daniel Pipes in 1990 – generated "dossiers" on professors and instructed students to report on purported anti-American and anti-Semitic statements made in the classroom. The David Project trained students to monitor anti-Israel/anti-Semitic speech and scholarship on university campuses. The David Project was a crucial player in the fight that unfolded at Columbia University about its "teaching of" Palestine and the Middle East in the years immediately prior to my tenure battle: it produced a film on what they claimed to be evidence of anti-Semitism among Columbia's Middle East faculty. And that film, *Columbia Unbecoming,* was designed to make the presumably secret crisis of anti-Semitism on campus public and to force the Columbia administration to respond – both internally and for the public at large.[5] Monitoring and intervening in campus speech on Israel/Palestine was the mandate of these groups. Smear campaigns, accusations of anti-Semitism, and very public efforts to intervene in hiring, promotion, and tenure decisions were their tactics. That was the context within which the campaign against my tenure emerged.

The Public Life of a Tenure Case

In August 2007, a petition titled "Deny Nadia Abu El-Haj Tenure" showed up online. By the end of the month it had approximately 1,900 signatories. Purportedly initiated by a Barnard College graduate-cum-West Bank settler, my tenure case was being adjudicated in the public domain. Over the next several months, *Jewish Week, The Boston Globe, The Forward,*

The Nation, and *The New York Times*, among other publications, printed articles or op-eds about the now so-called controversy.

The petition against my tenure, however, was not the start of this campaign; it had begun a year or more before. In May 2006, two Barnard alumnae, Diana Muir and Avigail Applebaum, a mother-daughter duo I did not know, wrote a review of my first book, *Facts on the Ground: Archaeological Practice and Territorial Self-fashioning in Israeli Society*. They began by equating me to a magician's assistant: "You know, the girl who stands on the stage looking so good that you watch her and miss the sleight of hand that lets the magician make a rabbit vanish into thin air." The rabbit that I make disappear is the very facts of Zionist claims to Palestine, "archaeological evidence of an ancient Jewish presence in the land [that] constitutes a compelling claim to Jewish indigeneity."[6] According to Muir and Applebaum, the book's sleight of hand operates through its theoretical-qua-epistemological commitments: *Facts on the Ground* is mired in "post-modern theory," they claim. It reduces Zionist claims to the land to the status of "mere myth" (meaning unabashed fabrication). The review then proceeds to refute what the authors understand to be my major historical claims and to reveal my not so hidden political agenda. Rather than rehearse the details of their argument here, however, I want to consider why Muir and Applebaum's reading had traction. And I do so by placing it within a broader field of conservative political polemics.

Criticisms of my scholarship rotated around a series of accusations: about competence (did I know Hebrew? Had I spent any time in Israel? Did I know anything about archaeology?) and about bias (Was the book ideologically driven? Was I distorting the facts? Can a Palestinian really write reliably about Israel?). This was a fight over the proper interpretation of the situation in Israel/Palestine – over the facts on the ground, so to speak. It was also, and quite crucially, a fight over who gets to speak and write authoritatively about the Israeli state. And that was not all: critics of my work spoke within the terms of a wider battle over authority and truth claims in the American academy. Over 20 years since the "culture wars" of the 1980s and a decade after the "science wars" had rocked the academy, acrimonious arguments over the canon versus post-positivist epistemological commitments, about post-colonial theory, identity politics, and scholarly authority had, by this time, deep roots in the academy and widespread resonance in the American public domain.

And it was into that larger political quagmire that not just my scholarship but also my integrity as a scholar were dragged. As summed up by James R. Russel, a professor of Armenian Studies at Harvard University, "*Facts on the Ground* fits firmly into the postmodern academic genre, in which facts and evidence are subordinate to, and mediated by, a 'discourse.' There is no right or wrong answer, just competitive discourses." With Edward Said as its father figure, not just Middle East Studies, but also "other branches of the humanities" have "fallen prey to ideology," Russel continued.[7] In the words of Aren Maier, "this book is a highly ideologically driven political manifesto, with a glaring lack of attention to details and to the broader context. In part, this perspective can be explained as the product of a postmodern/postcolonial deconstructionist approach to the social sciences." The other part, Maeir would claim, is my hostility to the Israeli state. "Throughout the book she repeatedly quotes anonymous archaeologists to support her contentions. Although it might be claimed that she does this to 'protect' her sources, one wonders whether the real purpose is to protect the verifiability of these statements."[8]

In the post-9/11 period, the question of Palestine has found itself at the vortex of the culture wars, now reconfigured around the threat of (Islamic) terror and the US war on it. *Facts on the Ground* is a book about Palestine and Israel, a conflict understood to harbor its own (Muslim) terrorists. And in terms of what it signaled in the latest culture wars, it was about much more than that. It is a book squarely situated within the legacy of post-colonial studies and, to boot, it takes its inspiration from a critical literature in the history and sociology of science.[9] As such, *Facts on the Ground* was the perfect object to be pulled into that post-9/11 storm. In Edward Said's terms,[10] it emerged as an "event," "part of the social world" in that time and place because it brought together a series of issues – political, epistemological, cultural – that spoke to ideological battles, political anxieties, and culture wars, old and new.

Coda: On the Fragility of Facts

Much of the attack on my work rotated around the status of facts: did I actually know any facts? Did I intentionally distort the facts for ideological purposes? For that matter, did I even believe in them? But what does it mean to believe (in) facts? More specifically, what work can facts do in the face of deeply held a priori political beliefs and commitments?

In the fall of 2008, that is, nearly a year after I received tenure, I was running the senior thesis seminar required for anthropology majors at Barnard College. Early in the year, a senior came to me to ask that she be reassigned: she didn't have a good working relationship with her advisor, she told me. I had one more spot in my group so I invited her to join. An orthodox Jewish student, I worked with her all year; over time, I became more and more impressed with her intellect, and we developed a great working relationship. She got an A on the thesis, and I recommended it for honors.

The following semester, she sent me an email asking for a recommendation for law school, which I was happy to write. When I opened her c.v. I discovered, much to my surprise and more than a little bit of consternation, that she had been working for the David Project[11] for a few years, including during the period of my tenure review. I wrote the letter, and to be clear, it was a spectacular letter, and I sent it off. And then I wrote her an email: I informed her the recommendations were in. And I wrote: now that I am done and no longer your professor, I feel the need to tell you how surprised I was to see the David Project on your c.v. I told her that I hoped that after working with me, she might have gained a critical perspective on their work – that their tactics are dirty, and their accusations untrue, acts of harassment and intimidation rather than reliable renderings of someone's scholarship, politics, and personal integrity. I trusted that in the future, she would know better, that she would question the veracity of the David Project's accusations of fraudulent scholarship, hidden agendas, and barely masked anti-Semitism leveled at scholars who dared to write critically about Israel and Zionism.

Her response? It was long and heartfelt; she told me how freaked out she had been when I reassigned her to my thesis group; how getting to know me had been revelatory; how I had been her favorite professor at college, the one from whom she had learned the most and who she respected the most; and she told me how bad she felt about what I had been put through. But what had she learned? Sometimes even the wrong people get caught up in the vortex of political causes that are nevertheless fundamentally right. In other words, the fact was they were wrong about me. But that fact did not lead her to consider that they are – or even that they might be – wrong about others. No facts – not even facts she herself had discovered or observed – could shake her belief in the virtue and importance of the David Project's mission. Face to face with facts to the contrary, she remained a true believer in the organization and its cause.

Notes

1. Parts of this chapter are excerpted and modified from a paper, "On Scholarly Texts and their (Occasional) Worldliness: Zionist Activism, Academic Freedom and Free Speech," forthcoming in Didier Fassin (ed.), *If Truth Be Told*.
2. Nadia Abu El-Haj, *Facts on the Ground. Archaeological Practice and Territorial Self-fashioning in Israeli Society* (Chicago: University of Chicago Press, 2001).
3. See Zachary Lockman, *Contending Visions of the Middle East: The History and Politics of Orientalism* (Cambridge: Cambridge University Press, 2010).
4. For a discussion of Perle and Wolfowitz, see Lockman, ibid., Chapter 7.
5. For a discussion of the David Project, the film, and what transpired at Columbia, see Jane Kramer, "The Petition. Israel, Palestine and a Tenure Battle at Barnard," *The New Yorker*, April 14 (2018). Also see Jonathan Cole, *The Great American University* (New York: Public Affairs, 2009). Based in Boston, MA, the David Project is an organization that specifically targets college and university campuses to recruit and train student agents "to improve sentiment towards Israel," with the express purpose of influencing future leaders to ensure that "the U.S. [remains] pro-Israel." The tactics for which they advocate include encouraging students to accuse professors critical of Israel of committing "academic malpractice" and funding pro-Israel students to influence campus leaders by building personal relationships with them and offering financial and other kinds of support. See the David Project's website, and their white paper, "A Burning Campus? Rethinking Israel Advocacy at America's Universities and Colleges," www. davidproject.org/wp-content/uploads/2012524-ABurningCampus-Rethink ingIsraelAdvocacyAmericasUniversitiesColleges.pdf.
6. This review first appeared in the summer of 2006. The only online version I can find of it now was one reprinted by the *History News Network* in 2007. See Diana Muir and Avigail Applebaum, "Review of Nadia Abu el-Haj's Facts on the Ground; Archaeological Practice and Territorial Self-fashioning in Israeli Society," *History News Network*, www.historynewsnetwork.org/blog/25976. All websites last accessed January 28, 2016.
7. James Russell, "Ideology over Integrity," *The Current*, Fall (2007).
8. Aren Maeir, *Facts on the Ground. Archaeological Practice and Territorial Self-fashioning in Israeli Society*, Book Review. *ISIS: Journal of the History of Science in Society*, 95, no. 3 (2004), pp. 523–4.
9. For an extensive discussion of my post-colonial/post-modern (they tend to be read as the same thing) *and* science studies commitments, see especially

Alexander H. Joffe, *Journal of Near Eastern Studies*, 64, no. 4, October (2005), pp. 297–304.

10. Edward W. Said, *The World, the Text, and the Critic* (Cambridge, MA: Harvard University Press, 1983), p. 4.

11. Editors' note: See note 5 above on the David Project; see also Abraham Greenhouse, "Anti-Palestinian Groups' Advice to Campus Activists Raises Serious Ethical, Legal Concerns," *Electronic Intifada*, March 25 (2013), https://electronicintifada.net/blogs/abraham-greenhouse/anti-palestinian-groups-advice-campus-activists-raises-serious-ethical.

12

Censoring and Sanctioning Students for Justice in Palestine

Max Geller

Editors' note: Local chapters of Students for Justice in Palestine, or SJP, have sprung up on hundreds of campuses across the United States as the student movement against Israeli apartheid and for Palestinian rights increasingly acquires the mass character of the anti-South African apartheid movement that stormed US university campuses in the 1980s and helped pressure the US government to end its support for the white supremacist regime. At the same time, however, and because of this upsurge in student activism, numerous SJP chapters have experienced harassment and persecution by Israeli advocacy organizations and university administrations.

Loyola University in Chicago, for instance, charged the SJP with conduct violations after some of its members lined up and attempted in 2014 to register at a tabling event in order to raise awareness about Birthright Israel's policy of excluding non-Jewish people. After receiving complaints from a Jewish student group, administrators opened an investigation into SJP, even though the organization had not sponsored the protest, and charged it with six violations, including bias-motivated misconduct, harassment and bullying, disruptive misconduct, and violating the university's demonstration policy by failing to register the event.

Also in 2014, Montclair State University's student government sanctioned and tried a campus SJP chapter after receiving complaints that the group handed out "offensive" pamphlets at a tabling event that provided statistics on illegal Israeli settlement activity and home demolitions and information on how students could get involved with SJP. The student government cut the SJP's budget, ordered it to cease all "political propaganda" and "focus [its] events on Palestinian culture," and denied SJP the opportunity to respond to the complaints or appeal the decision. Administrators at Florida Atlantic University subjected SJP members to a four-month investigation and disciplinary procedures after a student interrupted a speech by an Israeli colonel to read a statement about Israeli war crimes.

While such incidents of silencing are commonplace, perhaps the best-known case of an administration's attempts to repress the SJP is Northeastern University in Massachusetts. The administration, under heavy pressure from Israel lobby groups, put the campus SJP on probation in spring 2013 and ordered the organization to write a "civility statement" after some of its members staged a walkout at a campus event featuring an Israeli soldier – a protest that lasted all of one minute. Then in early 2014, the university suspended SJP after a mock eviction action it organized. The students had slipped flyers under the doors of student dorm rooms that stated that authorities had scheduled the dorm for demolition, accompanied by a note explaining that it was not a real eviction notice and contained facts about Israel's illegal demolition of Palestinian homes. Amidst a storm of national protest from free speech and civil rights groups, the university administration was forced to reinstate the SJP.

In the following, one of the SJP leaders on the Northeastern campus at the time discusses these events.

One thing Northeastern University in Boston has in common with the Zionist Organization of America is Robert Shillman as a major donor. Shillman is the largest living donor to Northeastern University and sits on the Board of Trustees. On the Northeastern campus, there is a building named after him and a life-sized bronze statue of him seated, stroking a cat. The Zionist Organization of America offers a fellowship in his name. Shillman fellows are tasked with combating pro-Palestinian initiatives on college campuses in the United States.

It is within this context that Northeastern's unfair and inconsistent treatment of the campus's chapter of Students for Justice in Palestine (SJP) must be understood.

When the university notified us that we would be the first SJP chapter in the country to be suspended, the reaction from the general body was one of universal fury. We were right to be angry. All we had done was distribute obviously fake eviction notices to neighbors in order to draw attention to the Israeli practice of demolishing Palestinian homes. We chose this form of action precisely because of administrative repression even before our official suspension. We had been constantly thwarted by campus administrators and deprived of funding; events were moved around at the last minute and all kinds of bureaucratic roadblocks were erected to deter us. In this context, the only kind of activity we really could engage in was direct action – where we didn't need university funding or even university space. That is why we decided to go door-to-door posting mock eviction notices.

There's an obvious question. How did it all come to this?

Political Repression On and Off Campus

Many campus chapters of SJP face repression. But Northeastern's relationship with Robert Shillman made it an ideal target for people like Charles Jacobs, who, with a slick media campaign, could bring things to a head between the administration and its most important donor. After leaving CAMERA,[1] Jacobs started the David Project and began to attack universities. The most famous case was that of Joseph Massad at Columbia University (included in this anthology), but he also compelled Harvard Divinity School to turn down a 5 million dollar gift from a resident of the United Arab Emirates, who wanted to endow a Chair of Islamic Studies.[2] With those successes, the David Project turned in a different direction. At that time, Jacobs left the David Project and started collaborating with Steven Emerson and the notorious far-right Israel activist David Horowitz, who leads Campus Watch. These three played lead roles in the unsuccessful campaign to stop the building of a mosque in Boston, known as the Roxbury Mosque, which they had accused, without any evidence, of being funded by "terrorists."[3] The David Project reacted to the blowback against the anti-mosque initiative and parted ways with Jacobs, which led to Jacobs' founding of Americans for Peace and Tolerance, a one-man video operation, which targeted pro-Palestinian scholars and organizers at Northeastern University specifically. He focused on two professors and the Muslim chaplain, calling the latter a "terrorist indoctrinator."[4] The school fired the chaplain, emboldening Jacobs to further action. For example, in one video, he made the incomprehensible accusation that SJP students were hijacking the Holocaust.[5] In addition, Jacobs, along with the Anti-Defamation League,[6] blamed the Northeastern SJP chapter for a December 2012 incident in which a campus menorah was knocked over. In fact, it was revealed that the perpetrators were two drunken fraternity members.

The university administration did its part to undermine us as well. We endured event cancelations just for making minor clerical errors, faced extreme scrutiny when attempting to access student activity funds, and even had police details sent to our academic events. For example, during Israeli Apartheid Week in 2012 – a series of Palestine awareness-raising activities and events held each year at universities around the world – the Northeastern administration canceled our "mock checkpoint" demonstration less than 24 hours before it was scheduled to begin. They claimed we had not filed our forms correctly.

That first instance of discrimination coincided with a smear campaign, primarily consisting of a series of videos, called "Shame on Northeastern University." Produced by Jacobs' shadowy organization, Americans for Peace and Tolerance (APT), the campaign claims that Northeastern supports anti-Semitism and Islamic extremism. APT's campaign was based on falsehoods that incorrectly conflated Palestine solidarity activism and criticism of Israeli government policies with anti-Semitism. False claims of anti-Semitism have been a favored tactic of Zionist organizations to silence criticism of the State of Israel in the United States. By misusing the history of discrimination and genocide against Jewish people, Zionist organizations claim to be defending Jewish populations against racism in the form of this new Jew hatred – which is, in reality, opposition to Israeli government policies, grounded in anti-racist politics.

APT spearheaded a concerted effort that, over the course of 18 months, would include more than 20 groups in more than 10 different media outlets – all of which were funded by some combination of major Zionist groups in the US – publishing dozens upon dozens of articles[7] attempting to chill Palestine speech on campus. The variety of sources hides the singularity of opinion in these articles. After months of sustained steady pounding of Northeastern with negative press, the university administrators sanctioned the school's SJP chapter. Clicking through some of the Zionist smears – keeping in mind the weekly barrage of such articles – provides a nice illustration of the long-standing strategy of the Zionist movement to equate Israel and Zionism with

Jews and Judaism, and then denounce criticisms of Israel or Zionism as attacks on Jewish people or Judaism.

The State of Israel and the global Zionist movement simultaneously promote the association of Jews with Israel, and then use the fact that Israel and Jews have become associated in popular imagination to claim that criticism of Israel is anti-Semitic. This blurring of the distinction between Jewish people and Israel is then used to claim that criticisms of Israel create an "unsafe" environment for Jews "threatened" by such criticism. In reality, the vast majority of criticism of Israel and Zionism is just that – criticism of the policies, practices, and racist propaganda of a political movement and a state. One cannot imagine white South African students studying in the United States in 1985 being able to get support behind a claim that criticism of South Africa's apartheid regime is racist and threatens their safety.

Within this context, it is perhaps easier to understand how Northeastern SJP's subsequent actions garnered so much attention and prompted such a draconian response.

In March 2013, the Israeli army did a presentation on the Northeastern campus, and the SJP staged a walkout at the event – a standard and widely accepted form of campus protest.[8] At that time, respected Palestinian researcher Salman Abu Sitta had been scheduled to come to the university the day after the walkout to give a talk sponsored by the SJP. The school canceled the event and sanctioned our SJP. This occurred in the context of a series of videos and articles and press releases given traction by an astro-turf network – a series of media institutions that essentially repeated nearly verbatim the same spurious claims.

After this sanctioning, the Northeastern administration forced the SJP to write a civility statement. The administration also placed it on probation. The SJP received no direction as to the content of the "civility statement" and wrote it according to its own understanding of civility. The administration rejected it and simply never followed up with the SJP. At this point the school had basically turned the SJP into a non-functional organization. We were subject to opaque "civility tests" for our events, were not allowed funds, and were told that if we wanted to do further events at the law school we would have to pay for our own security detail – a violation of the law. By July 2013, when no one was present at the school, the Zionist Organization of America sent us a letter, and Robert Shillman was copied on the letter.[9]

When the SJP returned to campus in September 2013, the letter was waiting for us, as well as its consequences. Charges of "Jewish students feeling unsafe" appeared on the local news. Meanwhile, the producer of that story was the exact same individual who was sued alongside Jacobs amidst their campaign to try to stop the construction of the Roxbury Mosque. Furthermore, the story quoted an individual from the ADL, who was the same person who represented them in the defamation suit that was tied to the campaign against the Roxbury Mosque. At the same point, the school was getting insistent calls about the news report, making it difficult to do other work.

On February 23, 2014, the Northeastern SJP distributed mock eviction notices at student dorm buildings, another widely performed bit of political theater. Within two days, Hillel was writing about how Jewish students felt targeted and demanded an official response. The administration in turn suspended the Northeastern SJP, a reflection of its official stance of opposing academic boycotts – which are indeed protected political speech – on the false grounds that they limit freedom of expression.

On February 25, 2014 the Northeastern University Police Department began a campaign of systematic interrogation of SJP members. By calling individual students on their private cell phones and showing up unannounced at students' homes, the university intimidated and coerced students they believed to be involved in this "mock eviction notice action" into speaking with them. It is important for us to note that the first and only students who were actually interrogated in connection with this investigation are members of the SJP with Muslim-sounding names. Following these two interrogations, every other student contacted by police declined to answer questions about this event without legal counsel present. Despite being informed by SJP members of our wishes to speak with our legal counsel, the police continued harassing students in the SJP.

For what it's worth, the Handbook guidelines on flyer distribution in dormitories are flouted, if not flatly ignored, by other student groups, as well as individuals on a regular basis. I assert that our suspension was due to the content of the flyers – the mock evictions that draw attention to the Palestinian plight – and not the responsible individuals' conduct (the alleged violation of university guidelines on flyer distribution). If the university was interested in applying equally its flyer policy, instead of holding the SJP to a double standard, the university would sanction its athletic team boosters, organizers of music and drama events, and fraternities, not to mention the myriad local businesses who leave unauthorized menus and flyers at dorms all the time, but obviously are never contacted by the Northeastern police – unless of course it's to place a lunch order. It is no coincidence, I suggest, that the university singles out speech consistent with SJP's views because important university benefactors consider such content objectionable, such as Robert Shillman.

A Strong Defense of Freedom On and Off Campus

One of the reasons we were able to combat our suspension was because we successfully channeled that fury into something constructive. Let me put it this way: the day we found out we were suspended, many of our members could have easily been talked into going into every bathroom on campus and writing "free SJP; the administration sucks!" This impulse, while perhaps cathartic, would have doomed our chapter. Instead, we took the weekend and began systematically preparing for a public onslaught. We went to work framing all of our online materials in a way that would be digestible to mainstream media coverage. For example, rather than explain that we were sanctioned by the university for "walking out of an event featuring Israeli war criminals," we stated that we got in trouble for walking out on "Israeli soldiers." (The thought process here was that those particular soldiers had not themselves been convicted in any international court, and we didn't want to give any outlet a pretext for not listening to us.)

In addition to targeting mainstream media outlets, we also gave interviews to sympathetic news organizations, like the Electronic Intifada, Mondoweiss, etc. (At this point you should be getting the strong feeling that we didn't get very much sleep that weekend.) Alongside the re-framing process, we set out to respond to each charge the university made against us, systematically refuting each one. We also created an "action packet" to email to supporters that included form emails to our administration as well as the phone numbers to individual university administrators. Several pro-Palestinian groups including the US Campaign to End the Israeli Occupation, the International Jewish Anti-Zionist Network, and Jewish Voice for Peace would mail this action packet to their hefty email listservs. The avalanche of phone calls and emails that followed apparently shut down the university switchboard and overwhelmed its servers. I consider the public outpouring to have been instrumental in our reinstatement.

Our hard work notwithstanding, it's unlikely that our suspension would have made national news had it not been for one very obvious mistake by the administration. Right before we were to go public with our action packet, our announcement about suspension and response to it, etc., the university informed two of my SJP colleagues, both young women of color, that they were being brought up on individual disciplinary charges related to the distribution of our mock eviction flyers. The university provided no rationale for singling out these two members. More than ten SJP members had participated equally, and yet the university was only disciplining two of us. So, moments before we were to go public, the university provided us with the shocking headline that would galvanize more than just our base: "Students Disciplined for Free Speech; Women of Color Singled-out!"

The reaction from the SJP and its local supporters was fast and strong. About 30 groups in Boston sponsored the march for free speech at Northeastern. Local steelworkers and school-bus drivers showed up, the fruit of SJP's work in supporting the drivers against Veolia, as well as the steelworkers' relationship with the drivers. At one point, even the Teamsters showed up with the giant inflatable rat. Local Palestine groups and local SJPs, including Harvard, Tufts, Boston University, UMass-Boston, as well as local anti-war group, Black and Pink, and the National Lawyer's Guild all participated. Phone calls began pouring into the administration – hundreds and hundreds every day to the point of shutting down the phone system. Due to a sophisticated media mobilization, the SJP got excellent media coverage from outlets such as NBC national news,[10] our members did over 100 interviews, and we placed an op-ed in the *Boston Globe*.[11]

The massive show of solidarity on both local and national scales led to our ultimate reinstatement, showing how a forceful grassroots campaign can reverse administrative decisions.

Reflections from Northeastern

The Northeastern SJP experience shows how right-wing media and billionaires were able to mount an escalating attack on the Northeastern chapter of Students for Justice in Palestine, to the point where the administration chose to indefinitely suspend the group. It also shows in minute detail the steps through which one multi-millionaire turned the university administration into an organic part of the repressive apparatus. More broadly, it evinces the capacity of Zionist networks to mount intense campaigns in order to remove SJP groups from college campuses. Such campaigns also work on a logic of escalation, creating a series of provocations, which, if not countered strongly enough at each stage, will snowball. They have multiple sources of information and material for defamation that they release strategically in order to create an atmosphere, which in turn contributes to the demonization of pro-Palestine political work.

But our case also tells the story of a massive, nation-wide media campaign, combined with community organizing and a strong student movement, which was able to push back against well-financed external pressure groups in order to restore the SJP chapter to good standing on campus. Our experience demonstrates that a strong media strategy coupled with and underpinned by a local organizing strategy which mobilizes a rainbow coalition of progressive forces, including pro-free speech liberals, can protect the space for anti-Zionist organizing.

Notes

1. Editors' note: CAMERA is a Zionist, non-profit organization dedicated to correcting what it perceives to be "anti-Israel bias" in the media. See "History of CAMERA" on their website, www.camera.org. According to Alex Beam of *The Boston Globe*, a senior member of CAMERA organized a campaign of more than 50 people to scour the popular website Wikipedia in order to "keep Israel-related entries ... from becoming tainted by anti-Israel editors." "War of the Virtual Wiki-worlds," *Boston.com*, May 3 (2008) (accessed January 20, 2016).
2. Charles Jacobs and Avi Goldwasser, "Being Pro-Israel Isn't Enough," *The Jewish Daily Forward*, March 2 (2012), http://forward.com/articles/152224/being-pro-israel-isnt-enough/ (accessed January 20, 2016).
3. Judy Rakowsky, "Lawsuits Dropped, But Battles Over Boston Mosque Continue," *The Jewish Daily Forward*, June 29 (2007), http://forward.com/articles/11052/lawsuits-dropped-but-battles-over-boston-mosque-c-/ (accessed January 20, 2016).
4. Charles Jacobs, "Video Exposes Northeastern University's Muslim Chaplain as an Islamic Extremist," *Family Security Matters*, September 7 (2012), https://

web.archive.org/web/20141219233338/http://www.familysecuritymatters.org/publications/detail/video-exposes-northeastern-universitys-muslim-chaplain-as-an-islamist-extremist (accessed February 26, 2014).

5. Americans for Peace and Tolerance On Campus, "Video: Northeastern University Professors Abusing Holocaust Remembrance," *Facebook*, April 2, 2012, www.facebook.com/APTonCampus/posts/299385463467855 (accessed February 22, 2015).

6. The Anti-Defamation League is a national lobby organization that takes as its mission "to stop the defamation of the Jewish people and to secure justice and fair treatment to all." However, the group is at the forefront of efforts to characterize any and all criticism of the State of Israel, its policies and practices as *ipso facto* anti-Semitic.

7. The following list represents just a small sampling of the many articles published in an attempt to mischaracterize, intimidate, and silence pro-Palestinian campus activists at Northeastern. September 21, 2011: Steve Emerson Investigative Project article about Charles Jacobs' APT video, re: Imam at Northeastern, www.investigativeproject.org/3352/university-mum-on-radical-chaplain. April 1, 2012: Charles Jacobs' APT releases video *Hijacking Holocaust Rembrance at Northeastern*, www.youtube.com/watch?v=x1kdsezcnek. September 5, 2012: Investigative Project on Terrorism chimes in about Northeastern chaplain that based entire article on APT press release/video, www.investigativeproject.org/3738/radical-imam-may-be-out-at-northeastern. September 14, 2012: Jacobs article for Boston Jewish advocate reprinted by Campus Watch, www.campus-watch.org/article/id/12550. September 27, 2012: Charles Jacobs' APT releases 32-minute video titled *Anti-Semitic Education at Northeastern*, featuring clips of SJP and two professors, www.youtube.com/watch?v=a9mmoilcda4#t=34. September 27, 2012: Israel National News runs Charles Jacobs' press release about APT "Exposing Northerastern" as news story, www.israelnationalnews.com/News/News.aspx/160347#.UoFqQ_msgyp. Stephen Schwartz, Executive Director of the Center for Islamic Pluralism, wrote for Campus Watch a project of the Middle East Forum. December 3, 2012: FrontPage mag article by Scholars for Peace in the Middle East President Richard L. Cravatts defaming Northeastern SJP, http://frontpagemag.com/2012/richard-l-cravatts/northeastern-us-students-for-justice-in-palestine-cheerlead-hamas-call-for-the-murder-of-jews/. December 12, 2012: Anti-Defamation League (ADL) press release alleging anti-Semitism at Northeastern: "several Jewish communities across the U.S. reported additional anti-Semitic acts, among them the vandalism of a menorah on the quad at Northeastern University, where anti-Semitic fliers were also discovered (same as ZOA letter), and anti-Jewish graffiti on Hanukkah displays in South Florida," www.adl.org/press-center/press-releases/miscellaneous/adl-highlights-top-10-issues.html. March 15, 2013: Jacobs in Front Page accusing Northeastern University of "Campus blood libel," http://frontpagemag.com/2013/charles-jacobs/israeli-apartheid-week-learn-

to-crush-it/?utm_source=feedburner&utm_medium=feed&utm_campaig
n=Feed%3A+FrontpageMag+%28FrontPage+Magazine+%C2%BB+FrontP
age%29 (accessed January 20, 2016).

8. Yvonne Abraham, "Stifling Student Voices," *The Boston Globe,* June 13
(2013), www.bostonglobe.com/metro/2013/06/12/stifling-student-protest-
northeastern-university/H7k5rk8VCsPlpWaJVS7eFI/story.html (accessed
February 22, 2015).

9. Morton Klein and Susan Tuchman, "Letter to President Aoun Regarding
SJP Suspension," *Zionist Organization of America,* March 12 (2014), http://
zoa.org/wp-content/uploads/2014/03/letter-to-President-Aoun-re-SJP-
suspension-3-12-14.pdf (accessed February 22, 2015).

10. Nona Willis Aronowitz, "Pro-Palestinian Students Charge Universities
with Censorship," *NBC News,* March 24 (2014), www.nbcnews.com/news/
education/pro-palestinian-students-charge-universities-censorship-n58896
(accessed February 22, 2015).

11. Max Geller, "Northeastern University Limits Free Speech," *The Boston
Globe,* April 7 (2004) www.bostonglobe.com/opinion/2014/04/07/limits-
free-speech/GD NRNljsyfnBUd3zWVNyOL/story.html (accessed February
22, 2015).

13

A So-called Self-hating, Anti-Semitic Jew Speaks Out

Lisa Rofel

Editors' note: Lisa Rofel is a distinguished Professor of Anthropology at the University of California at Santa Cruz who specializes in feminist anthropology and gender studies, with an area focus on contemporary China. As she describes in the following testimony, she has faced ongoing harassment as a result of her participation in several events on her campus critical of Israeli settler colonialism. She points out in her testimony that the Zionist charge leveled against her and others that Jewish critics of Israel are "self-hating Jews" ends up undermining the real struggle against anti-Semitism, and she discusses the implications of the Israel lobby's repression for academic freedom.

I first learned that I am a so-called self-hating Jew in 2008. The previous year I had organized two events on my campus. One was a symposium called "Alternative Histories Within and Beyond Zionism." David Theo Goldberg, Judith Butler, Terri Ginsberg, Hilton Obenzinger, and Ryvka Bar Zohar spoke. They collectively offered a clear and compelling critique of the illegal Israeli occupation of Palestinian land and Israeli settler colonialism that produces the ongoing oppression of Palestinians. They spoke about the racism that has been produced out of Zionism, both against Palestinians and among Jews in Israel, with the dominant European Ashkenazi group discriminating against Arab Mizrahi Jews. The second event was a speaker from the group of Israeli soldiers who are against the occupation. That group is called Breaking the Silence. At that time, I decided to invite all Jews to speak for two reasons: 1) Given the intense suppression in the United States of speech that is critical of Israel, and given that the Israeli oppression of Palestinians is done in the name of Jews around the world, I felt that Jews not only have an obligation to speak out but that other Jews might actually be able to hear what they have to say; and 2) I learned from my years of feminist activism and critiques by feminists of color that challenged White women to unlearn our racism, that White women need to speak about Whiteness and its privileges. My approach to discussions of Palestine/Israel is a form of "unlearning racism," that is, unlearning Jewish racism toward Palestinians and other Arabs and Arab/Mizrahi Jews.

In that spirit, I organized these two events in which Jews could speak about Israeli Jewish privilege that dispossesses Palestinians of their autonomy and their full human and civil rights. As a result of these events, I was put on a list posted on the internet, called Self-Hating Jews. There were about 2,000 of us. Judith Butler quipped that they had made it easier for us to find one another. Eventually, those at the forefront of this campaign decided this tactic was not a winning strategy, so they dropped it and went on to their current charges of anti-Semitism, which they find has more cachet.

Over the next two years I was also dragged through a number of formal and informal charges. Ilan Benjamin and Tammi Rossman-Benjamin, the first a faculty member and the second a lecturer on my campus who are part of the Israel lobby, protested the events I had organized.[1] After the events, they began their harassment campaign. First, under the California Public Records Act, they demanded to see all of my emails related to these events. I did not, in the end, turn over my emails to them. Second, they started an international email hate campaign. I received about 1,000 hate emails from people who did not attend the event, comparing me to the Nazis and accusing me of helping another Holocaust to take place. (I have since learned from Lisa Duggan, former president of the American Studies Association, to call these emails "BDS love letters".) Many departments and units on campus had contributed funds to co-sponsor these events. They also received these hate emails as did the event participants, the chair of my department and the chancellor.

Most of the letters were written with the exact same wording, which they had undoubtedly taken from the international call to do so. To quote just one of them:

"I was deeply disturbed by a state funded institution, an institution of higher learning presenting a conference that was biased, politically motivated and factually incorrect." Among the recommendations in the letter: "Develop mandatory sensitivity-training programs for faculty and students about anti-Semitism and its recent variant, anti-Zionism." This recommendation already presages the most current strategy to suppress speech that is critical of Israel, by equating that criticism with anti-Semitism.

The two people on our campus who were incensed by the events I organized, who were then active with Scholars for Peace in the Middle East – a group that is part of the Israel lobby – decided to bring me up on charges of having broken the rules of academic freedom. With no sense of irony, they claimed that the university's rules of academic freedom do not allow overt political speech on campus. They also claimed that state monies were not allowed to be used for such purposes. While they had brought pro-Israel speakers to campus, they did not seem to find any contradiction between their actions and my own. They brought these charges to our campus Committee on Academic Freedom. The chair of the committee, instead of finding me guilty, turned around and told them to stop harassing me. Not satisfied, they then brought the same charges to the chancellor's office and demanded that the chancellor punish me for supposedly having broken the rules of academic freedom. The lawyer for our campus, after having examined the case, told them I was fully within my rights to academic freedom of speech.

A few years later, the Civil Rights office of the Department of Education added "anti-Semitism" to their list of legally recognized racial discriminations, which I abhor not only because it was added with the explicit goal of silencing criticism of Israel but also because it racializes Jewishness – something my parents' generation were vehemently opposed to as a result of the Holocaust. But I guess in this, too, they are following Israeli state policies. One of the faculty had stopped public harassment activities, presumably because he became concerned with the effects of his actions on his own academic career. But the organization AMCHA, of which the lecturer who had harassed me is a leading member, then filed a legal complaint against our campus and several other UC campuses, charging these campuses with fostering a climate of anti-Semitism. The events I had organized (which took place prior to the law's effects) featured prominently in their complaint. After two years of investigation, the Department of Education's Civil Rights office quietly dropped the case, having found no basis for the charges. But AMCHA considers these actions a success, for the goal is harassment and silencing, not legal victory. Prior to this frivolous lawsuit, or what some are now calling "lawfare" action, then UC President Mark Yudof (currently chair of an Israel lobby group called Academic Engagement Network) made inflammatory remarks condemning peaceful protests on UC campuses against representatives of the Israeli government. He then commissioned a Jewish student campus climate report written by a prominent member of the Anti-Defamation League (ADL), a leading organization of the Israel lobby. Far from using standard social science techniques, failing to report even how many students were interviewed, the report essentially held one recommendation: censorship of speech critical of Israel.

Despite these various forms of harassment and attempts to suppress speech throughout the University of California system and on my campus, in some very important ways, I feel fortunate to be teaching on the Santa Cruz campus of the University of California, where a preponderance of the faculty in Humanities and Social Sciences hold progressive politics. I am sure that at another university I would have faced more serious consequences. While the two faculty who harassed me have managed to garner some small support from a few students, the vast majority of students and faculty on my campus support the academic freedom to engage in all kinds of speech, especially speech that does not line up with US State Department policies. (A propos of the latter, when the Bush administration named UC Santa Cruz as a campus to watch out for in the War on Terror, our then chancellor gave Bettina Aptheker and me $50,000 to organize a large speak-out against that war.) When some faculty heard of the harassment I was receiving even before the events took place, they showed up at these events to show their support of me. The administration has never harassed me for my criticism of the Israeli occupation and has shown support for my right to academic freedom. The two Israel lobbyists have alienated much of the faculty and administration with their extreme tactics.

On the other hand, only two other faculty members, Paul Lubeck and Christine Hong, have engaged in pro-active work to challenge the Israeli occupation. All of the other faculty have either not been interested, not willing, or are against having a public discussion of the illegal Israeli occupation. Our campus would undoubtedly not be able to pass any kind of resolution in the Academic Senate supporting speech critical of the Israeli occupation or condemning the recent California State Legislature resolution denouncing such speech as anti-Semitic. The administration has also never made any public pronouncements in support of me and against the harassment I have received, though they are quick to make pronouncements in support of students on our campus who complain that they are made to feel uncomfortable by the activities of Students for Justice in Palestine (SJP). (The administration has also never made statements condemning harassment of SJP or condemning Islamophobia.) Several faculty have criticized my involvement in the Boycott, Divestment, and Sanctions movement. One administrator admonished me for my activities with regard to Israel/Palestine, implying I would not get funds from the campus for these events in the future. I thus feel both supported and not supported simultaneously.

Academic freedom is the freedom of professors and students to reach conclusions that contradict previous dogma, whether within the academy or throughout the larger society. Academic freedom rests on the commitment to truth, wherever it takes us. Debate is one of the hallmarks of academic freedom. Time and again, those who wish to suppress speech critical of Israel have refused to engage in debate. One of the leading members of the ADL, an organization that also tries to suppress criticism of Israel, had agreed to engage in a debate on our campus with someone from the American Civil Liberties Union (ACLU) who works on defending critics of Israel. Prior to the event, the ADL leader received a great deal of pressure from those who take the position of what I call "Israel no matter what it does" not to engage in debate. They know that their myths about Israel would not hold up to scrutiny.

Academic freedom also means the freedom of the university from interference by the state. Recently, having not succeeded in suppressing speech critical of Israel on individual University of California campuses, those who wish to suppress such speech have addressed the state. Hence the unsuccessful civil rights case through the Department of Education. And hence the recent California legislature resolution condemning anti-Semitism on California university campuses. Most irksome about that resolution are three things: the fact that many of the politicians had not even read the resolution when they voted on it, presumably because they have to spend too much time on fundraising instead of a full discussion of academic freedom; second, that voting to condemn anti-Semitism has become one of those knee-jerk feel-good moves that is nearly meaningless and therefore holds the danger of making true anti-Semitism difficult to discern; and third, that the students who face the overwhelming amount of harassment today are those students protesting the Israeli occupation along with those students who face Islamophobia.

Recently, there has been pressure on the University of California, which is considering a redefinition of their tolerance policy, to highlight anti-Semitism, which the same lecturer who harassed me has tried to claim is rampant on the University of California campuses. The pressure is to adopt the US State Department definition of anti-Semitism. The State Department definition equates criticism of Israel with anti-Semitism. The State Department does have a caveat at the end of their list equating criticism of Israel with anti-Semitism. The caveat states: *However, criticism of Israel similar to that leveled against any other country cannot be regarded as anti-Semitic.* This caveat, though stuck at the end of the State Department statement, is in fact at the heart of the matter. Is criticism of Israel anti-Semitic prima facie or can we distinguish between criticism of Israel and anti-Semitism? The State Department obviously finds itself stuck in its own contradictions about the relationship between criticism of a nation-state and racism.

Ironically, although one of the charges listed is the spurious idea that Jews are more loyal to Israel than to their own nation, in this State Department definition, Israel is treated as an essential attribute of Jewish identity, an equation I categorically reject. In April 2012, then interim President of Cal State Northridge, Professor Harold Hellenbrand, stated the problem with this equation quite eloquently in a letter he issued defending Professor David Klein for posting his criticisms of Israel on his website: "[These] critics implicitly fuse the elected policy of the Israeli government with God's covenant with the Jews as a spiritual people and/or ethnic tribe. This consolidation empowers them to denounce, with the fury of Jeremiah, dissent to policy as if it were apostasy."

Rather than acknowledge the humanitarian disaster that the Israeli state has created in Palestine, rather than acknowledge that Israel is a settler colonial state, rather than acknowledge that the Israeli government has applied some of the same tactics to Palestinians that they experienced in Christian Europe, the State Department pretends there is an equivalence between Jews and Palestinians and thus states that we shouldn't blame Israel for all the political tensions. Leaving aside for the moment the statement that Israel is a democratic nation, when in fact it is democratic for Jews only, the State Department also inverts the fact that Israel is one of the only nations we do *not* hold to account for its consistent violation of international law. Hence, the use of the charge of anti-Semitism to try to silence that criticism. I am sick and tired of this opportunistic use of the charge of anti-Semitism precisely because I believe that anti-Semitism still exists and yet this opportunistic use of this charge makes it extremely difficult to discuss those cases as distinct from criticism of the Israeli occupation.

Academic freedom in the US academy today is situated within the increasing privatization of public education, and the increasing profitization of the academy in general, the inability of our students to get a college degree unless they take on a lifetime of debt, and the precariousness of many of our colleagues' working situations as adjunct lecturers with no security of employment. As my colleague Bob Meister has so perspicaciously analyzed, the University of California primarily acts as a profit-seeking, lending institution involved in the business of making profits from offering loans – to developers, financiers, and investors of all sorts. Chris Newfield in *Unmaking the Public University* argues that the end of affordable public education has been a long-time conservative campaign to end public education's democratizing influence. Neo-liberal profitization of everything thus means that those with most ability to make profits out of the university are those increasingly taking power into their hands to define the university. Thus we see across the country the power of donors but also of the boards of trustees who have been allocating to themselves increasing power to decide the curriculum of the university. And thus we see so many administrators either passively or actively suppressing controversial speech.

If we are going to have public universities become entirely reliant on capital investments and donor funds, if we are going to admit only students who can afford the tuition at public universities – thus returning to the original concept of the university as a place for elites only – in other words, if we are going to fully privatize public universities – then we cannot have unseemly behavior, uncivil effects that might create anxiety in parents, donors, and investors about the fact that students might learn that questioning and challenging often produces discomfort and knowledge that goes against their former ideas.

Academic freedom is, of course, more protected if one has security of employment – although even in this case that security can be annulled. Here we see the connections between the academy in the United States and the situation of Palestine/Israel. When I was an undergraduate, we were still in the midst of the Cold War. Any discussion of Marxism or communism could lead to a faculty member being denied tenure. Radical journals are filled with these ex-professors. As students, we organized illicit Marxist study groups. Today, generally speaking, we have no trouble within the academy offering a critique of capitalism. This is not to say that it is a simple matter or that critique is sufficient. And these faculty members certainly find it more difficult to gain the power and voice of a public intellectual who will be feted by mainstream media.

But the limit case of academic freedom in the United States today is not actually Marxism. The end of the Cold War and the supposed triumph of capitalism led the victors to feel self-satisfied and complacent. The limit case today of academic freedom is a discussion of the Palestine/Israel conflict. Or to be more precise, the limit case emerges when one voices criticism of Israel for its occupation and clear support for Palestinian rights. The speech about Palestine/Israel that is absolutely protected are those scurrilous, baseless accusations that have ruined people's professional lives. We need to acknowledge the toll these kinds of harassments take on everyone who speaks out in favor of Palestinian rights and who criticizes the racist ethnic cleansing perpetrated by the Israeli state. Those of us senior tenured faculty experience the toll of having to fight off investigations, challenges to our teaching, and the affective dimensions that are hard to ignore. But these are still not nearly as life shattering as those who are fired or denied tenure, or unhired, such as happened to Professors Norman Finkelstein and to Steven Salaita and several contributors to this volume. Or the international campaign – ultimately unsuccessful – to deny tenure to Nadia Abu El-Haj. Or those long-time tenured faculty with secure academic jobs who suddenly found themselves thrown into jail, kept in solitary confinement, and deported without ever having been found guilty of anything. That would be Professor Sami Al-Arian. These are all the more reasons for everyone to speak out in support of those who have taken these risks. Thus far, I have not heard of anyone experiencing these risks and harassments when they speak out in support of the Israeli occupation or in support of whatever the Israeli government does.

As employees in institutes of higher learning we have a particular interest in and responsibility to respond to the obstacles to the right to higher education that the Israeli state has created for Palestinians both inside Israel and in the Occupied Territories. As educators we have a responsibility to model forms of horizontal solidarity for our students, showing them that charity is not the only form of engagement they can have with the world.

Ashis Nandy once wrote that "the present is the 'historical' moment, the permanent yet shifting point of crisis and the time for choice." I take this present moment as a time for all of us who are working together to end the Israeli occupation, to once again choose social justice, which is the memory of the Shoah that should prevail but has been obscured.

Obviously, those who want to suppress criticism of Israel go to great lengths. Their ongoing efforts to suppress academic freedom when it pertains to criticism of Israel have led to programs being defunded, as we are witnessing with Middle East Studies programs. It has led to students being put on a list posted on the internet, in an effort to derail their future careers, as we witnessed last year at UC Riverside. These tactics remind us forcefully of the McCarthy era. These concerted efforts are well funded. But in spite of this ongoing harassment, we have to keep moving forward. Many amazing political accomplishments have happened in my lifetime that I never thought I would see. I look forward to thinking collectively about effective strategies to fight off this harassment on the one hand and fight for Palestinian rights on the other. I for one take this incredible level of harassment we face as a sign that we are winning in our fight for social justice for Palestinians.

Note

1. Tammi Rossman-Benjamin is a founder of AMCHA, a California-based Zionist group that targets critics of Israel on college and university campuses and on lobbying governmental agencies to repress these critics of Israel.

14

Interrupted Destinies: Before and After and Forthwith

Steven Salaita

Editors' note: Perhaps more than any other recent case of persecution by the Israel lobby, that of Steven Salaita has grabbed US and international public attention. Salaita, a Palestinian-Jordanian born in the United States, was a tenured professor of English and an award-winning scholar of American Indian Studies at Virginia Polytechnic Institute and State University when the University of Illinois at Urbana-Champaign (UIUC) hired him in fall 2013. The following summer, after he had resigned from Virginia Tech, and as he and his family prepared to move to Illinois, the Israeli military undertook another deadly assault on Gaza, Operation Protective Edge. The operation, involving air strikes and a ground invasion, left some 2,100 Palestinians dead (75 percent of them civilians), over 11,000 wounded (including 3,374 children), and displaced up to 30 percent of the Strip's two million residents. During the three-week siege, Professor Salaita published "tweets," or maximum 140-character posts on the social media site Twitter, criticizing the Israeli action, several of which were published in media outlets supportive of Israel. The faculty at UIUC initially defended him, stating that "faculty have a wide range of scholarly and political views, and we recognize the freedom-of-speech rights of all of our employees."

But then the lobby went into action. The Simon Wiesenthal Center wrote to UIUC calling Professor Salaita an "anti-Semite" and declaring that hiring him represented "a danger" to the university community and to Jewish students. In the following weeks, according to internal documents obtained under the Freedom of Information Act (FOIA), UIUC Chancellor Phyllis M. Wise and other university officials met with major donors who had threatened to withdraw their financial backing, including with a venture capitalist who served on the board of the Jewish Federation of Metropolitan Chicago and the University of Illinois Hillel Foundation. Chancellor Wise did not inform Professor Salaita of these meetings. Instead, just two weeks before the start of the academic year, she wrote to inform him that she would not recommend his appointment to the university's Board of Trustees – this after the university had already assigned Professor Salaita the courses he would teach, an email address, an office, and invited him to a faculty event on campus.

The university administration surely did not anticipate the outcry that the withdrawal of Professor Salaita's appointment would ignite. Condemnation of the university's disregard for free speech and academic freedom poured in from around the country and the world. More than 5,000 academics declared their intention to boycott UIUC and at least 16 UIUC departments passed a vote of no confidence in the administration. Numerous professional associations joined the protest, including the American Association of University Professors. A letter from dozens of law faculty stated: "The constitutional problem underlying the withdrawal of an offer of employment to Professor Salaita on account of his opinion on the Middle East affects not only him individually, but all current and prospective faculty at the University of Illinois insofar as it will have the predictable and inevitable effect of chilling speech – both inside and outside the classroom – by other academics." In reply to the university's charge that Professor Salaita's tweets were "anti-Semitic," a group of over 40 Jewish UIUC faculty and students signed a letter to Chancellor Wise protesting an unjustified conflation of "criticism of the Israeli state with anti-Semitism." In December 2014, the University Senate Committee on Academic Freedom and Tenure concluded that Professor Salaita's termination violated due process and the principles of academic freedom. Although the university chose to reject the Committee's recommendation that it reconsider his candidacy and that it take financial responsibility for its actions, Chancellor Wise was forced to resign from her post in August 2015 amidst the scandalous revelation that she colluded in hiding emails related to the rescinding of Professor Salaita's appointment.

Professor Salaita filed a federal lawsuit against the university in 2015 for violation of his constitutional rights, breach of contract, and other tort claims. The parties reached a settlement in November of that year that awarded Salaita a sizable payment for loss of income and legal expenses incurred in the trial. Professor Salaita currently teaches at the American University of Beirut. His story is chronicled in great detail, along with reflections on Palestine and academic freedom, in his 2015 book, *Uncivil Rights*. As a fitting conclusion to this collection, Professor Salaita has prepared an essay that reflects on the larger issues that the testimonials published here raise about Palestine, free speech, the commodification of higher education, academic freedom, academic repression, and the vitality of open debate and critical thinking in today's society.

I've had an unusual year. On August 2, 2014, I received an email from University of Illinois at Urbana-Champaign [now former] Chancellor Phyllis Wise informing me that I needn't turn up to begin my position as Associate Professor of American Indian Studies, which was to begin in 14 days and for which I had been under contract for nearly a year.

My hire took nearly two years to complete and a single email to terminate. During Operation Protective Edge, Israel's intensive attack on the Gaza Strip in the summer of 2014, I had sent a series of tweets harshly critical of the operation and those supporting it. Those tweets caught the attention of various rightwing and Zionist groups, which triggered a minor controversy that at the time seemed unexceptional. I didn't know, however, that behind the scenes, major donors to UIUC were threatening to withhold contributions should I turn up on campus.

The donors, as they nearly always do, prevailed. UIUC's upper administration, aware that I had already been hired and that cancelling my contract would likely result in a lawsuit, decided to fire me.

Wise's letter was stark and unceremonious. I had no idea it was coming. Shortly after news of the incident became public, a wide-ranging and often acrimonious debate commenced within and beyond academe about academic freedom, contract law, social media, professorial responsibilities, civility, and hiring protocol, framed by the participants' (wildly divergent) investment in the Israel-Palestine conflict.

Never could I imagine that I would one day be associated with so much high-stakes drama. Even when I received the termination letter from Wise, I didn't recognize its potential to mobilize so many. I did immediately recognize, however, that my chances of working as a tenured professor in US academe were suddenly miniscule. I was obviously wrong about the first recognition. I hope I am also wrong about the second.

I've given up trying to figure out why this story captured so much attention. I used to spend lots of time analyzing the discursive patterns, thinking about the conditions – seen and unseen – that inform the perception and performance of the rhetoric around civility and academic freedom. But now I just accept that my firing and the subsequent events became a story, and the story's origin is less important than its outcome. I still have my theories, sure, but I've come to realize that some things don't quite make sense according to either deduction or induction. We all have to learn at some point to accept the ambivalence of certainty.

Here are a few things about which I'm nonetheless reasonably certain:

- I never consciously set out to generate any sort of movement within or beyond academe. I simply didn't want to be treated like a chump by the upper administration of the University of Illinois. After having dismissed me, they attempted to buy my silence at a price that indicated nothing so much as pure contempt. The contemptuousness is common among the wealthy, who wish to punish subordinates for making the managerial class do oppressive things.
- There was never any question of foreclosing my interest in Palestine and retreating to some sort of monastic scholarly life in which I pretend to be disinterested or objective (though disinterest and objectivity are remarkably profitable strategies in academe).
- I smiled when the chancellor and provost of UIUC both, ahem, "resigned."
- Both the firing and the university's subsequent decisions and discourses should be read as a clear attack on the American Indian Studies Program and part of a larger pattern of managerial hostility to disciplines vested in critique of racism and colonization.
- The Palestine solidarity community in the United States (and worldwide) can no longer be ignored. It has been spectacularly effective in pressuring the university and its supporters.
- Academic freedom is often negligible when it comes to structural critique of racism, colonization, militarism, or state power. We must therefore position our analyses of academic freedom within the systemic phenomena that frame its definition and performance.

A final observation is worth some reflection: Boycott, Divestment, and Sanctions (BDS) has been a monumental factor throughout this affair. Indeed, BDS precedes my firing and will predominate long after whatever resolution occurs. I highlight BDS for two reasons: first, because I vocally advocated academic boycott in the years leading to my job offer from Illinois; and second, because it is by and large the organizers of BDS who refused to let the matter die.

My vocal support of BDS rendered me a target of recrimination well before I composed the tweets that supposedly got me fired. BDS has achieved a number of crucial victories in recent years, even in academe, a space where hostility to Palestine is as fundamental as underfunding, binge drinking, protracted committee meetings, and grumpy colleagues. With the slight shift of power away from uniform fealty to Zionism, those with a vested interest in maintaining a pro-Israel consensus reacted harshly to the emergence of a sustained, effective movement, the anxiety of a strong party perceived to be in decline – this sort of anxiety always produces a brutal outcome for the dispossessed. Many of us who work on academic boycott were targeted. For a variety of unfortunate factors, their campaign against me worked.

It is with great sadness that I offer the following observation: I certainly wasn't the first, and sadly will not be the last, professor fired for outspoken commitment to Palestinian liberation.

It's crucial to recognize that it's not merely ideological Zionism that leads the vast majority of upper administrators to support Israel – or, to be more precise, to entertain and normalize Zionist activism. Zionism is part and parcel of administrative repression. It lends itself to top-down decision-making, to suppression of anti-neoliberal activism, to restrictions on speech, to colonial governance, to corporatization and counterrevolution – in other words, Zionism behaves in universities precisely in the same way that it does in various geopolitical systems. Palestine solidarity represents democratization, grassroots organizing, anti-racism, and decolonization; it's deeply involved in ethnic studies and other subversive fields. An upper administrator needn't be ideologically inclined to West Bank settlement in order to make an advantageous selection when choosing sides.

I've spoken often of these matters. Let me then say a few things, if you're kind enough to indulge me, about what it means to exist in an economy in which one's ability to feed and clothe family is inseparable from his willingness to appease prevailing orthodoxies. This dilemma affects many people in academe, particularly those who exhibit no inclination toward either appeasement or orthodoxy. In US academe, standing up for Palestinian humanity or refusing to accept the probity of Zionism is a trenchant violation of civil etiquette.

It means, first of all, that the advocate of justice for Palestinians (or any other colonized group) must diffuse concerns about her biased scholarship, her polemical disposition, her appeals to emotion, her ability to behave professionally. She must assure her anxious superiors that she won't toss stones at Jewish students or facilitate class with a suicide bomb strapped to her torso. Please note that in this formula Jewish students are necessarily Zionist; those who identify as anti-Zionist escape the precious concern of the punctilious professoriate. They get expelled, as do all anti-colonialists, from the normative spaces of ethnonational consciousness.

If punishment for condemning Israel occurs, it is meant to be lifelong. Take my case, for example. Having dispensed of me, Zionist activists aren't content merely to wish themselves a job well done. If I am competitive for a tenured position in the future, the hiring process will need to be as low key as possible because if the folks who got me fired from Illinois get wind of another potential job opportunity they'll do exactly the same thing. That's one reason why – along with a surfeit of ignorant and racist suppositions – they were so perturbed to hear of my position at the American University of Beirut (AUB); they had no ability to torpedo the hire. Many Zionists detest the mere idea of a critic of Israel earning a living.

This perpetual diligence is concordant to the colonization they embrace. Of course they deliver lifetime punishments. Their worldview is dominated by the permanence of the histories from which they benefit. Colonization is irreversible. The United States, then, can never rightly be considered Indian Country because the American nation-building process is both manifest and linear. The same logic prevails in Israel. It leaves no room for the possibility of repossession or redress. It is in this context that the punishment for acts of decolonization must be permanent. The colonizer cannot abide a world in which his authority is less than categorical.

The effects of this strategy are wide-ranging. Beyond its codification of conquest as immutable, it results in increased corporate dominion on campus and both formal and informal limits on speech policed by the managerial class or by arbiters of uncritical convention.

This version of self-centered historicizing is why the argument that I wasn't really hired, proffered only by those with a deep affinity for Israel, is so dangerous. UIUC's supporters, these days numbering perhaps two or three dozen, won't simply say, "I hate his politics and therefore want him fired." They have to pretend that a higher purpose is in play, that their concern somehow portends the very survival of our profession. They must maintain a pretense of altruism and rectitude – of *standards*, a term that has played a critical role in the delegitimization of minority communities. Pretending to support my firing because of reasons other than political speech screws over everybody, not just critics of Israel. It creates new, arbitrary standards for academic hiring protocol; unsurprisingly, the beneficiaries of this new protocol are upper administrators and politicians.

I really wish, if only for the sake of their own happiness, that UIUC's apologists would just proclaim that they like to punish critics of Israel rather than sloshing around in disingenuous remonstration. People who work tirelessly to promote a politics they refuse to own must inhabit a remarkably sad existence.

This disingenuousness isn't random, however. It informs a specific iteration of power on campus. The humanistic discourses of tolerance and inclusion reify the colonial hierarchies that structure academic governance. We can generate useful analysis from these disparities between narrative and patronage. Such disparities, in fact, frame the inability of academic freedom to fulfill its promise. Shared governance and dissentient speech are fundamentally incompatible with the economies of today's corporate university.

* * *

As somebody who recently experienced the fallout of this incompatibility, I'd like to reflect on the implications of losing a job in this profession, especially when it happens so publicly.

First, those who organized to have me fired didn't merely take away my livelihood or disrupt a career trajectory. They took away a passion and a vocation. Being a professor is a strange sort of job, if one can even call it a job. It requires years of intense training, a rigorous interview process, an insanely competitive job market, and a constant attentiveness to trends and breakthroughs in our fields. An academic position is a commodity whose value cannot in any reasonable way be measured by salary. Tenure can provide security, but it also involves precariousness. Once a professor has been removed from a tenured appointment, it is extremely difficult to return to a position of equal or greater quality. So many things have to go well for a hire to come to fruition. The mere appearance of baggage, then, is enough to warn away even the most adventurous suitors. When that baggage involves unpopular political commitments, the opportunities for secure employment shrink from small to miniscule.

Our employment, in short, is a way of being, a distillation of life more than a description of lifestyle, easily disrupted and impossible to separate from personhood. In eliminating my job, the University of Illinois also destroyed my identity. And what does colonization desire more than the destruction of alien identities?

When I was a little boy, my father, a physics professor, used to call me "prof" because I begged to go to work with him. I adored the rational disarray of his office, the seriousness of all those big people carrying books and calculators, the dusty grooves on the chalk holder, the beige desktops attached to orange plastic chairs. He couldn't get rid of me. The other day, as I prepared to teach my first class at AUB, my three-year-old son insisted on coming to my office. He grabbed the side of my shirt and refused to loosen his grip, declaring that without his help I'll never find the office. He accompanied me to Building 37 and explored all the wonderful things that exist in academic buildings: photocopy machines, bookshelves, paperclips, keyboards, water coolers. He cried when I told him he couldn't join me in class. I cried when my father told me the same.

To this day, I answer my office phone with a gruff "Salaita" because that's how my father always answered his.

I knew from toddlerhood that I wanted to be a professor. I worked damn hard throughout my life to render that desire a reality. I always knew that my vocal support of Palestinian liberation would make it all the more difficult to earn a position in a profoundly restricted market. So, I abjured socializing and gossip and sycophancy and instead read and published as much as I could. It is this way for most ethnic, sexual, or racial minorities. We must be way better than mediocre, because mediocrity is generally reserved for the normative.

In the end, my stellar record still wasn't enough to prevent my ouster. But on the day my son cried, I felt a certain joy once I managed to suppress my own tears, because I knew in that conflicted moment that my ouster wasn't nearly enough to prevent the dream of liberation from flourishing.

* * *

Let me speak for a moment of pragmatic matters. What do we do? What *can* we do? How best to proceed? I have no universal answer to these questions because none exists. There are ways to prepare ourselves for struggle, however.

In order to produce any sort of victory against centers of power, one must absorb an extraordinary amount of public abuse and private turmoil. Agents of the powerful, pretending to uphold higher principles of human behavior, will spread lies about you, subject you to moralistic inquests, rally sites of state authority against you, and slander you as incompetent. They will scrutinize every word you've ever written in order to find a post hoc rationalization for your punishment. They will, in many cases, go so far as to dig up dirt on your loved ones. Challenging centers of power means risking criminalization. It means never winning awards. It means constantly being made to answer for other people's ethical shortcomings.

It means, above any of that, conducting yourself in the best tradition of humanity.

* * *

Restrictions on academic freedom are inseparable from the decline of the public university. I don't mean simply a decline of quality, which is a subjective judgment. I'm thinking about an erosion of the notion of "public" and its traditional meanings. The connotation of a public good has been privatized as an esoteric commodity.

It's a given that universities are increasingly corporatized. This means that governing boards have increased power; students are viewed as consumers; lobbyist groups often dictate programming and curricula; management provides itself exorbitant salaries; a permanent underclass assumes the burdens of labor; the inflow of capital motivates nearly all decision-making; and commitments to the public good slide into oblivion. Campus leaders make tremendous amounts of money, as do semi-private contractors in athletics departments and healthcare facilities. Banks earn billions on the interest from student loans, a burden that most graduates are ill-equipped to handle.

On whose behalf does the corporate university exist? There are many ways to answer this question. Most answers, unfortunately, lead to the inevitability of campus as a deeply private domain.

In this era of neoliberal graft, many universities barely pretend to care about the ideals upon which higher education was founded (though the ideals themselves are dubious and exclusionary). Sure, admins and PR wonks still prattle about dialogue and self-improvement and the life of the mind, but not even impressionable eighteen-year-olds believe the claptrap. They know just as well as their superiors that college is really about acquiring the mythical-but-measurable status conferred to them by a crisp sheet of cotton-bond paper.

Students, like all demographics, respond to discursive stimuli. As universities more and more resemble corporations in their governance, language, and outlook, students have become acutely brand conscious. Guardianship of the brand thus predominates and overwhelms the primacy of thought and analysis to which sites of education are nominally committed. Students no longer enter into places of learning. They pay outrageous prices to access the socioeconomic capital of affiliation with the most recognizable avatars, adorned magisterially with armor and pastoral creatures and Latin phrases.

Take that most sacred element of pedagogy, critical thinking. Many faculty, enamored as they are with the cartographies of their own gratification, don't know how to do it, never mind imparting instruction in the practice to those trying to learn it. (My conception of "critical thinking" includes acting in some way on the knowledge it produces, if only in the formulation of a dynamic ethical worldview.) Critical thinking encompasses numerous definitions, but one of the greatest skills it provides is the ability to recognize bullshit. In its better moments, it attempts to undermine whatever bullshit it recognizes. In short, if critical thinking is to be useful, it necessarily endows its practitioners with a reflexive desire to identify and understand the discourses, practices, beneficiaries, and disguises of power; in turn, it engenders a persistent focus on subversion. This sort of focus is low on the list of what universities want from students, just as critical thinking is a terribly undesirable quality in the corporate world, much more damning than selfishness or sycophancy.

Let us then be honest about critical thinking: on the tongues of cunning bureaucrats, it is little more than an additive to brand equity, the vainglorious pomp of smug, uptight automatons who like to use buzzwords in their PowerPoint presentations. Critical thinking by faculty is even more undesirable. In research institutions, we are paid to generate prestige and to amass grant money; in teaching-centered colleges, we enjoy excess enrollments according to fine-tuned equations that maximize the student-teacher ratio. (In elite liberal arts colleges, we pamper the kids with simulations of parental affection.) Critical thinking is especially harmful to adjuncts, reliant as they are for income on the munificence of well-paid bosses who cultivate a distended assemblage of expendable employees. Nowhere in our employment contracts does it say, "Challenge the unarticulated aspirations of the institution, especially when it acts as a conduit and expression of state violence; and please try your best to support justice for those on and off campus who are impoverished by neoliberalism." If we practice critical thinking, though, it is difficult to avoid these obligations.

Because of their high-minded rhetoric, it is tempting to believe that university managers care about ethics or maybe even about justice, but most managers care about neither. The exceptions, of course, deserve our praise – just don't poke around the highly ranked schools if you want to find them. The key to a successful managerial career isn't striving to be a good person, but developing enough instinct to cheat and charm in opportune moments. Whatever independence can be acquired in academe requires a fundamental distrust of authority, be it abstract or explicit.

The same is true of civic spaces in the United States. There were never pure epochs of uncorrupted democracy, but increasing corporate control disturbs greater sectors of American life, particularly on campus. The economies of injustice underline policymaking; those who make policy are therefore invested in the unjust. There is no choice anymore but to distrust authority. Management can reward us if we behave, but those rewards lead to the disenfranchisement of other human beings. There are better ways to conduct the practices of education.

*   *   *

Let's consider the state of academic freedom today. The popularity of social media combined with managerial emphasis on branding puts students and teachers in a tenuous position. It's useful to think of repression in academe as regenerative; social media and corporatization, then, are instruments of a long-standing phenomenon.

Remember that the banishment of Palestine from respectable academic spaces belongs to a long tradition of comparable suppression. Academe has always been hostile to deviant bodies and bodies of deviant ideas. Deviant ideas – though only political systems steeped in colonial violence consider liberation from military occupation to somehow be aberrant – do not merely offer negligible value to the corporate university; they offer negative value. It is fundamentally impossible for them to survive the marketplace of consumer-oriented pedagogy. In such conditions it is impossible for critical thinking to flourish. The very purpose of a useful education vanishes, replaced by a sort of vocational training to either conquer or concede the rigors of the capitalist marketplace.

Academic freedom increasingly is treated as a commodity rather than a right, a reflection of the values consecrated in the vocabulary of private enterprise: return on investment, efficiency, annual revenue, diversity, best practices, flipped classroom, digital literacy, buy-in, leverage, synergy, streamlining, sustainability, shareholders, survival strategies, scalability, stratcom, and paradigm shifts.

We see this process in the recent presidential search at the University of Iowa, where Bruce Harreld was awarded the job based on his executive experience at IBM and Boston Chicken. The regents who selected Harreld ignored the overwhelmingly negative response Harreld generated from students, faculty, and community members. That response was irrelevant, as it's clear that Harreld was brought aboard to wreck shop at the behest of a reactionary governor. He'll earn millions of dollars of taxpayer money for this task. Anybody who didn't know immediately that Harreld would win the job as soon as the four finalists, three qualified university administrators and this ridiculous outlier, were announced hasn't been paying attention to recent trends in higher education. Such is the condition of shared governance on more and more campuses today.

I urge us – student, faculty, administrator, community member – to dislodge pedagogy and scholarship from these venal exercises in neoliberal bean-counting. I don't simply mean in our practices of teaching and writing, but in our conceptions of what it means to educate and be educated. The vast majority of us love our vocation; in fact we view it as an avocation. Herein exists the most meaningful principle of university life. Without that principle, we simply have little love to impart and little left to love.

*   *   *

When I was an undergraduate, many moons ago, I was a shy, wiry youngster. I'm no longer wiry, but I do remain shy, painfully so at times. I was way too timid to speak in class, way too intimidated to challenge the views of folks with so many letters behind their last names.

In my silence, I learned lots of interesting things, though that silence disallowed me from educating the educators who themselves still had much to learn.

Here are some of the things I learned: my mother is a meek, submissive object devoid of agency; my father is an angry, irrational misogynist; my maternal ancestors never existed; I was genetically endowed with a propensity for violence; my sister needs to be saved from oppression by heroic Westerners; and without serious cultural deprogramming, my graduation into a world of terrorism is all but assured.

This kind of education wasn't unique to me. Many Arab and Muslim Americans learned the same things, certainly beyond the classroom if not inside it. Nobody has done a better job analyzing such representations than the man in whose name my position at AUB is endowed, Edward Said.

I think about this peculiar education whenever I hear upper administrators justify the suppression of ideas based on the need for student comfort and safety. It sounds like a given, student comfort and safety. Of course we want students to be comfortable and safe. But on whose behalf does this advocacy function?

When upper administrators ask us to prioritize student comfort and safety, they generally have in mind only a certain type of student, one wholly invented by the managerial desire to restrict ideas while maintaining an illusion of humanism. The student with whom management is most concerned is the one who provides cover for the prosecution of a neoliberal agenda.

Let me put it in simpler terms: one of the major justifications for my firing was the fact that Jewish students would supposedly be unsafe and uncomfortable in my classes. Never mind that in my teaching career

I've received exactly zero formal complaints about my pedagogy and that it's not a good look to evict academics based on claims entirely devoid of evidence when professing a pious commitment to maintaining academic standards.

The narrative does an enormous disservice to actual Jewish students, who are made to inhabit the identities of infantilized consumers concocted by management. In this formulation, Jewish students are necessarily one thing, beholden to one way of seeing the world, which is remarkably ironic considering it is nothing so much as a classically anti-Semitic proposition. "Jewish students," therefore, are but an exploited demographic formulated to rationalize managerial adherence to Zionism.

Let's return to the condition of the Arab and Muslim student in the American classroom. Take any of the countless Zionist ideologues running classrooms. It's possible, likely even, that they support, at least tacitly, ethnic cleansing, military occupation, displacement, home demolition, ethnocracy – in short, a profoundly undemocratic state whose violations of human rights are widespread and well documented.

How are Palestinian, Arab, or Muslim students to feel in one of their classes? Have you ever heard an upper administrator fret about the safety and comfort of these students?

What about Native American students? Or working class students? Or undocumented students?

The moment a university president publicly affirms the value of Palestinian life, then I might ascribe a semblance of credibility to his concern about Jewish students. The moment a university president offers a single peep about Israel's decimation of Palestinian academic freedom, rather than joining the executive chorus condemning BDS, then I might ascribe a semblance of honesty to her position. Until either happens – and they won't happen, because the structures university presidents inhabit don't allow them to happen – then we can feel free to treat apprehension about "the students" as yet another ethical debasement.

* * *

It's not too surprising that I've found something of a redemption at the American University of Beirut, where I came to teach in 2015. The institution has a distinguished history of hosting radical thought even amid its concomitant history of elitism and repression. It's a thrill for me to be here, working in and working out the contradictions that endow this campus and city with such intense, frenetic energy.

I've already met dozens of intelligent, insightful colleagues, people who take very seriously their mandate to speak and educate in the most honorable traditions of critical engagement. The students with whom I've interacted are lively and curious, exhibiting a terrific sense of irony and energy. And when sand particles aren't blocking the sky, the natural environment in Beirut is spectacular.

If I sound a bit too gushy for many of you, I understand completely. Last year, 2014–2015, was difficult. In addition to so publicly losing a job, I had to travel constantly in order to earn money and to take the fight to those who would love to un-employ so many of my colleagues on so many campuses. Being away from my beloved wife and young son was a mental and emotional torment. And to top it off, there was the real possibility that my career in academe was over before the age of forty. So, to be back on campus, amid the ornate buildings and green spaces and kinetic youngsters and quirky scholars, is a blessing I will never take for granted. I'm in a one-year visiting position here at AUB, so there's still considerable uncertainty about the future. But things are improving, and in this world any kind of improvement is simultaneously an act of affirmation and subversion.

I believe deeply in the idea of education for improvement – not merely economic improvement, but psychological, intellectual, spiritual, and ethical, as well. We cannot undertake this task in environments in which unpopular or unorthodox ideas are banished. The basic goal of a critical education is to vitiate the sacrosanct and demythologize the consecrated.

We do this by fighting. No theory is worth anything if it doesn't put us in a better position to eradicate injustice. No pedagogy is worth employing if it doesn't help students understand the transformative potential of theory. Insofar as the corporate university treats justice as a threat to brand equity, we must then seek the eradication of the corporate university.

List of Resources

There are many resources available to those who find themselves in the crosshairs of efforts to silence and repress any criticism of Israeli policies or support for Palestinian rights. Below we have listed just a few.

Further Reading

The report issued by the Center for Constitutional Rights and Palestine Legal, *The Palestine Exception to Free Speech: A Movement Under Attack*, https://ccrjustice.org/the-palestine-exception.

"Israeli Violations of Palestinian Academic Freedom and Access to Education," Institute for Middle East Understanding, http://imeu.org/article/israeli-violations-of-palestinian-academic-freedom-access-to-education.

Piya Chatterjee and Sunaina Maira (eds.), *The Imperial University: Academic Repression and Scholarly Dissent* (Minneapolis: Minnesota Press, 2014).

Beshara Doumani, *Academic Freedom after September 11* (Cambridge, MA: MIT Press, 2006).

Legal Resources

Palestine Legal, http://palestinelegal.org.

Center for Constitutional Rights: Palestinian Solidarity Project, https://ccrjustice.org/home/what-we-do/issues/palestinian-solidarity.

Activist and Professional Resources

The website for the US Campaign for the Academic and Cultural Boycott of Israel, www.usacbi.org/.

The website for Jewish Voice for Peace, https://jewishvoiceforpeace.org.

Consult the web for the contact information of your campus's Students for Justice in Palestine or your local Jewish Voice for Peace.

The link to the American Association of University Professors (AAUP) program, "Protecting Academic Freedom," www.aaup.org/our-work/protecting-academic-freedom.

The Electronic Intifada, an invaluable source for news and commentary on the Palestinian struggle for freedom, https://electronicintifada.net/.

Notes on Contributors

Rabab Ibrahim Abdulhadi is Associate Professor of Ethnic Studies/ Race and Resistance Studies at San Francisco State University (SFSU). She is Senior Scholar of the Arab and Muslim Ethnicities and Diasporas Initiative at SFSU, and editor and author of a number of books and articles.

Nadia Abu El-Haj is Associate Professor of Anthropology at Barnard College and the author of several award-winning books, among them, *Facts on the Ground: Archaeological Practice and Territorial Self-Fashioning in Israeli Society* (2002) and *The Genealogical Science: The Search for Jewish Origins and the Politics of Epistemology* (2012).

Richard Falk is Albert G. Milbank Professor of International Law, Emeritus, Princeton University, and served as Special Rapporteur for Occupied Palestine on behalf of the UN Human Rights Council from 2008–14. His most recent book is *Power Shift: On the New Global Order* (2016).

Max Geller is an organizer with the international Jewish Anti-Zionist Network. Now, based in New Orleans, Max is building a radical community based in opposition to the intersection of Zionism and anti-black racism. Much to his chagrin, Max is most famous for being the catalyst of the Renoir Sucks at Painting Movement.

Terri Ginsberg is Assistant Professor of Film, and Director of the Film Program, at The American University in Cairo. Her most recent book is *Visualizing the Palestinian Struggle: Towards a Critical Analytic of Palestine Solidarity Film* (2016). She is a member of the Organizing Collective of the US Campaign for the Academic and Cultural Boycott of Israel, and a Board member of the International Association of Contemporary Iraqi Studies.

David Theo Goldberg is Professor of Comparative Literature at the University of California, Irvine and director of the University of California Humanities Research Institute.

Maryam S. Griffin is a University of California (UC) President's Postdoctoral Fellow at UC Davis. She holds a Ph.D. in sociology from UC Santa Barbara and a J.D. from the UCLA School of Law with an emphasis in Critical Race Studies. She has been active in racial, gender, and economic justice initiatives and organizations across California for over a decade. She is currently working on a book manuscript that examines the politics of public transportation and mobility in Palestine.

Taher Herzallah is the Director of Outreach and Grassroots Organizing at American Muslims for Palestine and was one of eleven students criminalized for protesting then Israeli Ambassador, Michael Oren in 2010 at the University of California, Irvine, also known as the "Irvine 11." His work focuses on building Muslim and Palestinian community power to effect change in US policy towards Israel.

Persis Karim is a professor in the Department of English & Comparative Literature at San Jose State University. She teaches courses on world literature, ethnic literature and coordinates the Middle East Studies minor program and directs the Persian Studies program.

David Klein is Professor of Mathematics and Director of the Climate Science Program at California State University Northridge. He is a member of the Organizing Collective and a co-founder of the US Campaign for the Academic and Cultural Boycott of Israel, and is the author of the ebook, *Capitalism and Climate Change: The Science and Politics of Global Warming.*

Saree Makdisi is Professor of English and Comparative Literature at UCLA. His most recent book is *Reading William Blake* (2015).

Joseph Massad is Professor of Modern Arab Politics and Intellectual History at Columbia University. He is the author of *Colonial Effects: The Making of National Identity in Jordan* (2001), *The Persistence of the Palestinian Question* (2006), *Desiring Arabs* (2007) and *Islam in*

Liberalism (2015). Professor Massad's work has been translated to Arabic, French, Spanish, Portuguese, Japanese, Dutch, Swedish, Turkish, Italian, and German.

Cynthia McKinney served six terms in the United States Congress, from 1993 to 2003, and from 2005 to 2007, as the first black woman to represent the state of Georgia in the House of Representatives. She was eventually forced out of office in 2007 by congressional redistricting, known as gerrymandering, that reduced her voter base. The attacks against her were seen as punishment by her Democratic and Republican party opponents for her outspoken activism, including her efforts to pass numerous anti-war, anti-racist, and human rights bills in Congress and the introduction in 2006 of articles of impeachment against President George W. Bush. Since leaving Congress she has been a tireless champion of numerous peace and social justice struggles around the world. She earned her Ph.D. in Leadership and Change in 2015.

Kristofer J. Petersen-Overton is a doctoral candidate at the CUNY Graduate Center. His dissertation is a normative account of the concept of atrocity.

William I. Robinson is professor of sociology, global and international studies, and Latin American studies, at the University of California-Santa Barbara. He worked for a decade prior to entering academia as an investigative journalist in Central America and has lectured widely at universities around the world on the topics of the global economy, international politics, and contemporary world affairs. He is active in several social justice movements, including immigrant rights in the United States and justice for Palestine. Among his many award-winning books are *Global Capitalism and the Crisis of Humanity* (2014), and *Latin America and Global Capitalism* (2008). His web page is www.soc.ucsb. edu/faculty/robinson/.

Lisa Rofel is Professor of Anthropology and Director of the Center for Emerging Worlds at the University of California, Santa Cruz. She is also co-coordinator of the California Scholars for Academic Freedom and on the editorial collective of the Journal of Feminist Studies. She has written and co-edited five books and numerous articles on China, most recently a co-authored book (with Sylvia Yanagisako) entitled *Made in Translation: A Collaborative Ethnography of Italian-Chinese Global Fashion* (forthcoming).

Steven Salaita holds the Edward W. Said Chair of American Studies at the American University in Beirut and is the author of several books, among them *Israel's Dead Soul* (2011) and *Uncivil Rights* (2016).

Osama Shabaik, J.D. is a graduate of Harvard Law School and an alumnus of the University of California, Irvine, where he completed his bachelors and was arrested for his role in the "Irvine 11" protest.

David Delgado Shorter is Professor of World Arts and Cultures/Dance at the University of California, Los Angeles. His works include the book *We Will Dance Our Truth*, the film *Cutting the Cord*, and the website Wiki for Indigenous Languages. He is currently developing a digital platform for the sharing of ritual healing practices from around the globe.

Index